Praise

Trauma and the 12 Steps

"What I love about Jamie Marich's approach in *Trauma and the 12 Steps* is her flexibility in weaving together healing modalities that have worked for her, her clients, and the addiction and trauma communities she serves. She honors the twelve-step model, without accepting its orthodoxies at face value. She knows firsthand the value of twelve-step work in saving lives (her own included) and its flaws. Marich offers a compendium of practices that make using the twelve steps more effective in sustaining recovery. There are suggestions for including expressive arts, yoga breathing, meditation, prayer, and ceremony into the recovery plan, honoring above all the therapeutic relationship as the most potent agent of healing. *Trauma and the 12 Steps* belongs in the hands of everyone who serves those suffering from addiction."

—AMY WEINTRAUB, E-RYT-500, founder of LifeForce Yoga and
author of *Yoga for Depression* and *Yoga Skills for Therapists*

"Dr. Jamie Marich has a highly accessible and clear style of writing that engages the reader. In this new edition of *Trauma and the 12 Steps*, she updates and expands on her previous message of the importance of acknowledging the co-occurrence of problems with addictions with a history of trauma. She cogently explains the need to address both for a comprehensive recovery and creatively integrates attention to trauma in twelve-step work. This is a book that I will continue to wholeheartedly recommend!"

—CHRISTINE A. COURTOIS, PhD, ABPP, author of *Healing the
Incest Wound: Adult Survivors in Therapy* and coauthor of *Treatment
of Complex Trauma: A Sequenced, Relationship-Based Approach* (with
Julian Ford)

"Dr. Jamie Marich has written the book to address a complex and seemingly intransigent issue. With a compassionate yet defiant and stern voice she exposes the river of trauma running through the twelve-step experience in which so many are drowning. Clearly an admirer of the twelve-step philosophy, Marich brings understanding and a cogent critique of the culture with clarity and her own personal experiences to help those in recovery navigate the tumultuous waters of trauma in all of the ways they affect our lives. Her deep love and respect for people who are suffering shines in this book. What I love most about this book is that it is built around a well-thought-out solution—one that is accessible and straightforward guided by years of collective wisdom and experience, and most especially pain—pain that is transformed into a whole new way of living."

—DAN GRIFFIN, MA, author of *A Man's Way through the Twelve Steps;*
A Man's Way through Relationships: Learning to Love and Be Loved, and
coauthor of *Helping Men Recover: A Man's Workbook*

Trauma and the 12 Steps enhances our understanding of the role of unresolved PTSD as an invisible force that fuels addictions. Her expertise is offered in an accessible tone that leaves you feeling as if you've just sat across the table with a cup of tea with a beloved friend, sponsor, mentor, and skilled therapist. Dr. Marich is brazenly unafraid to challenge her readers to let go of our own intellectual theories and to join her in a real and raw pursuit of human presence. Undoubtedly, we come away from this book both clinically informed and spiritually enriched as we discover a strength-based approach to caring for individuals who suffer from addictions."

—ARIELLE SCHWARTZ, PhD, author of *The Complex PTSD Workbook: A Mind–Body Approach to Regaining Emotional Control and Becoming Whole; The Post Traumatic Growth Guidebook: Practical Mind–Body Tools to Heal Trauma, Foster Resilience and Awaken Your Potential;* and *EMDR Therapy and Somatic Psychology: Interventions to Enhance Embodiment in Trauma Treatment*

Jeff, the recovering trauma survivor whose case opened this chapter, shared: "Steps four and five allow you to identify the causes and conditions of your disease and all that has happened as a result of it. These steps allow you to identify old ideas, so many of which happened as a result of trauma. What's interesting is that so many people don't even realize that they have been traumatized by their addiction until they do steps four and five." Jeff's insights are powerful in explaining the potential for growth that working these steps can offer, if the recovering person chooses to work them.

Although steps four and five are the clearest examples of how the power of catharsis can help, in a broader sense, all of the steps can play some type of role in catharsis. Each allows the recovering person to get something out and work it through. Every night before I go to sleep, I offer my prayers using the tenth and eleventh steps as guides. I go through my day with God, admit where I could have done better, and turn stressors over, asking God to reveal their will to me. Speaking purely from my experience, strength, and hope, this ritual is a form of daily catharsis that I cannot live without.

As Jeff's story highlights, outside of working the steps, there are ample opportunities in twelve-step fellowships or other types of recovery groups for a person to experience catharsis by telling their story. Whether you're in a restaurant having coffee with your sponsor and some friends after a meeting, talking to a member of your support group on the phone in a moment of emotional revelation, or getting up to the podium and sharing your story publicly at a meeting, healing can occur. At least this idea is what Bill Wilson and Bob Smith tapped into when they founded Alcoholics Anonymous. It's no wonder that there is a great deal of buzz in trauma treatment circles about an approach to treatment called narrative therapy, or healing through telling the story, formally developed by Michael White and David Epston in 1990. Narrative-style therapy is an approach that AA, other twelve-step groups, and many other recovery programs have been incorporating all along to facilitate healing.

Other Gems

Two therapies that have garnered a great deal of attention in recent years are dialectical behavior therapy (DBT), an approach that combines cognitive behavioral therapy approaches with principles of Zen Buddhist meditation; and acceptance and commitment therapy (ACT), a similar approach using principles of mindfulness. Although I like and use aspects of both, I chuckle, as someone who has worked a twelve-step program for quite some time. Both of these therapies contain rebranded applications of many sobriety strategies that AA and other twelve-step programs have long incorporated. One of the central skills in both of these therapies is the importance of radical acceptance, a concept that receives a great deal of attention in the book *Alcoholics Anonymous.*

Practicing acceptance is a strategy that the steps do not directly reference, although the steps certainly can help with this process. A classic passage in the book *Alcoholics Anonymous* simply yet completely defines acceptance and how to practice it as a recovery tool:

> *And acceptance is the answer to all my problems today. When I am disturbed, it is because I find some person, place, thing or situation—some fact of my life—unacceptable to me, and I can find no serenity until I accept that person, place, thing, or situation as being exactly the way it is supposed to be at this moment. Nothing, absolutely nothing happens in God's world by mistake. Until I could accept my alcoholism, I could not stay sober; unless I accept life completely on life's terms, I cannot be happy. I need to concentrate not so much on what needs to be changed in the world as on what needs to be changed in me and in my attitudes.*[7]

If read, studied, and applied, this passage offers an ideal solution for helping a trauma survivor move out of victim mode and into survivor mode.

Accepting something, someone, or some situation does *not* mean that you have to like it. You don't even have to embrace the spiritually saccharine idea that *everything happens for a reason.* All the principle of acceptance asks you to do is to acknowledge that it happened, and there's nothing you can do to change the fact that it happened. So often, people struggle with their past, especially the difficult relationships that the past may contain. They beat themselves up with self-talk in the vein of, "If only things could have been different," or, "If only she would (or could) just change." In essence, the trauma survivor is putting all the power on the other person. Practicing acceptance facilitates personal empowerment. Although you're not letting the person off the hook for what might have occurred, you are making a conscious choice to take your life back and focus on what you can control when you practice acceptance.

Consider the case of Frances. A young woman in her early twenties, Frances grew up in a broken home with an alcoholic mother, in addition to surviving severe childhood bullying in her Catholic elementary school. For years prior to entering recovery for her own alcoholism, Frances was admittedly "other-focused." Frances shares:

> I would spend so much mental energy, trying to will my mother into changing, or trying to will my boyfriend into loving me more. I would say things like, "Things will get better when she changes," or "My life will be fine once he makes those changes," and I stayed miserable, drinking to cope with it all, just waiting around for them. In my early months in the program, I was introduced to the concept of acceptance, specifically the line that acceptance is the answer to all my problems today. For me, it felt like the most radical piece of advice I ever received. Suddenly it dawned on me, "They just are who they are. Accept it. Now it's up to you to change you and live your life without waiting for them."

Frances's story is a prime example of how acceptance can be a helpful concept with both addiction recovery and trauma recovery, especially if one can embrace acceptance as a measure of empowerment and pathway to freedom.

Another classic suggestion presented in the book *Alcoholics Anonymous* and used in other fellowships is about dealing with resentments. Resentment comes from the Latin roots *re* and *sentire*, which literally mean "to feel again." Resentments are the grudges that we hold against other people or situations. Not being able to let go of them can be harder than it seems if the root cause of the resentment was a traumatic experience, the aftereffects of which stayed locked in that limbic brain we discussed in chapter 3. A very powerful suggestion appears in the book, *Alcoholics Anonymous:*

> *If you have resentment you want to be free of, if you will pray for the person or thing that you resent, you will be free. If you will ask in prayer for every-thing you want for yourself to be given to them, you will be free. Ask for their health, their prosperity, their happiness, and you will be free. Even when you don't really want it for them and your prayers are only words and you don't mean it, go ahead and do it anyway. Do it every day for two weeks, and you will find you have come to mean it and to want it for them, and you will realize that where you used to feel bitterness and resentment and hatred, you now feel compassionate understanding and love.*[8]

Once again, this is a suggestion and not an absolute; trauma survivors do not have to follow these suggestions if they do not feel prepared.

I find that this spiritual solution has great power if a person is willing to try it. What is remarkably flexible about this suggestion is it tells you that even if you don't mean the prayer for the person, you still do it. This speaks to the power of intention, a concept used in many facets of spirituality, to begin changing our bodies and our lives just by speaking something into existence.

Frances, who shared about the power of acceptance, also remarked how working this resentment prayer with the people in her life against whom she held the biggest grudges—specifically her father—worked for her:

> *When I started praying it, it seemed a little bit weird to me. I was raised thinking you couldn't pray for a person unless you meant it. I stepped out of my comfort zone and gave this a try. When I first started praying it for my father, I didn't mean a word of it, and I even got a little feisty with God. "Dear God," I would pray, "Please help that evil man and give him every prosperity that I want for myself." I would even throw in a few choice swear words here and there! It took a lot longer than two weeks on the big ones, like my dad or one of my other abusers, but even-tually, I found that this prayer helped me release the power these people held in my head.*

Praying the resentment prayer is not for everyone when first entering a recovery program, and it may be a tough sell on some trauma survivors. However, with time and some willingness, if a person chooses to try it, it can be very empowering because the person praying it actively releases the grip this other person has over her. Thus, she can become free to live a life without the abuser still wielding conscious control. I see this resentment prayer strategy as the power of the pardon in action.

If these directly spiritual solutions like prayer or intention don't quite work for you, considering how you can use the first three steps may help you address resentment. You can take any person, place, or thing that you resent through the steps. Replace *I am powerless over alcohol, drugs, etc.* with that person, place, or thing you resent, and work it through the first three steps. Remember, doing this does not mean you endorse or validate what an abusive person may have done to you. Admitting powerlessness simply means you cannot change the person or what happened, and can be another way of practicing healthy acceptance. Use verbal strategies or writing strategies, and check in with your sponsor or guide as you would on any other working through the steps, especially if you find this suggestion activating in any way.

If you encounter difficulty practicing acceptance or working through resentments using these suggestions from the program, you are not alone. These difficulties may be the sign of more significant trauma-related blocks that will need to be addressed with outside help and modalities geared toward trauma resolution. In my own experience, I've needed a fusion of these daily style practices of acceptance and spiritually addressing resentments in addition to trauma therapy to help heal some of my deepest wounds.

Whatever Works

Although I personally endorse twelve-step principles, I realistically admit that twelve-step programming will not work for everyone. There are dozens of recovery programs and paths available in the modern era that offer alternatives to the twelve-step approach. As a professional, I am looking for two major elements should one of my clients seek out an alternative fellowship: One, does the program promote healthy lifestyle change within the individual person, helping them reach and maintain their recovery goals? And two, is the program helping the person reach their recovery goals in a way that is not shaming, taking into account the sum total of their life experiences, including any traumatic elements? If you are inclined to seek out these elements for your own benefit or for the benefit of those you work with, I encourage you to use these two questions as a guide.

The internet is filled with resources for pointing you and the people you work with toward twelve-step alternatives for recovery within your community. Simply entering "twelve-step alternatives" into a search engine will offer many possibilities. The online meeting portal In The Rooms, founded by men in long-term recovery named Ken Pomerance and Ron Tannebaum, is a favorite resource for inclusive recovery. All the equipment you need is speakers for listening and, if you wish to share, a microphone or some type of webcam (optional). Not only do they offer hundreds of meetings each week in the traditional twelve-step fellowships, they also offer space to alternative fellowships and different styles of meetings on a regular basis. They were the first to provide a home for a meeting based on the *Trauma and the 12 Steps* content in 2016.

Many alternative recovery programs promote themselves in a way that puts down twelve steps or reliance on a Higher Power, and I generally get concerned whenever I see this level of negativity. It feels like the religion or political ideology promotes what they have to offer simply by putting down the other side. Look for programs that are positive in their language. However, be aware of programs that not only put down twelve steps or traditional recovery but also promise to offer quick solutions that seem too good to be true.

TOOLKIT STRATEGY:
EVALUATING TWELVE-STEP ALTERNATIVES

Enter "twelve-step alternatives" or "AA alternatives" into an internet search engine of your choice and scan your search results, choosing a program that jumps out at you (e.g., SMART Recovery, Rational Recovery, LifeRing, Celebrate Recovery, Moderation Management, Refuge Recovery, etc.). Take a few moments to explore the program you chose, reading the program's philosophy and approach. Then, apply the "litmus test" questions presented in this chapter to what you found:

◆ *Does this program have the potential to promote healthy lifestyle change and help a person reach and maintain their recovery goals?*

◆ *Does this program have the potential to help a person reach their recovery goals in a way that is not shaming, taking into account the sum total of their life experiences, including any traumatic elements?*

A major component of trauma-informed recovery is honoring the individual's choice. Even if you are an adamant twelve-step proponent, consider how offering twelve-step meetings as part of a larger array of choices is not only trauma informed, it can also make participation in twelve-step programs seem less forced or coercive.

5

Where Twelve-Step Recovery Can (and Often Does) Go Wrong

Imagine that you grew up in a home where *don't talk, don't trust, and don't feel* were the unwritten rules. You witnessed unspeakable abuse between your father and your mother. Even though you had so many emotional needs, your mother raged whenever you sought help. She yelled if you cried. She belittled you if you spoke up. So even though you were experiencing horrific abuse at the hands of an uncle, who was a respected leader in the church your family attended, you dared not speak. The feelings were unbearable, and they had no way to get out. In fact, you believed that letting out your feelings might put your life in danger. So in your early teens, when several of your peers at school invited you to try a little alcohol and weed with them, you quickly learned that these substances not only helped you deal with the feelings, they also allowed you to better cope with the pressure of having to hold in so many feelings. Eventually, because your body was vulnerable to developing the disease of addiction (your family history with the disease was extensive), the alcohol and cannabis turned into daily use of cocaine, and soon heroin entered the mix.

Now twenty-two, you enter your first treatment program for addiction after getting into some legal problems. As part of your program, you are required to attend Alcoholics Anonymous (AA) meetings. At your first meeting, populated by many "old-timers" and traditionalists, you hear this phrase: "Take the cotton out of your ears and put it into your mouth." Unaware of the intention behind that statement, you start to panic, start to feel that same uncomfortable, "here we go again" experience. I'm not allowed to speak up. So instead of paying attention to the meeting, you zone out, flooded by so many memories of the past. Countless times, you wanted to open your mouth and speak up about the horrors you experienced and witnessed. Certainly you would be punished for it. Now here you are, at a program designed to help you, and they are telling you to do the same thing.

Traditionalists may have good *intentions* when they relay such "tough love" slogans. And yet so many slogans that people in twelve-step and other recovery programs use that may seem helpful to the rational mind may do more harm than good to those with unresolved traumatic memories.

As Nancy shared in chapter 2, those who have been affected by trauma "can't put anything into proper perspective." Thus, if someone introduces one of the slogans or steps to a newcomer out of context, which often happens at recovery meetings, re-wounding can occur. Pejorative slogans are just one facet of recovery programs that may prove problematic for those struggling with traumatic stress issues. This chapter fully explores some of these problem areas, as well as problems with step work and issues with unhealthy or dictatorial meeting styles and sponsorship as they relate to individuals affected by trauma.

Mind the Slogans and Recovery Small Talk

Most of the slogans heard at recovery meetings are not actually in basic texts or major pieces of literature associated with an individual fellowship. Slogans can be described as sayings, mottoes, or bite-size pieces of wisdom that have trickled down through the years in the rooms of recovery fellowships. A slogan can be helpful, especially if it resonates or "clicks" with a person. Additionally, newcomers and old-timers alike may be much more likely to remember a small saying like "Let go and let God" during a troubled moment, whereas an entire book passage or step may seem overwhelming.

The benefit that slogans can provide because they are so compact can also prove detrimental. The word *slogan* comes from the same Gaelic root as the word *slew,* as in "a short jab or application of brute force during a time of war." This word origin is interesting because, for a newcomer struggling with trauma issues, so many slogans can be received as little jabs that can prove retraumatizing if the meaning, intention, and context are not explained.

The following slogans tend to be most problematic for recovering individuals struggling with unresolved trauma:

- Just for Today/One Day at a Time
- Think, Think, Think/Think the Drink Through
- Your Best Thinking Got You Here/Stinkin' Thinkin'
- We Are Only as Sick as Our Secrets
- Take the Cotton out of Your Ears and Put It in Your Mouth
- Our Feelings Are Not Facts
- Keep It Simple Stupid (K.I.S.S.)
- Your Picker Is Broken

Let's take a look at each slogan, consider its original intention, and discuss how each slogan may be counterproductive or otherwise problematic to a person with unresolved trauma. If any of these slogans worked for you in your recovery process, there's nothing wrong with that. Please consider, however, that what worked for you may not work for others.

JUST FOR TODAY OR ONE DAY AT A TIME. The concept sounds incredibly simple—stay in today. One could argue that mindfulness practices ask us to do the same thing with even more of a micro focus—stay in the moment. Many people who suffer dwell notoriously in the past or project into the future. "One day at a time" is arguably the one twelve-step slogan that people outside of twelve-step fellowships most commonly associate with recovery programs. No doubt, living in today, staying in today, operating just for today, or taking life one day at a time are excellent goals to work toward.

Here is the problem. Living in today can be nearly impossible for a person with unresolved trauma because what happened ten, twenty, or even fifty years ago can seem just as real as if it were happening today. Remember what chapter 3 teaches about the limbic brain having no rational sense of time. A teacher once explained to me that the amygdala, a major component of the limbic brain, has no clock. So, when a person new to recovery who has yet to work through their issues with unresolved trauma cannot stay in today, there is a valid reason for it. A person can work on living "*one day at a time*" as a goal, although to a newcomer it isn't the instant solution that we can make it out to be.

THINK, THINK, THINK OR THINK THE DRINK THROUGH. Like so many slogans, the cognitive behavioral intention here is noble. Wouldn't it be nice if, when faced with the temptation to drink or use, we could all just calmly, rationally sit down and intelligently examine the consequences of our impulsive actions? However, basic understanding of how triggers work in the limbic brain with both unresolved trauma and addiction teaches us that thinking has very little to do with the drive to use.

The *thinking* or cognitive-only strategies, as solutions in and of themselves, are simply not adequate, especially for people who are in crisis or who are grappling with unresolved trauma. Remember, when a person is triggered, the reptilian and limbic brains take over (survival and emotion). The neocortex, which contains our rational brain, can go offline. So while we may have awareness of what's happening, we have little to no ability to make sense of it during periods of activation or pain when we need to protect ourselves. When a person is triggered, activated, or in some state of emotional overdrive, appealing to the rational brain is a fruitless exercise *unless* some measures have been taken to first address the limbic-level activity (more on this in chapter 6).

YOUR BEST THINKING GOT YOU HERE OR STINKIN' THINKIN'. While we're on the subject of thinking, let's discuss these well-intentioned yet problematic slogans. A newcomer may hear, "Hmm, on one hand they're telling me to think the drink through, but on the other hand they're telling me that I'm full of stinkin' thinkin' ... well, which is it?"

Once again, the intention is good. We often describe the thinking patterns that fuel addictive processes—especially the defense mechanisms of rationalization, intellectualizing, and minimizing—as problematic. However, these slogans can seem like all-or-nothing proclamations to people in early recovery. They often hear, "my thinking is all screwed up, it's all bad." The reality is that, for many survivors of trauma, thinking on their toes after first learning to cope with some heavy emotional experiences was necessary to stay alive. While serving in Bosnia, I heard countless stories of how people trapped in Sarajevo during the four-year siege of the city managed to feed themselves and carry out the basic functions of survival. These testimonies to the survivor spirit continue to astonish me. Indeed, the reality of a traumatized existence can lead to some pretty creative thinking, fueled by that survival drive.

Consider the teenage daughter whose mother was always out of the house drinking and using. Abandoned and left with a world of emotional hurt, she resorted to any measure to keep her three younger siblings fed, including theft, or as she got a little bit older, dealing weed to her friends. This teenage daughter knew how to cook, clean, and help the younger children with their homework, showing a great deal of resilience and smart thinking to keep everything in the house afloat. Although she went on to develop a series of problems with substance abuse and interpersonal relationships, there was a lot she did that was *right* in her thinking to keep herself and her siblings functioning. Trauma survivors often have a great deal of pride in the thinking they mustered, albeit fueled by limbic survival drives. Hearing the nature of their thinking criticized in meetings or treatment groups, especially when done in the form of an out-of-context jab like in these slogans, can be hurtful and alienating.

WE ARE ONLY AS SICK AS OUR SECRETS. The intention of this slogan is to teach that whatever we hold in—emotions, shame-based details of our past, fears—will inevitably keep us stuck and unable to move forward in recovery. If you consider the information on trauma processing covered in chapter 3, this idea makes a great deal of sense. Once again, the problem is with the semantics of this slogan and its delivery to the newcomer. For survivors of trauma, keeping secrets is often an essential component of survival. One of the greatest tactics used by abusers is some variation of the line, "If you tell anyone at all, then I'm going to (insert threat here)." People in twelve-step meetings, or even those who work in treatment centers, can fail to consider the power of the word *secret*. And how we are vulnerable to hearing a message that we are inherently defective or sick because of what we are carrying. Yes, an ultimate goal for healthy recovery would be for those dark, shame-filled secrets to be released in a healthy context (e.g., with a sponsor, counselor, or through a fifth step). Please be sensitive to the survival-laden context of "keeping a secret" to many newcomers struggling with unresolved trauma. We must be gentle and refrain from delivering this well-intended wisdom as an insulting jab.

TAKE THE COTTON OUT OF YOUR EARS AND PUT IT IN YOUR MOUTH. The intention of this slogan is that in early recovery, listening is important. However, its wording and delivery are downright insulting. For one young woman that participated in a major research project I conducted, hearing this slogan upon entering treatment or meetings immediately caused her to shut down. In this slogan, she heard that what she had to say was not important. The messages of *don't talk, don't trust, and don't feel* that were given to her in her alcoholic home of origin were further reinforced.

I'm not discounting the importance of having newcomers gently mentored in distinguishing between what is appropriate and not appropriate to share at meetings. Nor am I opposed to having newcomers appropriately challenged about when they may be using too much talk to avoid addressing some deep issues and emotions. I am asking you to consider how degrading this slogan can sound to a person who is struggling to cope and work through a legacy of trauma. Taking it a step further, what if a trauma survivor was placed in a situation where they were quite literally gagged or restrained (common with many survivors of sexual abuse)? What if a sexual abuse survivor was ever put in a situation of being forced to perform oral sex? Consider what hearing such a slogan out of context may mean to such an individual.

The other issue to address with this slogan is that we encourage recovering individuals to open up about their emotional lives, especially in treatment. Many newcomers to recovery come into treatment programs or meetings needing to unload a heavy burden. Meetings, step work, treatment programs, and various other modalities can be ideal in helping the newcomer do this; and yes, newcomers need guidance on which forums are best for opening up about which elements of their lives. However, it is important to consider how hearing this slogan at the wrong time, delivered in the wrong manner, might cause a person to shut down and perhaps never again feel safe sharing in a recovery setting.

OUR FEELINGS ARE NOT FACTS.   This slogan has been making the rounds in both treatment and meeting culture with greater intensity over the last two decades. Like any other slogans, the intention is solid—avoid overidentifying with your feelings because they will pass. In yoga culture, we might explain this as you are not your feelings. Feelings are something you experience that can be released; they are not meant to define you.

Yet think of what you've learned so far about the limbic brain and its lack of a rational time scale. When you are in the middle of an intense emotional experience and the limbic brain is in control, the rational teachings you've learned about *this too shall pass* may be inaccessible. The moment you are experiencing that emotion or feeling that feeling is all consuming. At times in my career when I've tried using *your feelings are not facts* with folks to try to teach disidentification and impermanence, I've usually been met with, "Bullshit. The fact of the moment is that this feeling is real."

Point very well taken.

KEEP IT SIMPLE STUPID (K.I.S.S.)   Learning to focus on the simple steps one may need to take in early recovery to keep from obsessing over the big picture and things out of one's control is a solid skill. This slogan is designed to teach such a time-honored idea, and the addition of the stupid part just to make the acronym nice and neat is unnecessary. There is never a place for name-calling in recovery, even when you may be addressing unhealthy or harmful behaviors.

Although we can all feel stupid from time to time, especially when poor decisions end up affecting us, believing that you *are* a stupid person can keep you stuck in a shame rut. Self-injury is a significant part of my clinical history. Often when I would hurt myself, I punctuated the injury with "You're so stupid, Jamie." The self-injury became a tangible form of punishment I inflicted upon myself for this internalized belief. As a solid best practice, refrain from calling people stupid—even if it's just in the context of a seemingly harmless acronym.

YOUR PICKER IS BROKEN.   This is a classic slogan used in many Al-Anon Family Group meetings, and it can be heard in other fellowships too. Yes, people in recovery with unhealed trauma have a tendency to get into unhealthy relationships. I've met very few people who have entered the rooms of recovery absent some type of relationship drama, either in the present or at some point in the not–too-distant past. I am a long-termer and have been married and divorced twice while in recovery. According to the wisdom given to me by Denise S., a recovering friend who left this world much too soon, "I think that our relational lives can be the last thing to heal because they were the first thing to get broken."

The drama that people in recovery face in their romantic or intimate relationships can be dismissed with, "Your picker is broken." I went to the funeral of a friend in recovery shortly after my second divorce, where I had a chance to connect with folks I hadn't seen in a while. When I told them of my news, I was avalanched with that slogan and it made me feel gross inside.

"I'm working on it," was the best response I could muster.

Years ago I heard a woman criticize the slogan at an Al-Anon conference and I was so glad. She validated us, relaying her belief that our ability to love such difficult people is a testament to the beauty of our hearts. We cannot choose whom we love, although recovery may ask us to do a great deal of work around setting boundaries and learning to love ourselves with the same vigor. And think of the wonderful fruits that can result from difficult situations, namely children that may be born of dysfunctional situations or lessons that can be learned to move us forward in our journey. Hearing such a nasty slogan can feel shaming for those who have worked to find the hidden blessing in the mess.

This list of slogans is by no means exhaustive. Just about any recovery slogan can be problematic for a newcomer struggling with unresolved trauma who does not understand the context of the slogan. Furthermore, newcomers may feel like they are trying to voice a legitimate concern and they find themselves being "cut off" and placated with a slogan. If this experience happens in a public way during a meeting or treatment group itself, it can feel even more shaming to the individual.

Also consider how some individuals who are not ready, willing, or prepared to entertain the spiritual principles of twelve-step recovery or other faith-based recovery programs may also feel barraged if they constantly hear spiritual slogans. Some other problematic slogans that I have heard for traumatized people struggling with spirituality (especially those whose unresolved trauma may stem from an experience in a religious denomination, with a clergy member, or with an overzealous parent) include "Let go and let God," "This too shall pass," and "Nothing happens in God's world by mistake."

And don't get me started on "God never gives us anything more than we can handle." First of all, it's theologically incorrect. Just ask anyone who has ever gone through a "dark night of the soul" experience. Secondly, it's invalidating and dishonoring of a person's struggle. Much more on all things spiritual in chapter 12.

Potential Pitfalls in the Twelve Steps

The twelve steps themselves do not require significant alteration for addicted survivors of trauma. However, the steps may be a harder sell on those with unresolved trauma either because of language or because of what the step is asking a person to do. Some light modification, especially in wording, may be required. At the very least, proper and trauma-informed guidance through the intention of the step is warranted.

Problems of misinterpretation are common, especially because of trauma survivors' tendency to be sensitive to triggering stimuli, and because those with unresolved trauma often lack the ability to put new learning into proper perspective. Also consider how rigid application of each step may be counterproductive if we do not take a trauma survivor's unique concerns into account. I offer more possible solutions for what to do about these various concerns in chapter 6, although it's important to first explore what the potential problems are:

STEP 1: WE ADMITTED THAT WE WERE POWERLESS OVER ALCOHOL AND THAT OUR LIVES HAD BECOME UNMANAGEABLE. By its very nature, a traumatic experience can render a person powerless. If the residual effects of the trauma are not resolved, a person can find themselves living in a pervasive state of powerlessness, helplessness, or paralyzing fear. The language of powerlessness in this step poses one of the greatest concerns of mental health professionals who work with people in recovery. As a colleague of mine once expressed, "Our job is to get a trauma survivor to tap into her personal sense of power, and here this step is telling her that she is powerless." My colleague's comments echo those that I hear from many trauma survivors trying to work a twelve-step program.

Thus results one of the great semantic debates of recovery: What does it mean to be *powerless*? Are we asking the individual to admit powerlessness just over drugs and alcohol, or over everything else in their life? And if they only admit they're powerless over drugs, alcohol, or other problematic behaviors, isn't that a belittling idea that goes against the very essence of empowerment?

These questions are very deep and can make one's head spin with frustration, and a full philosophical discussion could take up its own book! Most important to emphasize is that survivors of trauma coming into twelve-step recovery regularly ask themselves some variations of these questions. Without proper guidance to make sense of it all, the confusion can be alienating. Proper guidance in working the step is one of the solutions discussed in chapter 6. Giving the person the space to ask their questions and have them respectfully entertained is imperative throughout twelve-step recovery, especially on something as tricky as step one.

The other word that trauma survivors often struggle with is *unmanageability*. Those who truly see themselves as *survivors*—people who have been able to muddle through, cope, and stay alive despite the odds placed against them—can have the greatest difficulty with this wording. Survivors may take offense to others calling their lives unmanageable. Additionally, those individuals who have been able to succeed in many areas of their life despite the bad things that have happened to them, even though the drinking or using may be wreaking havoc on other areas of their life, tend to interpret the unmanageability concept in an "all or nothing" manner and get offended by the word. There are ample cases of Holocaust survivors or Vietnam veterans who have gone on to forge successful careers in medicine, the arts, or other professional arenas … and have also developed a drinking problem that gets in the way of interpersonal effectiveness with family and others. The unmanageability concept may be a hard sell with such individuals because they come into twelve-step recovery feeling a great deal of pride in having been able to rise above their trauma, even if it involved some maladaptive coping skills.

Although it is not directly written into the wording, step one is often described as one of surrender, or raising that proverbial white flag: "I've had enough, the addiction is stronger than me, it wins." For survivors of trauma, *fight, flight,* and *freeze* may form the fabric of life reactions. Survivors of trauma may have to use *fight* as their primary mechanism of survival. Thus, many people in this situation approach their problematic drinking or using behaviors as something that they can *fight.* This logic makes total sense to them because the neurobiological fight response that was set off at the time of the trauma has crystallized into a chief mechanism of survival. Once again, surrendering to the power of an addiction may be a solid, workable goal for someone who struggles to deal with trauma. Such a goal may be a hard sell at first because it goes against what they have long experienced as familiar. Helping people frame the first step as a goal, rather than an edict, might be the necessary modification a trauma survivor needs.

STEP 2: CAME TO BELIEVE THAT A POWER GREATER THAN OURSELVES COULD RESTORE US TO SANITY. A great struggle with this step is the element of spirituality it introduces, even for those newcomers to twelve-step programming who do not identify unresolved trauma as a major issue. However, if a trauma survivor relied on the fight of self-sufficiency to get through the trauma and cope over the years, it may be very difficult for them to accept (at first) that something outside of themselves is going to help them heal from the addiction. Even if the individual believes in God and is open to spirituality, reliance on something other than self may be problematic for a trauma survivor. The word sanity also poses an interesting challenge. If we need to be "restored to sanity," then we must be insane! If a newcomer, especially a trauma survivor, reads this step without having the root meanings of insanity and sanity properly explained or at least explored, there is a greater risk for insult-induced triggering that can happen, just as with some of the slogans we discussed.

The saying that "insanity is trying the same thing over and over again while expecting different results" is often used by professionals or counselors to explore insanity versus sanity. It's long been disproven as a saying of Albert Einstein; as a scientist, trial and error certainly would have been part of his process. So once again I go to word origin—*sane* comes from the Latin root *sanus* meaning "healthy." Individuals may find it more empowering to frame the constructs as unhealthy versus healthy, and that through the step, we are asking to be restored to health.

STEP 3: MADE A DECISION TO TURN OUR WILL AND OUR LIVES OVER TO THE CARE OF GOD *AS WE UNDERSTOOD HIM*. I admire the wording of this step because it permits a great deal of flexibility for the person to conceptualize God or Higher Power as they see fit. For so many individuals who grew up in religious institutions with a punishing or inaccessible God, this step honors a person's individual sense of spirituality. However, the sticking point here for survivors of trauma, regardless of where they stand spiritually, can be the notion of surrender or turning one's will over to some outside entity. As discussed in step two, for people who have learned to rely on or trust themselves only, especially if this learning resulted from a traumatic experience, the idea of "turning it over" may seem impossible, insulting, or too risky. Chapter 12 explores more modifications that ought to be accepted when working this step if the fellowships and treatment centers steeped in twelve-step philosophies want to be more inclusive.

STEP 4: MADE A SEARCHING AND FEARLESS MORAL INVENTORY OF OURSELVES.

STEP 5: ADMITTED TO GOD, TO OURSELVES, AND TO ANOTHER HUMAN BEING THE EXACT NATURE OF OUR WRONGS. Steps four and five in a twelve-step program are no doubt the gauntlet, for these steps ask us to make an inventory of our rights and wrongs (preferably in writing), and then share these findings with another human being. As Nancy explained in chapter 2, doing a fourth and fifth step can be a nearly impossible task for an individual with unresolved trauma issues. For her and many others, the challenge comes in their inability to put life into proper perspective. Reflecting on her past evoked such visceral and body-level responses, Nancy found herself unable to cope with the intensity. Individuals with traumatic stress concerns need extra help with these steps, and we discuss these solutions in chapter 6.

Many individuals struggle with the word *moral,* especially if they grew up in religious environments; or they automatically associate the word *immoral* with the idea that they are defective. People need proper guidance to do this step in a sensitive manner. Another struggle that individuals often have with steps four and five is writing it down and sharing it with someone else. Although solutions are offered in the next chapter, consider these legitimate concerns. When she was fourteen years old, one of my former clients decided to journal extensively about the abuse she experienced from a stepparent. She believed that journaling might help her sort out her feelings. One day, when her mother was cleaning her room, she found the journal and severely punished the client for writing such things. As a result, this client was justifiably skittish when it came to writing things down, in fear that the wrong person might find it.

I have also addressed this same struggle with many public safety personnel. Past experience teaches many in those professions that if caught with something in writing, they are much more likely to get in trouble for it. Similarly valid concerns exist with the fifth step. What if I get into trouble? What will the person I'm speaking with think of me? What if it gets out? So many traumatized individuals who feel that others made them do unspeakably horrible things operate with such fear of judgment, they strive to avoid the fifth step at all costs. Much of this results from a core, trauma-informed belief that they are defective, shameful, or some unique brand of crazy.

Another slogan that resounds in the rooms of twelve-step recovery is, "If you don't do a fifth (step), you're likely to pick up a fifth (of whiskey)." Sadly, I have seen this be the case. So many people are scared at the thought of doing a fourth or fifth step, they would rather avoid it, even if that means going back to drinking, using, or engaging in problematic behaviors to avoid really looking at themselves. Steps four and five are tricky. Often described as the hardest steps to get through, the gauntlet can prove to be especially challenging for those with unresolved trauma. Challenging, but not impossible—if proper preparation has taken place. More on potential solutions for creating a trauma-informed context in which to do step work follows in chapter 6.

STEP 6: WERE ENTIRELY READY TO HAVE GOD REMOVE ALL THESE DEFECTS OF CHARACTER.

STEP 7: HUMBLY ASKED HIM TO REMOVE OUR SHORTCOMINGS. People often work steps six and seven together, or very closely together. Although these steps no doubt come with their share of spiritual challenges, for many the greatest conceptual challenge of these steps is the idea of character defects. In so much of the criticism about twelve-step recovery, many constantly circle back to this idea that twelve-step recovery places too much emphasis on character defects and humility, and not enough emphasis on empowerment.

If a person with unresolved trauma has worked through the first five steps in a properly guided manner, hopefully these steps do not have to be as big of a gauntlet as steps four and five. Nonetheless, if a trauma survivor is still harboring deep-seated negative beliefs about himself such as "I am shameful," "I am worthless," or "I should have done something," the phrase *character defects* can trigger these beliefs and cause a person to get defensive or fall into a greater sense of despair about his selfhood. The word *defect* is what I find to be the potentially problematic sticking point for many survivors, since so many operate with the core belief, "I am defective."

The wording in step six is rife with many potential problems; it is naturally the step where I most emphasize the need for modification. For instance, in the basic text of the Workaholics Anonymous fellowship, an allowance is made to replace *character defect* with *negative coping skill.* These generally develop as a result of unhealed trauma or wounding. The addictive substance or behavior of choice simply amplifies the behavioral evidence that the wound(s) in question manifests.

STEP 8: MADE A LIST OF ALL PERSONS WE HAD HARMED, AND BECAME WILLING TO MAKE AMENDS TO THEM ALL.

STEP 9: MADE DIRECT AMENDS TO SUCH PEOPLE WHEREVER POSSIBLE, EXCEPT WHEN TO DO SO WOULD INJURE THEM OR OTHERS. Steps eight and nine, often referred to as the "making things right" steps, usher in their own unique set of challenges. With proper guidance and a productive working through of the previous seven steps, these paired amends steps do not have to be as scary as they seem. We must address the common concerns that come up with trauma survivors. I remember that my greatest struggle when I first worked step eight was a deep sense of anger I harbored because some of the people on my list (for stealing money) were some of the same people who injured me. I argued with my sponsor, "They owe me more of an amends than I owe them!" Such frustrations are common with those in recovery. A memorable client from an inpatient facility once told me, as she sat in my office weeping, "I feel that my parents need to be here just as much. Maybe even more than I do." Although it may be easy to write this off as a rationalization or excuse, after hearing her story and the abuse she endured for decades, it was difficult to disagree with her.

Without proper guidance, working these steps can be a disaster for someone in recovery who has not fully addressed issues of unresolved trauma, especially if people on the *amends list* (step eight) are some of the same people who inflicted the trauma. If traumatized individuals have not yet taken sufficient steps to reprocess the trauma (either in twelve-step recovery or through professional counseling), the likelihood is very high that they will be emotionally ill-equipped to determine what constitutes harm to self or others in making amends. The greatest emotional disasters I have seen with people working steps eight and nine are when they refuse to heed the guidance of a sponsor and/or counselor. I've seen many cases of people in recovery who have gone to abusive parents or an abusive spouse and dumped everything for the sake of making things right. Yet the other party may not have the emotional capacity to reason, especially if that other party is still inflicting trauma on others. Thus, further shaming can result from the process of doing steps eight and nine, which is not the intention of the step. *Proper guidance* is the theme of the solution chapter that follows. It is important to note that the lack of proper guidance is a major factor in how working some of these later steps can be retraumatizing.

STEP 10: CONTINUED TO TAKE PERSONAL INVENTORY AND WHEN WE WERE WRONG PROMPTLY ADMITTED IT.

STEP 11: SOUGHT THROUGH PRAYER AND MEDITATION TO IMPROVE OUR CONSCIOUS CONTACT WITH GOD *AS WE UNDERSTOOD HIM*, PRAYING ONLY FOR KNOWLEDGE OF HIS WILL FOR US AND THE POWER TO CARRY THAT OUT.

STEP 12: HAVING HAD A SPIRITUAL AWAKENING AS THE RESULT OF THESE STEPS, WE TRIED TO CARRY THIS MESSAGE TO ALCOHOLICS AND TO PRACTICE THESE PRINCIPLES IN ALL OUR AFFAIRS. People often discuss steps ten, eleven, and twelve together as the maintenance steps. In other words, a recovering person has done all of this restoration work in the first nine steps, and now it is time to make sure that proper upkeep on the restoration takes place. Of course, steps ten, eleven, and twelve often prove to be more rigorous than simple maintenance, since the steps continue to challenge those who work them with a series of tough tasks. These tasks might prove especially tough for survivors who have not yet worked through the trauma.

Admitting wrongdoing (the challenge of step ten) can prove difficult for those easily triggered by traumatic stimuli. Defensiveness can run high.

One of the best places for an individual in early recovery to practice step ten is on the job. I remember in my early recovery, I found it so hard to admit when I was wrong at work because I took every bit of feedback, or every legitimate critique of my performance, as a personal insult. The more I addressed my trauma issues, the less and less I became triggered upon being criticized. I was thus better able to work step ten on a daily basis.

Step eleven issues what is perhaps the greatest spiritual challenge of twelve-step recovery: "praying only for knowledge of God's will and the power to carry it out."[9] Many of the struggles trauma survivors face in this step tend to be spiritual in nature. Some people battle with the spiritual aspects of recovery for quite some time, so they may still encounter the same challenges presented by steps two and three with letting go of their self-sufficiency. Another problem for trauma survivors can show up in this step: the intricacy of God's will. Or the very concept of God to begin with, which I discuss further in chapter 12.

Many trauma survivors have trouble with the concept of God's will because it may be nearly impossible to wrap their understanding around the notion that the traumatic experiences they endured were somehow God's will. Until I worked through my traumatic stress issues with several reprocessing therapies, I found the *will of God* to be something that was very shady. As a result, I had great difficulty working step eleven. I can only imagine how difficult this step may be for someone who does not believe in traditional conceptualizations of God, or may still be coming to terms with their beliefs.

In step twelve, the word concept of *principles* seems to be the sticking point for many. Step twelve challenges those who work it to take the lessons learned in the previous eleven steps and apply them to every facet of their lives. There are several potential difficulties here for trauma survivors, especially if they had to resort to doing certain things that were illegal, immoral, or at the very least unhealthy, to survive the legacy of trauma. Learning a new set of principles, a new way of living, is a shift in perspective. For many survivors of trauma, this includes the difficult process of exchanging the old scripts of existence (which the negative cognitions left by the trauma likely instilled), for a newer, healthier, more principled way of living.

Some of the people who seem to have the hardest time with principles of recovery, even if they have worked all twelve steps, are those who continue to struggle with core shame. Shame can often leave people with the message, "You are such a bad person at the core, no matter what you do you're just going to screw it up anyway, so why bother?" This level of shame typically suggests the presence of unresolved trauma. I have seen people who use their job or their material possessions as a way to somehow prove to the world that they are good enough to be here, when deep down inside they battle a shameful existence. Thus, they end up doing whatever they need to do to keep their job or maintain this material wealth and its accompanied status, even if it involves lying, cheating, manipulating, or other interferences to the principled living that twelve-step recovery suggests.

For people in recovery dealing with codependency or unhealthy drives of attachment and being accepted by others, step twelve can reinforce the script of *fixer* that so many are trying to shake. Yes, a big part of step twelve is to carry the message to others who suffer. This does not mean that you become solely responsible for another's life or recovery. The step is not an open invitation for you to forget working on yourself as a sacrifice to others. The purpose of the twelfth step has always been to keep the person working it sober. Yet I've seen many people in recovery get caught up in the trap of reaching out to others in service at the expense of their own recovery. This is a problem we don't talk about enough in recovery settings and we need to address it more fully. The culprit is likely (you guessed it) unhealed trauma.

Meeting and Sponsorship Culture

All you have to do is go on the internet to find a host of people who have blogged, vlogged, or otherwise posted about their negative experiences in AA, other twelve-step fellowships, and even the alternative programs. One of the most common complaints is that even though twelve-step fellowships seem to present themselves as welcoming, they quickly become unfriendly, hostile environments if you don't follow the respective recovery program the way they suggest. People who have had negative experiences in recovery programs are often quick to label them "cultish." The guidelines of the entire AA program, many of the spin-off fellowships, and several of the alternatives are meant only to be suggestive. And yet something has happened in the way that meetings are set up and in the manner in which people conduct themselves at meetings that can allow recovery programs to project this cultish, "our way or the highway" mentality.

One can easily write off these critics as people who are resistant, or who sport a large chip on their shoulder because they couldn't follow the suggestions of a twelve-step program. Some of these critics have a point—not everyone who walks through the doors of a recovery group has a positive experience. Clients have shared with me a variety of experiences, everything from going to a first meeting and feeling preached at or belittled, to such horrible experiences as being sexually assaulted in the parking lot after a meeting by a recovery fellowship member. We are turning a blind eye if we choose to ignore that such things can and do happen. Moreover, I have heard a multitude of stories from my patients and clients about negative experiences with sponsorship, ranging from militaristic sponsors who use belittling tactics, to unethical sponsors who ended up cheating with the spouses of sponsees. As much as those of us in recovery programs may not want to hear about these experiences, *knowing that they don't represent what recovery programs mean to promote,* we must acknowledge that such experiences have caused some people to write off recovery programs completely.

We must also keep two words in mind—*flexibility* and *safety*—if we are serious about creating as welcoming and trauma-informed of an atmosphere as possible in meetings and in professional treatment. The best way to look at flexibility in a trauma-sensitive context is that it represents the ability to meet newcomers where they are *at* in the recovery or change process. Flexibility is the opposite of rigidity, and rigidity is a trait on display at so many recovery meetings and in many treatment centers. Rigidity manifests itself in a variety of ways in meetings, usually as absolute letter-of-the-law adherence to the twelve traditions. Like the steps, they are meant to be suggestive only. One of the most disturbing ways that I see rigidity at meetings is when home group members at certain meetings get absolutely fundamentalist about the fact that you can only talk about alcohol at AA meetings, or that you can only talk about narcotics at NA meetings. God forbid, if you are at an AA meeting and happen to mention how drugs relate to your story, or if you should mention the role that trauma or mental health concerns play in your addiction, you may be subjecting yourself to a public scolding by home-group members.

There is also a tendency in twelve-step meetings to shun those on medication-assisted treatment (MAT) that seems to be an even bigger problem than when I wrote the earlier edition. Many tales abound of people on Suboxone, methadone, or other pharmaceuticals not being welcome at meetings or not being allowed to share at meetings. Meetings that set this guideline are clearly ignorant of the tradition that "the only requirement for membership is the desire to stop drinking," etc. As a result, in many communities, people on MAT have risen up to create their own meetings and safe spaces. I'm glad to see this level of adaptability happening while I'm also very upset that it needs to happen in the first place.

Another issue that must be addressed with meetings is the culture of forced hugging or touching. I've been to several meetings in my time when I go to extend a hand to shake, I'm met with, "We hug around here." There are certain meetings in some fellowships where that is an anthem. If we are serious about being trauma informed and welcoming to even more people, it needs to stop. Respecting the fact that not everyone likes to be hugged, it's long been my protocol at meetings to extend my hand. If the person then extends or gestures me in for a hug, I oblige. Setting this boundary keeps me safe as well. Yet one day I was met with a response that horrified me.

After I extended my hand to an old-timer male, he got up from his chair and pulled me in, saying, "Enough with the handshakes, I wanna feel me some boob."

As he embraced me, I froze.

I wanted to chastise him in disgust for his harassing and wholly inappropriate comment. I wanted to tell him that I was there for my recovery, not to be objectified or have my body used as passing, sexualized comfort. I wanted to tell him—scream it to the whole table—that perverts like him are the reason that women don't feel safe coming to meetings. No woman should ever be exposed to comments like these or be treated in this manner at a twelve-step meeting as if she were at a bar.

Yet as is typical in my trauma response, I froze. As I'd been socialized to do, I decided not to make a big deal of it and I took my seat. I was fortunately able to work on this incident (which happened when I was about ten years sober) in my own healing and therapy, and this has since allowed me to be more vocal when I notice offenses like this take place. We must continue to challenge assumptions that just because something is one way for you (e.g., liking touch and hugs), doesn't mean it's that way for everyone else, especially the most vulnerable. And it's a special kind of offense to take advantage of or sexualize touch in a recovery setting.

Even the tendency we have to hug or touch people who begin to cry or show emotion must be examined. If someone is crying as they share at a discussion meeting, don't assume that patting or rubbing them on the back (if you're sitting next to them) is the most helpful course of action. Err on the side of no touch until you know the person and what works best for them, or be able to have a really good read of the vibe or energy of the situation. Speaking for myself, I generally dislike being hugged— especially by people I don't know well—when I'm crying heavily. I find it smothering, not comforting. I'm all for the hugs after I've released what I need to release. During the experience, however, I need my space even if I find the presence of others comforting. We all have our different styles that need to be respected in meeting culture.

Fortunately, not all meetings are created equally. Some display more tolerance, realism, and flexibility toward sharing about other addictions or problems, as they relate to the primary focus of the fellowship. Imagine that you are an individual going to your first meeting. Your defenses are already up, not only because of the addiction, but also due to your legacy of trauma. When you speak to someone at the meeting and mention that you're addicted to pills and alcohol and they gruffly cut you off with, "We don't talk about drugs here, just alcohol," that sends the message, "you're not welcome here unless you do it our way."

This mentality tends to manifest itself in sponsorship styles as well. Many recovering folks jokingly call certain twelve-step sponsors "AA Nazis" or "Big Book Thumpers" because they so rigidly follow the letter of the law and may not even consider sponsoring you unless you take all of their suggestions, period. I don't want to make a blanket criticism of such sponsors, because a very select number of people in recovery programs respond well to this style. However, I argue that most newcomers who come to recovery fellowships with unresolved trauma are more often harmed than helped—especially in the long run—by such an approach.

I remember something one of my former twelve-step sponsors once shared with me. When she first came to a twelve-step fellowship, she asked a woman to sponsor her, and the woman responded that she would only agree to it if "you do everything my way. If not, then I'm not your sponsor."

My former sponsor couldn't do it. She said it felt like her home of origin. For many of us who have struggled with trauma concerns, something that feels too much like home is not optimal for healthy recovery.

I am not advocating that we have to be goody-goody and treat all newcomers who have had horrible pasts with kid gloves. We must, however, remember that twelve-step recovery is meant to be suggestive *only*. Twelve-step sponsors are meant to be guides or mentors—not professional clinicians, ministers, or dictators. We ought to deliver our help to others in that spirit of making suggestions based on our experience, strength, and hope. We should not be using our roles as recovery sponsors (or counselors who operate from a twelve-step paradigm) as a way to meet our need to be in charge! Even if you feel like you are being a "Big Book Thumper" because tough love worked for you, don't assume that it will work for everyone. Yes, some people may respond well to it. And most who have unresolved trauma concerns will likely not feel safe with that style.

Safety is the other key element that we need to consider in looking at trauma-sensitive recovery. In meetings, in our sponsorship styles, in our treatment centers, and in our support circles, are we doing all we can to make sure newcomers feel safe enough? I do not believe a person can meaningfully recover until they feel safe to do so, yet so many people come to meetings where they feel threatened or unwelcome. Even though it is unrealistic to expect a perfect sense of safety at every twelve-step recovery meeting, some simple safety precautions often go unheeded. For one, there is absolutely no place for the public shaming that goes on in many recovery meetings, be they twelve-step or alternative meetings. One of my former clients had an unfortunate experience that describes my general concern.

Even though she had sensed for a while that she had a problem with alcohol and sleeping pills, Brandalyn was ultimately court ordered to treatment for possession of cocaine—a substance she had only begun using one year prior to her arrest. A strong-willed woman with an extensive history of childhood sexual abuse, she was initially scared off from going to AA meetings because someone had told her that "drug addicts weren't welcome," even though alcohol was her first drug of choice. Thus, Brandalyn decided to attend NA meetings. She had a pretty good experience, feeling optimistic about her membership in that fellowship following two weeks of attendance. Then, at an NA discussion meeting, she decided to end her share with a poem that her treatment counselor had given about the power of surrender, unaware that you are not supposed to share materials that aren't *conference-approved literature* (a term that meant nothing to her as a newcomer) at an NA meeting. An NA member tore into her before she finished, telling her that the poem had no business at an NA meeting. Upon hearing him scream at her, she panicked, and the old feeling of being scolded for doing something that she had no idea was "wrong" came flooding back. Even though the member was technically correct, what he could have done (preferably with another female member of the fellowship), was approach Brandalyn after the meeting and explain to her the difference between conference-approved literature and general recovery literature, noting that conference-approved literature is the only type of literature that gets shared within the meeting itself.

Brandalyn came back to treatment flustered, feeling unwelcome and unsafe in AA as well as NA because of both experiences. She was able to keep an open mind in treatment for a couple more weeks. When she was feeling stronger, she agreed to try some new AA and NA meetings to see if her experience would be different elsewhere. Fortunately, it was. Brandalyn was able to work through her steps. One of the key factors that helped Brandalyn stick with twelve-step recovery was seeking out an encouraging support team with the help of her counselor, who understood the uniqueness of her situation as a cross-addicted female with issues of unresolved childhood sexual trauma. To this day, I believe that if Brandalyn had not found the sponsor and cosponsor that she did—women with solid recovery who were able to meet Brandalyn in her recovery process and gently explain the steps and traditions to her—she never would have stuck with a twelve-step recovery program.

Solid sponsorship can make all the difference between whether or not a person, especially a traumatized person, sticks around and gives a recovery program a chance to work. Sponsors who publicly shame or are dictatorial in their styles, as we've discussed throughout this section, can be problematic. Another major area of offense that clearly violates safety in twelve-step recovery, is when sponsors attempt to work too far outside their scope of experience. Many times, sponsors attempt to play counselor to clients about matters that would be more appropriately handled by a professional. Remember that the AA Big Book texts from other fellowships do acknowledge that sometimes outside help is needed. More dangerously, sponsors will advise a person with mental health concerns to go off of their psychotropic medications because all they need is to work the twelve steps. I have no patience for this, and I have seen this attitude cause more harm than good to countless people who took this advice literally.

Many times, especially when people live in an area where ample sponsorship is not available, people feel backed into a corner about sponsorship. Sometimes those sponsors who are trauma informed or otherwise responsive to issues around mental health may not be available to take on more sponsees. If you are a person in recovery, you may have to get creative. For instance, maybe the person who is most available to work you through the steps can just take you through the steps, and you feel better about taking issues with the rest of your life to your professional or others in your support group who feel more accepting. Maybe the sponsor you struggle with has openness to reading this book or other resources you share with them about trauma or mental health. Since the publication of the earlier edition, I've received many messages about readers giving this book to their sponsors with good outcomes.

This chapter may be a hard read for you, especially if your sponsorship or clinical style resembles some of the problem areas I described. I validate that you may simply be carrying on customs and interpretations of the program that worked for you. While that can be very normal, it is no longer sufficient. In their purest form, the design of these fellowships is not to deal with the plethora of issues that people experience in modern times. The reality is that most newcomers entering twelve-step recovery today are coming in with those issues weighing them down. If we turn a blind eye to other issues and stay rigid just for the sake of tradition (or whatever unmet ego needs of ours we're trying to satisfy), we will be alienating a whole new generation of people. The people we will alienate the most are those with serious trauma wounds who most stand to benefit from what recovery programs can provide. In the next chapter, I tie together all that we have discussed so far and spell out specific ideas for how we can put trauma-informed twelve-step recovery into action, whether we are professionals or members of twelve-step fellowships ourselves.

TOOLKIT STRATEGY:
HONORING THE EXPERIENCE OF THE PERSON

Empathy is often defined as the experience of stepping into the shoes of another in order to see the world from their perspective. Many people who are in twelve-step fellowships or work as professionals have been accused of lacking empathy. The good news is that even if you struggle with being empathetic, you can work on building it.

- ◆ *Looking back on your time working with others, what are some of the greatest "horror stories" you have heard from your clients or sponsees about negative experiences they had in recovery meetings or treatment groups? If you'd like, take a few minutes to jot some of those down.*

- ◆ *Then consider how you, as a professional or sponsor, addressed these concerns when the person brought them to your attention. Looking back on it now, would you have done anything differently?*

Please go to the www.traumamadesimple.com resources site for an audio recording called "Step into Their Shoes" to further work this skill. There are versions for both professionals and sponsors.

6

Working with Others in a Trauma-Sensitive Manner

My first sponsor Janet exemplified the art of compassion during my early days in recovery. I was resistant, bullheaded, and prideful despite my obvious outreach to her for help. There were so many things she did that, I believe, set a good example of what recovery could offer. In my work as a professional today, I get so disheartened when I hear people share about negative experiences with addiction recovery programs, thinking to myself, "If only you could have had someone like Janet...."

Janet did not get hung up on whether I chose to identify myself as an alcoholic or addict. When I first sought out recovery, I had no problem admitting that I was an addict. I couldn't quite accept that I was an alcoholic. In the Herzegovinian town where I was living at the time, there were only AA meetings. She told me to come to the meetings and if I heard the word *alcohol*, just replace it with *drugs*.

"It's all gonna kill you anyway," she told me in her pronounced, Kentucky drawl. This simple action made such an impression because it taught me that I did not have to force myself to identify or fit in. By not preaching to me from the onset, she paved the way for me to go to meetings with an open mind. In my healing brain, it eventually clicked that I was both a drug addict and an alcoholic.

Another powerful way that Janet helped to meet me on the road of recovery was by demonstrating an understanding of my past and how it affected me. One time, something my boss said to me made me cry so hard, I was almost at the point of convulsing. Janet said simply, "This isn't just tears, Jamie, this is a post-traumatic reaction." Such a simple validation, and yet it allowed me to feel safe with her in exploring why my boss's behavior so deeply affected me. Janet did not let me sit in self-pity. She validated me first, then challenged me to action. Her classic line was, "Jamie, after everything you've been through, no wonder you're feeling this way. So what are you going to do about it now?" The sensitive combination of acceptance and challenge helped me work through my issue of both addiction recovery and unresolved trauma in those early days when hearing one wrong thing could have turned me off to recovery forever.

Like many a newcomer to recovery and supportive fellowships, I challenged Janet on just about everything I heard. "What do you mean, I'm powerless?" I would taunt as she attempted to explain the first step to me. "I spent years taking care of myself emotionally. Not to mention I'm an overachiever and I always succeed when I put my mind to something." She validated my concerns in an appropriate manner, not making me feel stupid for bringing up the objection. She then asked me to consider another spin on the concept of *powerlessness*. I also challenged Janet about why it was important to go to meetings (and go to so many of them), why she felt it was necessary for me to stay out of a romantic relationship, and why I had to change every aspect of my lifestyle if I was going to stay sober long term. Janet didn't spoon-feed me recovery. She let me hit some bumps along the way and reminded me that she was there for me when I was ready. And after a year of trial and error, when I finally took my last drink and became ready to take suggestions, I knew she would be the one to help me, so positive was the impression that she left on me in the craziness of early sobriety.

In this chapter, we explore how honoring the ideas of safety and flexibility is the most important feature of working with others in a trauma-sensitive manner. I explain the importance of safety to a traumatized person and share best practices for helping a person feel safe. Then we will explore how the stages of change model—widely used in the addiction treatment field—can help all of us better understand how to work with others in a flexible manner. Finally, we discuss some of the language problems with the twelve steps and time-honored recovery slogans uncovered in chapter 5 and how you can help to address reactions that traumatized newcomers may have upon encountering these difficulties. In this section, we'll learn that the best answer to newcomers' struggles with recovery may be to stop the *recoveryspeak*—the slogans, steps, and therapeutic clichés that abound in meetings and treatment literature—and simply validate their concerns.

Meet Them Where They're At

So much of what made Janet an exemplary recovery sponsor was that in her professional life, she had been a social worker and chemical dependency counselor. Thus, she was knowledgeable about what the fields of psychology, science, and medicine have to teach about addiction. This knowledge meant she understood the realities of traumatic stress and how it can interfere with learning new ways of living and embracing recovery. Her knowledge about addiction as a brain disease and the phenomena of craving also informed her that it's futile to get hung up on one specific drug as a prerequisite to attend and benefit from meetings. At the level of the limbic brain, addiction is addiction, and acceptance of people with cross-addiction issues is vital in all forms of recovery meetings today.

You do not have to be a social worker or drug and alcohol counselor to be an exemplary twelve-step sponsor or mentor/leader in another type of recovery program. The message in this chapter is that to be a trauma-sensitive professional or sponsor/recovery program leader, you need to honor certain principles, particularly safety and flexibility. Embrace the phrase *meet them where they're at* and let this phrase guide you. Although it may seem cliché or even trite, this phrase is important if we are going to make trauma-informed addiction care a reality. The spirit of its wisdom still needs to be more widely practiced in modern recovery so that traumatized people are not alienated as a result of being retraumatized by rigid professionals, sponsors, or community members.

Safety

People with unresolved trauma issues tend to live life on full alert. One commonly held belief is, I am not safe in the world. Sometimes, trauma survivors try to function while battling the belief, *I am not safe with myself.* The very prospect of change can seem unsafe: meetings, therapy, reaching out to people, and the process of self-exploration are risks. Making a decision to take these risks can be scary. Thus, as people positioned to help newcomers affected by trauma, we must recognize how important it is to create an environment that is as safe as possible in order for the change process to take place. When an individual affected by trauma does not feel safe, their tendency is to run. We must recognize this connection as a potential reason traumatized newcomers do not stay around long enough to give recovery a full chance to work.

Professionals who treat PTSD and other trauma-related issues consistently agree that establishing a sense of safety and a modicum of stabilization or preparation is the necessary first stage of treatment. In my early training, the words of John Briere and Catherine Scott, in their seminal text *Principles of Trauma Therapy,* made a special impression. Citing the work of pioneers like Judith Herman and Lisa Najavits (creator of the Seeking Safety treatment model), they clarify two important points about what safety means to people and what those of us who work with such people should and should not do:

- "Because trauma is about vulnerability to danger, safety is a crucial issue for trauma survivors. It is often only in perceived safe environments that those who have been exposed to danger can let down their guard and experience the relative luxury of introspection and connection."[10]

- "Psychological safety … means that the client will not perceive himself or herself to be criticized, humiliated, rejected, dramatically misunderstood, needlessly interrupted, or laughed at during the treatment process."[11]

Although these passages target counselors and professionals, they convey a general wisdom applicable to anyone working with addicted individuals.

Ensuring that people in your service feel safe is not about saying things like, "You're in a safe place," or "You're safe with me." Such statements are generally counterproductive to establishing a sense of safety for individuals because you are telling them what to feel. Safety is something that people have to navigate on their own. They may still be testing you, a treatment center, or a meeting, to determine if they are safe enough to engage. If in the middle of this investigative process they are told what to feel, their experience is invalidated and they may shut down further. Many well-intentioned folks I've met in all areas of service go to the default, *You're in a safe place,* in trying to educate a person on what it means to be someplace safe. And yet safety differs from person to person. What feels or seems safe to you may not to them.

There are certain best practices that can increase your chances for helping people feel safe enough in your care, in your treatment center, or at your meeting. Notice usage of the phrase *safe enough.* Some people, especially if they have not yet processed the fullness of their traumatic experience, may not believe it's even possible to feel one hundred percent safe in any setting. So know that, as a professional or a person working with traumatized individuals, meeting some perfect benchmark for safety may not be feasible. Following these best practices will help you do your best in providing as safe an environment as possible for healing to occur:

▸ **Do *not* retraumatize.** Sometimes, well-intentioned professionals and sponsors retraumatize without even realizing it. This tends to occur when we pressure people for too much detail about the nature of their traumatic experience before they are ready to give it. If we act like interrogators or pressure them to "get it all out," especially in meetings or groups where they may feel unsafe or unready, people may shut down, get activated, or stay away from the help they need. Retraumatization also occurs when we invalidate a person's experience by making comments such as, "You need to show some gratitude, there's always someone out there who has it worse." Even though that gratitude-based statement may be true and may eventually serve as a solution, bluntly saying it to a person without first validating the experience can open an old wound. Going into *recoveryspeak* or conveying toxic positivity when people need space to feel what they must feel in the moment is not helpful, especially when they feel cut off. Militaristic or dictatorial styles in sponsorship or counseling may also be part of the retraumatization culprit.

▶ **Do consider the role of shame in both addiction and trauma.** Shame is that essential belief that, at my core I am a bad person. An often-made distinction is that guilt is feeling bad about things you have *done,* and shame is feeling bad about who you *are.* The vast majority of people seeking treatment for addiction struggle with shame, and the complexity of this shame compounds if we add negative beliefs resulting from trauma into a person's cognitive mix. The toxicity of unaddressed shame is a major factor in why some of our most time-honored "helpful" comments can seem retraumatizing. Whether you realize it or not, as a professional, sponsor, or other leader, you are in a position of power to a vulnerable person. Your comments can make a powerful impact in reinforcing the shame scripts, or helping people to see new truths about themselves.

▶ **Do be nonjudgmental.** Being nonjudgmental does not mean that we should endorse unhealthy, illegal, or immoral behavior. However, it does mean that we ought to refrain from name-calling or other shaming, "hot seat" techniques that sometimes occur in addiction treatment centers or twelve-step meetings. We can call out or challenge the behaviors while always respecting the dignity of the person. Another major aspect of being nonjudgmental involves recognizing that such behaviors do not occur in a vacuum—they are generally a response to some unhealed wound or unmet need that needs treatment.

▶ **Do be genuine as you build rapport.** Respecting the dignity of a person does not mean that you have to be fake, phony, or saccharine. Addicted people and survivors of trauma can pick up on a fake person a mile away! Be the best, most genuine and most compassionate version of yourself possible. The more you've done your own work, the more naturally the relational process will flow when engaging others.

▶ **Ask open-ended questions.** Although this is a suggestion typically given to professionals, sponsors can benefit from it, too. An open-ended question is one that requires more than a simple yes or no answer. Open-ended questions typically avoid the word *why*, since the answer we tend to get with *why* questions is "I don't know." If a person genuinely doesn't know what compels her to engage in a certain destructive behavior, being asked *why* can come across as more shaming. Solid, open-ended questions typically begin with the words *what* or *how*. Examples include, "What were things like for you growing up?" or "How did that affect you?" Such questions invite new clients or sponsees to give you as much or as little detail as they are ready to give at any given point.

▶ **Do convey experience, strength, and hope.** In twelve-step circles, giving directives to people is not encouraged. Rather, sharing experience, strength, and hope is emphasized. Following this suggestion is massively important in conveying safety. Trauma survivors are much more likely to feel safe with us if we refrain from telling them what to do. And if a person does ask for a direct suggestion, still reply from that place of your own experience, strength, and hope. We should convey a sense—based on our own experiences—that hope for recovery is possible. We must be careful not to minimize in using this strategy. For example, avoid saying things like, "Well, everyone in this room has been through that, you'll get through it." First honor the struggle and then convey a message of hope that others on the path have gotten through it before. People can come into recovery feeling that they are some unique brand of crazy, defective, and terrible. Validate their feelings and then show them they are not.

▶ **Do have closure strategies ready.** This is an imperative best practice for professionals that is also useful to sponsors and other members of the public working with addicted individuals. One of the greatest errors I see in trauma treatment is when professionals let people leave a session while they are still overly activated, anxious, and jumpy, or the other end of the spectrum, shut down or dissociated. Hastily ending a session—a one-on-one meeting or a telephone call with a sponsee—with someone not reasonably grounded may put that person at risk for engaging in self-destructive behavior. At the end of a challenging session or phone call we can bring the conversation back to lighter, more general banter, or suggest that the person take some breaths or engage in some body-based action (e.g., go outside and take a walk, get into a hot bath, go and pick up your kids as you committed to do). Knowing some general grounding strategies, covered fully in chapters 7 and 9, can help. Using these strategies, we are helping bring the person back to a sense of equilibrium.

Flexibility and the Stages of Change

James Prochaska and Carlo DiClemente's stages of change model is often used in the addiction treatment field to conceptualize cases. Many professionals teach this model to the people they serve so they can get a better sense of where they are *at* in their change processes. The stages are:

- ▸ *Precontemplation:* The person is not prepared to take any action at this time or in the foreseeable future.

- ▸ *Contemplation:* The person is intending to change soon.

- ▸ *Preparation:* The person is intending to make a change in the immediate future.

- ▸ *Action:* The person is making significant changes in their lifestyle.

- ▸ *Maintenance:* The person is working to prevent relapse.

- ▸ *Termination:* The person has achieved one hundred percent self-efficacy, and the relapse potential is near zero. Most followers of twelve-step philosophy argue that a recovering addict is always in maintenance, and that stage six is not relevant. However, this stage is significant in other approaches to addiction recovery.

The stages of change can powerfully guide us in the approaches we take when working with people. They can help us from falling into the one-size-fits-all trap.

One of the most counterproductive approaches we can take, for instance, is to bombard a person who is precontemplative with a series of action-oriented interventions, such as, *Go to ninety meetings in ninety days,* or, *It's time to start working your steps.* Also, avoid the directive, *If it worked for me, it can work for anybody.* In the following table, we take a look at each stage of change, characteristics of people in each stage, and approaches that work best with people—especially addicted survivors of trauma—at each stage.

STAGE OF CHANGE	COMMONLY ENCOUNTERED ATTITUDES ABOUT RECOVERY	SUGGESTED APPROACHES
Precontemplation	"I don't have a problem, but other people say I do."	• supportive listening • invite to attend a meeting or support group just to "check it out"
Contemplation	"I'm thinking that it might be a good idea if I cut back on my drinking. I'm starting to get too depressed."	• supportive listening • invite to check out a meeting or support group, explain how meetings can benefit
Preparation	"Well, what my counselor says and what I hear at meetings makes sense; I just don't know if I'm ready to really commit."	• supportive listening with sharing of experience, strength, and hope—if listener is receptive • make the suggestion for more regular meeting attendance and getting to know more people in recovery

(continues)

STAGE OF CHANGE	COMMONLY ENCOUNTERED ATTITUDES ABOUT RECOVERY	SUGGESTED APPROACHES
Action	"I've gotta stop. I'm ready to take suggestions and listen."	• make the suggestion for regular meetings (typically ninety meetings in the first ninety days is suggested, but a minimum of three to four a week may be sufficient depending on the person) • make the suggestion to begin step work with the guidance of a sponsor • advise building a support group
Maintenance	"Recovery is a way of life for me."	• as a sponsor or a support figure, work out a plan with the person to determine number of meetings, best possible recovery tools, and if needed, outside help for long-term wellness
Termination	"I don't have a problem with drinking or drugs anymore, it's all in the past. I am recovered."	• supportive listening • ask about quality of life, and, if appropriate, suggest that checking out some meetings again or connecting with others in recovery may enhance wellness

This table is here to serve you as a general guide to the nature of our approach in working with newcomers. People who are new to recovery, especially those who are still jumpy around anything different due to the residual effects of trauma, need to be worked with in a flexible manner. This approach is important while they determine if recovery, specifically recovery groups and people, are safe for them. Honoring their needs for safety and flexibility will have a positive impact on retention in the long run. An often-quoted recovery slogan shared with newcomers is, "Don't leave before the miracle happens." We must consider that our behaviors can impact whether or not a person sticks around.

Addressing the Language Problems with Slogans and Steps

Comprehending the language of recovery can be a difficult task for any newcomer, especially one who has experienced language as a means of wounding. Think about verbal or emotional abuse survivors in particular—the least little saying delivered in the wrong tone can trigger a profound reaction. This is not to say that those of us in positions of guidance need to mind every little word we say with newcomers; that wouldn't be realistic. There are, however, two points to consider. When sharing new knowledge like slogans and steps with those first coming into recovery programs, pay attention to your delivery and tone. From my experience working with clients, so many trauma survivors are alienated from twelve-step meetings or other support groups because people came across to them as know-it-alls or they felt others were talking down to them.

The other major point to keep in mind is that resistance to new knowledge is completely normal for someone going through the lifestyle changes required for recovery. A person emotionally reacting to a certain slogan or step is not necessarily a negative development, nor does it mean that recovery and the people who are part of recovery groups have failed that person. It usually means that a newcomer will need support as they experience and work through the reaction. A sponsor or counselor can explain the intention of the slogan and entertain some dialogue if the person is open to it.

The key is to validate (honoring the emotional or limbic brain) before appealing to reason (the neocortex or rational brain). Let's take as an example the slogan, "You're only as sick as your secrets," reviewed in chapter 5. Chances are high that a vulnerable person will still be exposed to it. Here is a sample dialogue that demonstrates how a professional or a counselor (helper) may best address the traumatized newcomer's reaction to the slogan:

Newcomer: *I'm not too crazy about something an old lady told me at the Wednesday afternoon discussion meeting. I was talking about how hard it was for me to even come to these meetings because of all this shame I have about my past, and she said, in a real nasty way, "You're only as sick as your secrets."*

Helper: *Oh dear.*

Newcomer: *That really pissed me off.*

Helper: *Well, I can certainly see why it would.*

Newcomer: *I mean, she doesn't know me at all.*

Helper: *Can you tell me what upset you so much about hearing that?*

Newcomer: *Yeah, it's like, who the heck is she, to say something like that—she doesn't know me! She doesn't know that if I didn't keep secret all those things that my stepfather did to us, our mother would have put us out.*

Helper: *So, for you, keeping secrets really was a matter of survival.*

Newcomer: *Um, yeah.*

Helper: *Now I can definitely see why hearing that slogan upset you so much.*

Newcomer: *It's like she was calling me sick for doing what I had to do.*

Helper: *Well, yeah. Was there anything else about the meeting that bothered you?*

Newcomer: *Not really.*

Helper: *Okay. I definitely think what that lady at the meeting did to you was not cool, just saying the slogan like that in front of everybody without really knowing you. I'm certainly not a fan of that slogan and how it's worded. However, the intention behind "You're only as sick as your secrets" may have some value as it applies to recovery. Are you willing to let me explain?*

Newcomer: *Sure.*

Helper: *"You're only as sick as your secrets" doesn't mean that you have to spill your guts to everyone about your past. It does mean that all those things you've been holding in over the years have kept you stuck—maybe stuck is a better word than sick—and they will eventually need to come out in order for you to move forward in your recovery and feel better about yourself. Only when you're ready, and only with the people you deem trustworthy.*

Newcomer: *Hmm … well, that makes a lot more sense. I don't think I would have overreacted so much if she had explained it that way. Can we talk about what I need to do to get ready?*

Helper: *Absolutely.*

Although not all conversations will go this smoothly, this is a general guideline for validating first in order to lead to a more productive path for reasoning. This method can work with just about any problem a newcomer has with a slogan or language in the steps: validate, then explain. You will typically find that the newcomer is open to further exploration. Proper guidance delivered with respect for where people find themselves in the stages of change is crucial.

Let's take a look at other examples of potential problem areas that a newcomer with a history of trauma may experience, this time using the steps. Here is how a dialogue may play out with someone having difficulty surrounding step one:

Newcomer: *Powerless. I hate that word powerless.*

Helper: *What do you hate about it?*

Newcomer: *I don't know … it's like saying that I'm giving up. I'm not the kind of person to quit.*

Helper: *Knowing what I know about your history, you're definitely not a quitter, you're a survivor.*

Newcomer: *So I don't like admitting that I'm powerless.*

109

Helper: *Well, can I make a suggestion that might help?*

Newcomer: *Sure.*

Helper: *The step just asks us to admit that we're powerless over alcohol, not that we're powerless people.*

Newcomer: *What's the difference?*

Helper: *Admitting that we're powerless over alcohol, or whatever the drug may be, is simply admitting that when we drink or use, our lives go to hell. The alcohol and the drugs will always win. That's all the step is saying. It doesn't say that we're powerless people. Actually, it kind of gives us a way to take our power back.*

Newcomer: *What do you mean? Isn't that a contradiction?*

Helper: *You're right, it does seem like an oxymoron or a contradiction. And I had the same struggle when I came into recovery. I eventually learned that in admitting that the alcohol would always win and not even trying to fight that fight, the real power inside of me—the power I possessed to survive and to make good decisions—was able to come through.*

Newcomer: *I still don't know if I fully understand it, but the way you explained it makes a lot more sense.*

Another notorious problem area is with steps four and five. Let's see how these difficulties may be worked through in a trauma-responsive manner:

Newcomer: *I hate step four. Every time I've tried doing this recovery thing before, this is where I quit.*

Helper: *May I ask what's made it difficult?*

Newcomer: *One time I had a sponsor, a real by-the-book type of person, make me do it the way they do it in the Big Book. And it made no sense to me at all taking inventory by listing my resentments and looking at "my part in it." I mean, I can see where that applies for some things, but how am I supposed to look at "my part in it" when some of the people on my resentment list are people who abused me?*

Helper: *I get it. That's a problem for a lot of us and I really don't like how some people in the program badger trauma survivors with "What's your part in it?"*

Newcomer: *Well that's good to hear. So you're not going to make me do it the way it's done in the Big Book?*

Helper: *Not if that doesn't seem to work for you and makes you avoid the step.*

Newcomer: *I also tried doing NA once and those workbooks they use for the steps are no better. I did exactly as they suggested and they just made me realize what a worthless piece of shit I am.*

Helper: *So based on your past experiences, what would you need to safely work a fourth and fifth step?*

Newcomer: *Well, if you can help me through my writing that would be a plus. I also had another sponsor who said "Don't call me again until your fourth step is written out," so needless to say I never called them again.*

Helper: *Yup. So would it help if you could call or text me to check in when you're feeling stuck with your writing?*

Newcomer: *Sure thing.*

Helper: *If I may, something I found helpful when I wrote out my fourth step was the advice my sponsor gave me to "Just do it as best as you can for now—it doesn't have to be perfect." And also, remember that part of taking inventory is jotting down the good, helpful qualities about yourself too. There are lots of different ways to take inventory—you can just do some free-writing. What's in the books and workbooks are just suggestions. But if that way keeps you from taking an honest look at yourself and your behavior—which is really the point of the step—try another way. I'll give you some feedback as you go if it seems like you may be blocking or avoiding.*

Newcomer: *Wow, you mean we can do the step that way?*

Helper: *Sure thing. And remember that a lot of the behaviors that you may take responsibility for in the step are just things you did in response to trauma. Things that helped you survive. And if you are noticing that there are patterns* *coming up about that, you probably want to address those things with your therapist as part of your deeper work.*

Newcomer: *So when it comes time to do the fifth, can I use my therapist? Or you? Because when I was in treatment I seemed to get the message that a minister was the best person to hear it. And that is not going to work for me.*

Helper: *The step just says, another human being. That is your choice, as long as you pick the person you can feel safe enough talking to as you get vulnerable. We can cross that bridge of helping you decide when you come to it.*

You can address all the language problems that newcomers may encounter in the twelve steps or other recovery approaches using this method of *validate-explain-discuss.* Of course, you'll need to account for individual differences in experience and temperament. The more effectively you're able to do that, the more effectively you'll be able to work with the newcomer. If a person is having a hard time connecting with the 1930s language of the book *Alcoholics Anonymous* or other texts, consider having them look at other books that may cover the sample principles in modern language. Take a look at some of the websites and other reading recommendations in the Appendix.

No Program Knows It All

A vital aspect of trauma-sensitive recovery is acknowledging that no recovery program can be a panacea or cure-all. So often, people new to recovery encounter this attitude from others and it's unfortunate. Comments like, "You don't need those psych meds, all you need are the twelve steps of recovery," or, "You're complicating it by going to all those shrinks; you gotta keep it simple and work the program" abound. Even though self-help groups and their members are not bound to the same professional ethics as those working in treatment, it is truly troubling to hear that such attitudes are common in recovery groups. Whether the people who make these comments realize it or not, they are actually doing more harm than good to the reputation of recovery programs in the community. Moreover, they are going against the guidance that Bill Wilson himself made in writing *Alcoholics Anonymous,* in which he stressed the value of outside help and guidance.

Beth sought out services at a local counseling agency where a therapist specialized in the integrated treatment of trauma in addicted women. Eager to work on some issues related to Beth's past, her counselor did a preliminary screening of her safety needs and asked if she was going to meetings and had a sponsor. Beth replied, "Well, I'm doing about eight meetings a week. There aren't too many sober women in my town, and I asked the one with the most sobriety to sponsor me. But every time we talk, she always brings it back to how I shouldn't be on so many psych meds. We haven't even gotten to any steps yet because that's all she wants to talk about."

After a few preliminary sessions, Beth and her counselor mutually concluded that it would be best to seek out a new sponsor. Beth's psychiatric symptoms, which included a long history of PTSD and suicide attempts, were stable. The psychotropic medications she was taking for maintenance were not considered addictive. When Beth found a sponsor who understood mental illness and didn't always insist on bringing their discussion back to her medications, Beth was able to work the steps and obtain the support she needed. Both activities helped her more fully invest in the counseling process. Eventually, her PTSD symptoms went into remission, her suicidal ideations totally disappeared, and with a year of sobriety she began attending a technical college.

Sometimes, the best approach you can take in working with a person struggling with recovery is to put down the *recoveryspeak*. So often, people just need a human connection when in distress and don't need to have solutions immediately thrown at them. Consider this sharing from author Kiera Van Gelder, author of *The Buddha and the Borderline*. A woman in long-term recovery through Narcotics Anonymous who found herself on disability for mental illness, Kiera in this portion of her memoir puts this problem into sobering perspective:

Whenever I'm in pain, falling apart, or in crisis, [my father] gives me slogans: Easy does it. First things first. Keep it simple. Ask your higher power for help. Go to a meeting. If I were to call him and tell him I've just split up with Bennet, I doubt I'd get sympathy. He'd probably just suggest I do another moral inventory. F*&% moral inventories.[12]

Although a twelve-step purist may read Kiera's words and accuse her of being resistant, take her perspective into consideration. Her voice reflects the views of so many who struggle with both trauma and addiction recovery.

If you are a sponsor, and a newcomer with trauma concerns is not connecting after you make attempts at the guidance style offered in this chapter, it may be a sign that what *Alcoholics Anonymous* calls "outside help" may be needed. Depending on a person's needs, outside help can refer to a counselor, clinical social worker, psychologist, psychiatrist, pastoral counselor, minister, or alternative health care provider (e.g., acupuncturist, massage therapist, bodywork specialist, yoga teacher, or therapist). AA and the other fellowships endorse the use of outside help when warranted and needed. Newcomers with traumatic stress concerns may benefit from outside help at various points in early recovery, especially if they are struggling with fourth- and fifth-step work. Seeking outside help with twelve-step recovery is not just for the newcomer. People with years in recovery often seek outside help from professionals if too many issues surface, affecting quality of life, that the twelve steps alone cannot address.

Affirming a person's need for this wide range of help is necessary and supported by the core teachings of twelve-step programs. Discouraging such help continues to happen at an alarming rate, and it remains one of the greatest stains on the reputation of twelve-step meetings and sponsors among mental health professionals. No one program and no one person knows it all. Strengthening the quality of recovery services for our new generations means accepting that we are all in this together, continuing to build those bridges and tear down the walls.

TOOLKIT STRATEGY:
THE STAGES OF CHANGE

In this toolkit strategy, you are invited to use the stages of change model to help you better understand the people you serve:

- *If you are currently working with clients that have both addiction and trauma concerns, or if you are presently sponsoring recovering individuals in some type of recovery group, take a few moments and jot down the names or initials of those individuals.*

- *Go through the list, evaluate where each person is "at" in the stages of change model. Consider whether your approach with that individual is appropriate for where they are in the stages of change. If not, how can you modify your approach?*

- *Reflect back and recall what you were like as you passed through each stage of change in early recovery. What can reflecting on your own experiences teach you about what these folks may be experiencing, especially the ones you find to be resistant?*

Bring Your Butt, the Rest Will Follow—The Importance of Honoring the Body in Addiction Recovery

One day, Janet declared in her thick, memorable Kentucky accent, "Remember, Jamie, chapter 6 of the (AA) Big Book is called *Into Action,* not *Into Thinking*." She then shared with me another recovery saying: "It's easier to act your way into better thinking than to think your way into better acting." She reminded me that if people are unable to go through the motions of action with sincerity, then they should *act as if.* Sometimes when I would make myself frantic by overthinking a situation, she would say: "Too much analysis leads to paralysis."

While sayings and slogans can have their down sides, many of them encapsulate some trauma-focused wisdom. Those slogans that encourage action instead of thinking are, indeed, on to something....

Remember what we covered in chapter 3—our human, triune brain is three brains working together as one: the reptilian (survival) brain, the limbic (emotional) brain, and the neocortical (rational) brain. If you recall, when the survival and emotional brains are in the metaphorical driver's seat (which typically happens when some stimulus triggers a person), the rational brain goes offline. Although the rational brain is what makes us uniquely human, it is also the most complex to access of the three brains. Hence, we can think about, talk about, and analyze a problem until we are blue in the face. Unless we access those lower brains as well, it is hard for the new information to truly integrate. The best interventions when a person is activated (short term) or stuck (long term) are those that work from the bottom of the brain and move upward, not the other way around. Working with the downstairs brain is not as hard as it seems—it responds well to action and movement. The higher, neocortical brain is what responds to and works with speech or talk, logic, and yes—thinking.

Let's take a look at a pure recovery example to further illuminate this point. One of the classic twelve-step recovery tools is using the phone. If triggered, tempted, or otherwise overwhelmed, people are advised to call their sponsor or other members of their support group. Although many people in these situations report that talking to someone in recovery can be a lifesaver, the primary action at work may not be the talking. To call a sponsor or another support figure, you first need to pick up the phone—a clear action step. Then, you need to dial the numbers—another action step. Once the person answers the phone, a connection occurs. As a result of that connection, you may experience a calming response whether or not either of you speak a word. This relational connection is the limbic brain at work. If your sponsor allows you to vent and then provides validation, the rational brain is not particularly involved. Once more, the relational potency governed by the limbic brain—where we are injured but where we can deeply heal—is at play. Thus, even if the conversation does reveal excellent, rational insight to you or any other person making the call, several action steps took place first that allowed your brains to be more open to rational guidance and reasoning.

Using the rational brain to cope is not all negative. Many people in recovery from both trauma and addiction wish to operate more from their rational minds and less with their emotional minds. However, true recovery requires integrating the two and allowing them to work together. The best chance for success comes by using the lower brain as an access point for healing, certainly not by avoiding it. Put simply, take the action first; the thoughts and words will follow. The best trauma therapies utilize this logic. This understanding can blend elegantly with many of the tools and philosophies of twelve-step recovery. In this chapter, I look at the elements of twelve-step recovery philosophies that already take this action-oriented approach to heart. Then we look at simple, body-based strategies from the psychotherapeutic and other healing traditions such as grounding, breathing, muscle relaxation, mindfulness, and other embodied approaches. I present the most trauma-informed way for people to learn these strategies and integrate them into their daily recovery programs. Such body-based strategies are essential to those with trauma issues who may have a difficult time sitting still in meetings or tolerating the intense emotion that comes along with step work.

Into Action, Not into Thinking

The physical steps required to pick up a telephone and reach out are action-based steps that can aid in recovery. Several other examples of action-based steps that twelve-step recovery promotes may prove especially useful to the recovering person with unresolved trauma. I already covered how use of the telephone is an excellent, action-based step. Let's take a look at some others.

GOING TO MEETINGS.　Many people report that in the early days of recovery, not much from the meetings really "sank in." However, the mere action of having to be somewhere, interact with others, and sit still for an hour or so was a form of therapy in and of itself. Sometimes when I go to a meeting, I don't get much out of it—I don't connect with the speaker or I don't have much to contribute to the discussion. Yet the act of committing to sit still for an hour is also the art of me practicing, or putting into action, the mindfulness attitude of patience. Sometimes it's a practice in distress tolerance, which I need plenty of in both my recovery and in life generally. While I don't advocate that people go to meetings where they feel repeatedly retraumatized or insulted, learning to sit with a healthy amount of unpleasantness, boredom, or discomfort helps to build our distress tolerance muscles.

Thus, I can honestly say that I take something out of every meeting, even if it is what I gain in the way of patience or distress tolerance. Taking the actions over time will make a difference. If you are a sponsor or counselor working with new clients in recovery, it is critical to emphasize the importance of such action steps. Let the people you work with know that even if things don't seem to be sinking in at the rational brain level at first, that's fine—in fact, it's normal in a brain recovering from the impact of addiction, trauma and/or dissociation, or their interplay. By taking action, we are taking steps to help ourselves.

REACHING OUT TO OTHERS. For newcomers, especially those used to isolating themselves, reaching out to others may seem as scary as walking down a set of train tracks in the black of night with no one around to guide you. If you are working with newcomers, emphasize the importance of small steps. Going around and shaking people's hands at meetings, even if they aren't making meaningful connections, is an action step. If shaking hands or hugging is not your style, still consider walking up to people and saying hello. Joining other people from the fellowship for coffee after a meeting, even if they just hang around and listen at first, is still an action step. Taking the action lays the groundwork for meaningful connections with others to eventually take place.

PRAYER AND OTHER SPIRITUAL EXERCISES. If a person is open to the spiritual aspects of a recovery program, there are ample opportunities for action. One of the reasons so many religious traditions incorporate ritual is that for many, the actions of ritual or ceremony help in connecting with a Higher Power. It is no coincidence that rituals involve action.

Prayers can be done in a variety of forms, and most of those forms involve some type of action. Whether you are getting down on your knees and folding your hands to say prayers in the morning, driving in your car and shouting out at God, or sitting through a religious service, the body is on some level taking action. Even if there are no experiences of spiritual connection, taking action can serve as a powerful coping mechanism to get through difficult moments. When performed over time, they can serve a function in helping people develop new, more positive habits.

Consider the case of Gary, a working-class man who entered twelve-step recovery in his mid-forties. His sponsor suggested that he start praying to ask the God of his understanding to keep him sober. Gary was resistant.

Then, his sponsor asked Gary if he'd be willing to get on his knees every morning and say, "God, help me to stay sober today," and to get on his knees every night and say, "God, thank you for keeping me sober today." These tasks were not a spiritual exercise per se, but a "trick" he could try to help him stay sober, because so many people had done it before. Gary felt he had nothing to lose, and the first week or so, he reported that the words meant nothing. He decided to stick with it. Midway through the second week, he came to mean it, and at the end of the month, he surprised even himself when he realized he was still sober. What initially started as a "fake it 'til you make it" action process eventually helped Gary develop spirituality, and he is in long-term recovery today.

Various twelve-step fellowships and other recovery publishers have made a wide variety of daily meditation books available, also excellent mechanisms to help a person take action-oriented steps along a spiritual path. I have a very personal connection to this ritual. When I first came into recovery, I had no problem believing in God. I did have a problem disciplining myself with morning prayer. Janet suggested that I place one of my daily meditation books on the toilet seat so that when I woke up in the morning, I had to pick up the book in order to lift the toilet seat! Thus, I would have it in my hands and it would remind me to start my day on a spiritual note, reading the meditation and saying a little prayer. By the end of thirty days of my toilet meditations, I formed a new habit. To this day, I cannot even dream of starting my day without at least a little prayer and meditation reading. Although I no longer keep the meditation book on the toilet seat, I do still keep it in my bathroom or at my bedside.

Recovery fellowships pass along many spiritual techniques that incorporate action components, even if these principles aren't in the books or spoken about widely at meetings. Another favorite of mine is the "God Box." With this technique, you simply get an old shoebox, jar, or other container and put it in a special place, designating it as your God Box. Whenever a problem or issue cannot stop swirling around in your head, get out a piece of paper and write down what's bothering you. Then, fold the paper as much as you can. I like to keep folding the paper over until I can't fold it anymore—it helps to work out the frustration more physically—and then place it in the

God Box. For many of us, the act of writing it down and getting it out is a key part of the healing. And it's clearly action-oriented. If, later in the day, the person, place, or situation starts swirling around again, remind yourself, "I put it in the God Box; it's out of my hands now," and bring up the visual of putting the paper in the box. You can also use whatever spiritual principles or nonspiritual principle you like as a variation to this exercise (for example, call it a "universe capsule," instead of the God Box).

Once the box gets full, choose another action-based activity to further the ritual or ceremony. Some people like to clean out their God boxes every time they fill up, and read through the slips of paper. Many of us are surprised that the things that we stressed over six months ago have long resolved. At that point, you can take those slips of paper out of the God Box and keep them in a separate *thank you* box. Some people take great comfort in burning them (outside, of course), with the smoke rising up to the sky representing a thanksgiving. Some people flush them down the toilet as a symbol of release. The options are endless, as long as they are meaningful to the person carrying out the ritual.

WRITING AND EXPRESSION. Whether it's jotting down a simple statement and placing it in a God Box or spilling out your soul into an entire novel, writing provides a means of emotional release for many people in recovery. The quality of what you write is not important. Taking the embodied, actionable step of writing to get stuff out is the imperative. That stuff can include obsessions, emotional angst, resentments, past memories that you're holding on to, or simply a list of stressors that may just need to come out and be visible on paper. When clients are resistant to journaling, I often tell them that I'm not going to grade them like I would an English paper, and they don't even have to keep what they write if they don't want it. After you write a journal entry, you have every right to rip it up. This act of ripping or tearing the pages can be therapeutic in a body-based sense. These actions can further the process of working out the stress, especially if ripping up symbolizes "I don't want this anymore."

Another journal-based writing exercise that can be helpful is the gratitude list. A piece of folk knowledge in twelve-step recovery is that the best way out of self-pity is to foster an internal sense of gratitude. Although this may be a hard sell for people new to recovery with a difficult life due to trauma or other circumstances, if presented lovingly by a trusted sponsor, this technique can be quite effective. With the gratitude list, a person writes down at least ten things they are grateful for at any given time. I encourage my clients to get as specific as, "I have a place to live right now," or, "I have food to eat." Other popular entries include, "I still have my children in my life," or, "I have been able to stay sober this long." The action-oriented process of writing down the positives can be therapeutic. Tangibly seeing the entries on paper can help people refocus on the positives in their life in a way that just thinking about them cannot.

For the same reasons that writing out a gratitude list can be helpful (instead of just thinking about it), so too can writing out step work facilitate the process of mental retention. Different sponsors have various approaches to guiding sponsees through the twelve steps, and many choose to have sponsees write out inventories (as in step four) or make lists (as in step eight). Some fellowships like NA use workbook sheets to help members work each step in depth, and incorporate writing as a main mechanism for the step work. Although writing out the steps is not for everyone, the action that writing requires can be a beneficial part of the process, especially if it helps individuals to take further, healthier action as they work the steps.

As an expressive arts therapist with an artistic soul, I've long allowed my clients and sponsees the modification of using the arts in places where writing traditionally may be recommended. For instance, making a gratitude collage, playlist, or other art piece may feel much more nourishing and helpful than just writing down a list. And you always have the option of further embodying your practice by dancing to any playlists you create! Songwriting is another avenue of expression that may work for people in recovery. I didn't even realize I could write a song until I learned the guitar as a way to counteract the boredom of early sobriety. As I learned to play chords, I eventually started pairing these with some of the ideas and poems I'd written in my journal and voilà—songs emerged! Singing those songs also allowed emotions and experiences to pass through my body and be released in a healthy way.

The practice of visual journaling is becoming increasingly popular, and it is a favorite among my students and members of the Dancing Mindfulness and Institute for Creative Mindfulness communities. As the name suggests, in visual journaling, you keep a series of drawings, paintings, and mixed-media work in a journal-style book as a means of process. While you can certainly mix writing into the visual journaling process, opening the pathway to more than one medium of expression is vital for people who find the directive to just write it out too confining or impractical.

REPETITION OR RITUAL STRATEGIES.   A few other folkways of recovery are worth mentioning because they incorporate strong, body-based components. I discussed the importance of using the phone earlier in the chapter. An issue that often comes up with newcomers is, "What if I can't reach someone, especially my sponsor, on the phone?" The simple answer to this legitimate question is to keep calling. Even if they dial ten numbers collected at meetings and no one is there, keep pressing ahead with the action, picking up the phone and dialing the number.

The expanding presences of recovery resources or groups on social media can make it easier for people with access to connect in a way that wasn't available when the earlier edition came out. While the pros and cons of the internet as a means of connection can be debated at length, I believe that these online resources are true lifelines for people who may not be able to connect in any other way. Even if a person doesn't end up connecting with someone on the phone or online, taking five to ten minutes to get busy with their body in the simple, healthy action of dialing may be just enough time for the craving or trigger to pass.

Many people find similar relief in doing household tasks, especially scrubbing and cleaning, as a coping skill. This action makes perfect sense because it uses the body, not the mind. As a friend of mine once shared, "During my first year of sobriety, I had the cleanest toilet bowl in town. I must have scrubbed it twice a day as a coping thing!"

Gifts of coins, chips, and key chains in many fellowships mark milestones in recovery. Many people proudly carry around their thirty-day chip or nine-year coin (or whatever the item may be) as a form of security, a physical reminder of all they have accomplished. These physical tokens often help for coping and grounding. For instance, during a rough day, a person may pull a coin out of her purse and just hold it in her hand for a few minutes. The physical sensation of the coin brings the body into her process of practicing distress tolerance.

A humorous and actually helpful saying that circulates in meetings when someone receives a coin or a chip is, "Now, if you ever think about drinking, put that coin on your tongue. When it dissolves, then you can have a drink." This strategy has worked for many people I know, and from a trauma-sensitive, neurological perspective, it makes sense because there is such power in the physical, as opposed to the cognitive, reminder. Please be mindful not to choke on the coin!

Mindful, Bodyful Coping Strategies

When I do trainings on trauma-sensitive addiction treatment, I use the phrase *coping skills* a hundred times because the phrase is so important. The reality of recovery—especially for someone with trauma concerns—is that more unpleasant emotions, thoughts, and issues will surface, the longer the alcohol or drugs have been out of the system. This idea makes total sense to anyone who has ever gone through recovery or watched people go through the process. If you take away people's numbing agent, they are going to start feeling and experiencing with full force, and having healthy coping skills to deal with that process is essential. If the phrase *coping skills* doesn't sit well with you, synonyms include *distress tolerance strategies, self-soothing,* or *affect regulation techniques*. Whatever you call the actions you require in order to manage and handle what life throws at you in as healthy and adaptive a manner as possible, they will work. Although many of the twelve-step ideas discussed in the previous section can serve as positive coping skills to help a recovering person stay stable through adjustments, more help is often needed for coping. Skills that make use of the whole self—especially the body, and as many senses as possible—are the most successful.

In this section I cover and give examples of the major skill categories I teach my clients—grounding, breath work, pressure points, muscle relaxation, mindfulness, yoga, other embodied approaches, and the expressive arts. If you are a clinician with a willingness to first practice these skills yourself, my hope is that you can integrate these tools into your practice immediately. Most if not all can be taught in groups, as long as you allow time for some questions and discussions afterward about how people may need to modify the skills. The number one thing that makes a skill trauma-informed is your willingness to modify it for the person you serve. Reading skills out of a book only goes so far. These scripts usually don't take the individual experience of the person into account. For example, an exercise you found online may have you do a certain breath with a particular hold strategy for eight to ten repetitions. The person may only be able to do one or two repetitions at first without the hold, and that is more than okay. Start with what a person can do and then work from there.

All these skills are also appropriate for sponsors or general members of recovery fellowships to share with others. The imperative is that you first try them yourselves and if you feel in over your head with certain skills, know when it's best to have a person consult with a professional like a therapist or a yoga or meditation teacher in the community. The best practices for sharing the skills that follow in a trauma-informed setting include:

- Eyes can stay open during all of the exercises.

- Time in the exercise is variable—even if a description you read says five minutes or eight to ten rounds of a practice, know that you can cut down the time so people can adjust.

- Let people know how long the exercise, specifically the silence, will last—they can create more anxiety for themselves if they don't know how long something takes.

- Clarify any misconceptions or misinformation about what mindfulness or meditation means (more on this in the section on mindfulness).

- Be open to variations in practice—don't assume that just because something works for you, that it will work the exact same way for everyone else.

▶ Avoid any prolonged holding with breath exercises, especially when a person is first learning breath.

▶ Have your own practice—this will help you modify if what you read out of a book seems to fail you.

If you get stuck with learning or adapting any of these skills from the book, please visit my complimentary resources website at www.traumamadesimple .com for video instruction in all of these skills.

GROUNDING. Grounding is the practice of using all available senses and experiences to come into or remain in the here and now. People who are struggling with unhealed trauma can have a very difficult time staying present in the moment and in their bodies. While it's imperative to teach grounding skills to all individuals seeking recovery, it's especially important if dissociation is part of the person's experience. The practices of grounding may seem elementary on the surface, yet for people who struggle to be present, learning to ground can be radically life changing.

There are many different ways to ground and these are just a few. Grounding can be as simple as holding a rock or recovery coin, sensing into the texture of a delightfully soft blanket, or smelling your favorite essential oil—anything that helps you to know you are here, now, and present. You can literally hug a tree if you find this helpful, or take a walk around the block or down the road, paying attention to the sensation of your feet hitting the pavement. I heard a speaker at a twelve-step meeting once share, "One of my favorite things to do is look down at my feet. I've learned my feet will not lie to me. When I'm stressed it's usually because I'm feeling the pull of the past or obsessing about the future. But my feet always tell me exactly where I am."

If these strategies don't quite resonate with you, try these classic techniques for grounding:

▶ Take a look around the space that you are in right now. Start naming the different things that you see. Be as specific as possible, for instance, "I see the carpet below my feet. The carpet is blue with some bits of brown in the thread. I see the lamp on the desk. The base of the lamp is brown glass and the shade is beige."

- ▶ Keep going for as long as you need, until you feel fully present in the space.

- ▶ If you need, move on to the other senses: What are you hearing (or not hearing) in this moment, in this space? Observe and describe. What are you smelling? What are you tasting? Then, use your hands and either touch your clothes or make contact with the chair or the table. Observe and describe touch sensation.

However you proceed with the rest of these skills, start with grounding first. If you or the people you work with feel uneasy or unsafe in any way during these other techniques, think of returning to basic grounding as a home base. You will also discover that it becomes easier to approach these other skills if you first feel sufficiently grounded.

BREATH WORK.   We all need breath to live, yet so many of us don't take the time or spend the energy that we need to breathe deeply and fully. For those living with the aftereffects of trauma, it can seem like we are moving through life in a state of holding our breaths. Breathing— although a tremendous resource that can help restore balance to the body—can also be a trigger. Our bodies may not know how to handle breathing so deeply and feeling relaxed. A client once mentioned to me, "Wow, that breathing exercise you showed me is really working. I'm relaxed but I don't like that—now I can't protect myself."

I validated her experience, returned her to grounding, and asked if she'd like to try again but more slowly. So we proceeded with her just doing one or two breaths at a time, then returning to grounding, then having her continue to explore breath. Spending just a few minutes a day on some mindful, concentrated breathing can help the body and the mind more effectively cooperate with each other. Remember that it may not be as easy for some people to learn, so that's why modifications and options are necessary.

Here is a simple way to begin breath work. As a start, pay attention to your normal breathing for thirty seconds to a minute. If your mind starts to drift, that's okay, just bring the focus back to your breath. A whole minute can be a challenge to start; not to worry, start slowly and be gentle with yourself. If you can eventually work your breath practice up to three minutes, you will find that your breath will be there for you to help you calm yourself when you need it most. It takes practice. If you need the extra help, consider using this classic mantra as a guide, saying to yourself as you breathe: "As I breathe in, I know I'm breathing in—as I breathe out, I know I'm breathing out." A simple "in-out" will also do.

Once you can stay with your natural breath for at least a minute, consider experimenting with some of these other breaths and notice if you (or those you work with) find them helpful:

Diaphragmatic breathing: Otherwise known as belly breathing— breathe in through your nose and out through your mouth or nose, focusing on the rise and fall of the upper belly and the extension it creates around your entire midsection. This will help you to notice the diaphragmatic muscle (the dome-shape muscle at the bottom of your rib cage) as the source of deeper breathing. Expand your belly as far as it will go (without forcing or striving) as you inhale. As you exhale, release the air and notice the belly pull back in toward your center. If it will help you, put one or both hands on your stomach to concentrate on this rise and fall motion. Keep the inhales and exhales even when you begin, although you may eventually notice that a longer exhale may feel better in the body.

Complete breathing (three-part): In this strategy, begin by engaging a belly breath. This time, continue the inhale motion up into the ribs and chest, noticing an expansion. This is a deeper inhale that may feel a little too much at first, so be sure to go slowly. Keep the inhales and exhales even when you begin, although you may eventually notice that a longer exhale may feel better in the body. Experiment with the exhales. You can try pursing the lips as if you are blowing out through a straw, allowing for a slower and more deliberate exhale that helps many people reduce symptoms of anxiety. You can also experiment with a quicker, more rapid "sigh of relief" to your exhale. Don't be afraid to really make a sound of letting go!

***Ujjayi* breathing ("ocean breathing" or "Darth Vader breathing"):** This breath, which literally means "victorious breath," can be highly effective as an affect regulator during moments of high stress or intensity. In the most basic technique, think of it as a noisy in-through-the-nose, out-through-the-nose breath. The mouth should stay closed during this breath, pursing the lips slightly. If possible, focus on constricting the muscles in the back of the throat to make the sound louder. Keep the inhales and exhales even when you begin, although you may eventually notice that a longer exhale may feel better in the body. Don't be afraid to get loud, hearing the sound of the ocean within your own head!

These breaths are a sample and ought to be the foundation of any coping skills toolkit. There are dozens of different techniques and variations that you and those you work with can attempt, many of them appearing on www .traumamadesimple.com and other resources provided in the Appendix.

Trial and error with respect to safety is the key. Find which breath or combination of breaths will work the best for you and those you serve. Keep a few precautions in mind. First, start slowly. Although breathing may seem like common sense, many traumatic responses involve halted breath. Very often, trauma survivors continue living their lives breathing in a shallow manner. Thus, stopping to pay attention to taking deep, deliberate breaths can be a new and scary experience. Don't overwhelm yourself, and be mindful that those you work with may be initially apprehensive. Taking only a couple breaths at first and focusing on an even inhale-to-exhale ratio will usually prevent any uncomfortable lightheadedness. Another precaution is that you do not have to close your eyes for breath work to be effective. The darkness of closed eyes can produce a claustrophobic, traumatic response in some. A sudden sense of vulnerability can catch a person off guard, and this may happen when a person gets more relaxed than normal in the dark.

MUSCLE RELAXATION. Just as breath is an inherent resource that we all have the potential to access, so too are our muscles. In this section, we learn how the simple act of tensing muscle groups, relaxing them, and noticing the sensations of release can produce a powerful relaxation response. "Letting go" is a concept that twelve-step and other approaches to recovery emphasize. One of the classic twelve-step slogans is "Let go and let God," and many of the steps (especially four–five and eight–nine) are designed to help people let go of the past. Sometimes, letting go is a tough concept for alcoholics and addicts. From my experience, you can talk to a person until you are blue in the face about the benefits of letting go and how good it can feel, or you can use the body to demonstrate it. Using muscle clenching and releasing exercises offers an ideal solution. Try this powerful exercise called Clench and Release:

▶ Start with your hands if they are available to you. Clench your fists together and notice your edge. Do not hurt yourself. Once you feel you're squeezing as tightly as possible, begin to notice your nails make contact with your skin. Notice the tension. As you do this, bring to mind a person, place, or thing that is causing you distress.

▶ Hold the clench as long as you can, at least ten to twenty seconds.

▶ When you feel like you no longer want to hold on, slowly release the grip of the fists. Feel each finger unlock and spread out. Notice the sensation of letting go and how you experience that in your body.

▶ Take a couple of breaths of your choice as you notice the sensations of release.

▶ Repeat as many times as necessary until you are at your desired level of relaxation about the stressor.

▶ *Optional:* You can also choose to take a deep breath in with the fist clench and hold it as you clench your fists. Release the breath as you release the fists. Only do this if you feel comfortable enough holding the breath.

▶ *Variation:* Some people are not able to make fists due to medical conditions like rheumatoid arthritis, or it may not be considered culturally appropriate. Know that any muscle group can be tensed and released, including the shoulder, the stomach, the forearms, the thighs, or the feet.

I very often clench and release my feet, especially when I'm in public settings where it wouldn't be acceptable to start making fists. This Clench and Release exercise is based on classic progressive muscle relaxation techniques that can be helpful in helping people fall asleep. In a full progressive muscle relaxation exercise, the Clench and Release strategy is applied one muscle group at a time (e.g., start with left fist, then left arm, left shoulder, chest, right shoulder, etc.). By cycling through the muscle groups and noticing the relaxation response in each release, sleep may come more easily. I recommend the modification (Clench and Release) and the full skill (Progressive Muscle Relaxation) to anyone I serve who struggles with falling or staying asleep. This is as example of how, in early recovery, we can learn to replace self-medicating responses to distress with behaviors that are more natural and helpful in the long run.

PRESSURE POINTS.   You may associate the idea of pressure points with Eastern practices like acupuncture. You can use knowledge from such healing arts to get blood flowing to the parts of your body where it can help you relax, calm, and soothe yourself. Although my explanation of how pressure points work may be overly simplistic, this presentation is what makes the most sense to me and to many of my clients. I am not offering these strategies as a complete system of energy healing like you might get from a qualified Eastern medicine practitioner. Rather, they are an embodied practice you can use to ride the wave of distress until it passes. If you end up liking these and find them helpful, you may consider consulting with someone who practices acupuncture, acupressure, reflexology, or Eastern medicine forms for more personalized practice suggestions.

Take a look at the following photos with explanations of how to use each pressure point. To begin, hold each pressure point for about two minutes as you engage the breath of your choice. I find it best if you can focus on your breath as you hold the pressure point—it can enhance the relaxation response. Like with many of these skills, experiment and explore. Not all of these pressure points will work for you equally well. Find the one or two that may work the best for you. Although there are more pressure points you can learn (see further reading and other resources in the Appendix), I've highlighted the ones that can best impact anxiety or other symptoms we normally associate with traumatic stress.

Karate Chop Point—This point assists with relaxation, and it is very handy to use if you are in a stressful setting or feeling anxious at a meeting. You can use this pressure point and go relatively unnoticed. Try alternating left and right hands and see where you notice the most impact.

Inner Gate—Use this point just below the base of your wrist, as it is an excellent point for the relief of tension and anxiety. Try alternating left and right hands and see where you notice the most impact.

Sea of Tranquility Point—This point is located at the base of the breastbone, over the heart, and can be a very good pressure point for the relief of anxiety and panic. Move it around a little bit until you find the spot that is softest or resonates the most. You do not have to directly touch the body if this feels unpleasant in any way. Simply linger the hand above the breastbone.

Letting Go Points—Many like these points because you are essentially giving yourself a hug as you apply the pressure, which can add another soothing element. As the name of the points suggest, these are excellent to use when you need to release or let go of a particular stress or tension.

Gates of Consciousness Points—Think of applying pressure with your thumbs to the base of the skull. These points are very good for the release of tension, panic, and anxiety, and they can also have some effect in the relief of stress headaches, irritability, or hypertension.

Clear Mind Point (Variation 1)—Take a look at this photo. It probably looks like something that you do anyway during stress. Next time, try holding it and breathing with it for the full two minutes, and you may be surprised how it may help you soothe or regulate intense emotions.

Clear Mind Point (Variation 2)—Use this pressure point right in the center of your forehead if you are looking for an increased sense of concentration. This place in the center of your brain is associated with mindful awareness.

MINDFULNESS AND BODYFULNESS.   Mindfulness is a buzzword in the clinical professions. Considered the heart of Buddhist meditation although not uniquely Buddhist as a concept, a simple definition of mindfulness offered by Jon Kabat-Zinn explains: "Mindfulness means paying attention in a particular way: on purpose, in the presence of the moment, and non-judgmentally."[13] Mindfulness is one of those practices that sounds simple and yet is not easy. If practiced consistently (as little as a few minutes a day to start), people in recovery generally find that it helps orient them to the present moment and the idea of one day, one moment at a time.

One of the simplest ways to begin practicing mindfulness is to pick an object in your space that captures your attention—it can be anything, from a picture of a daisy on the wall to the fan blowing in the corner. Try for a minute to stay focused only on that object. What does it look like? What colors do you notice? What textures are you picking up on? Is there a sound, smell, taste, or any other type of sensation that goes along with the object you selected? If so, notice those. Use all of your senses in the process. Be gentle with yourself. If you can start with only a minute, that is wonderful. As you become more comfortable with practicing mindfulness, you may find that you are able to engage in this meditative practice longer.

If your attention starts to wander, it does not mean that you have failed mindfulness. Indeed, the practice is in the coming back to full awareness when you notice that you are no longer paying attention. The English word *mindfulness* comes from an Eastern word, *smiriti* (from Sanskrit), meaning "to come back to awareness." This suggests that awareness is our natural state and that everything about the world we live in will try to take us out of awareness. The practice is in the coming back. So the next time that you or people you work with say things like, "I can't pay attention, I can't sit still," consider responding, "Sitting still and paying attention isn't a requirement. You use the practice to help you get there."

You may encounter mindfulness or meditation practitioners in other traditions of meditation on your journey, who sit for anywhere from twenty-five minutes to hours at a time. They may even go on days-long silent retreats. Know that this is not where you have to begin, or even end up, in order to develop a mindfulness practice, and also be assured that mindfulness and meditation practices can look different for everyone. In the words of one of my favorite teachers, Krishna Das, "The best practice for you is the one that you do."

Another variation for working on a mindfulness practice is to pick any activity you do on a daily basis and set your intention to do it with full attention. It could be folding laundry, washing dishes, taking a shower, or brushing your teeth. After years of practicing meditation I still struggle with brushing my teeth mindfully. In the two to three minutes of brushing, I've been known to pick out my clothes, check my phone, and do many other things to pull me aware from total awareness. This can be meditation and working on being in the moment—it doesn't have to involve sitting on a cushion.

Although mindfulness may conjure up images of sitting meditation only, it's important to recognize that the entire body must be brought into the process of awareness. Since the earlier edition of *Trauma and the 12 Steps,* a writer and somatic scholar, Christine Caldwell, coined the term *bodyfulness* that speaks to this importance. Concerned that many meditation teachers give lip service to honoring the body yet shy away from using it in cultivating present moment awareness, Caldwell's terminology calls for an even wider embrace of the body's wisdom. She recognized that practices like yoga, *T'ai Chi, Qi Gong,* dance, and other forms of movement are legitimate paths for practicing meditation. They can be even more powerful vehicles for tapping into mind–body fusion. I've long believed in and taught this idea in my work, especially as an expressive arts therapist, yoga teacher, and developer of a practice called Dancing Mindfulness.

I often suggest more active mindfulness and bodyfulness strategies for clients who have problems staying focused during meetings. One of my clients carries a marble in her pocket at all times. If she notices herself getting anxious or feels triggered at a meeting, she pulls the marble out of her pocket. She notices its dominant blue color and other hues within the glass. As she rubs the marble between her fingers, she feels the coolness of the glass and the smoothness of the texture. Then, she experiments with rolling the marble between the palms of both of her hands, just noticing, nonjudgmentally. Typically, after about two to three minutes of this practice, she feels much more relaxed and ultimately is better able to focus on her twelve-step meeting.

It is important for twelve-step group members who are sponsors or who have been around for a while to recognize that trauma survivors may need to engage in such simple practices in order to stay present at meetings. Furthermore, it may also be helpful for newer members who experience high levels of anxiety at meetings to step out of the main meeting room for a few minutes and practice mindful breathing. This suggestion does not give newcomers an excuse to miss the whole meeting and stand outside smoking cigarettes (which happens). My hope is to raise our collective awareness in twelve-step meetings that sometimes people need to step out for a while in order to stabilize, return, and then actually get something out of the meeting.

YOGA AND CONSCIOUS MOVEMENT. Yoga is an ancient practice that originated in India. Yoga means a "yoking," or "union." When I first began practicing yoga, I understood the union to be that of body, mind, and spirit. The more I've deepened my study and practice of yoga's art and science, I've learned that the ultimate purpose of yoga is for an individual to return to the source of who they really are—to the truth of the Self. The union refers to uniting the person I think I am as a human being navigating the stressors of this world and all its accompanying thoughts, feelings, and experiences with the essence of my Divine or Higher self. A prayer from the Upanishads used in the primary yoga lineage I study asks us to be led from the unreal (who I think I am) to the real (who I really am). That's much deeper than just stretching, breathing, and getting a workout, right?

I often wonder what the ancient yogis would think about the modern-day yoga industry that exists in the West. Despite the billion-dollar industry of yoga apparel, videos, and classes that have sprung up, yoga's potential as a healing art is what makes it of utmost interest to many recovering individuals. Because its integrative properties are vast, yoga is excellent at helping a person master the modifications of the mind. In classical yoga, there are eight limbs of practice that help a person do this, with *asanas* (poses) and *pranayama* (breath work) being just two of them. Although much of the yoga taught in the West focuses on just these two limbs, the good news is that they all tie together. So even a very modern, Western instructor can work in wisdom from the other limbs on ethical practice, withdrawal of the senses, concentration, meditation, and living in unified bliss into a practice that meets Westerners where they are at.

Many treatment centers now offer yoga as part of their programming, and a wide variety of recovery yoga programs and classics continue to develop in our communities. I personally studied with Nikki Myers, the developer of Yoga of 12-Step Recovery. I still integrate some of her approach into recovery yoga classes I teach at conferences and in our local recovery community.

There is no shortage of trauma-informed and recovery yoga training programs available that equip practitioners in the helping professions with tools to safely share the principles and practices of yoga with those they serve.

Even without these specialty classes, a person working a recovery program can benefit from many standard yoga classes offered in the community. Classical yoga philosophy and twelve-step paths are remarkably complementary. I make some related recommendations in the Appendix if you wish to further your study.

New students of yoga in recovery are generally advised to first talk to a yoga teacher at a local school or gym to make sure that the class is appropriate for the student. As the helper, you may consider getting to know the yoga scene in your area. Sometimes, people get repulsed by yoga when they're put into a "power" or "hot" yoga class, when what their body (and their recovery) most needs at the moment is a gentle or restorative yoga class. There is even a sleep-based meditative practice within yoga called *yoga nidra,* which allows people to practice the art of non-doing. *Yoga nidra* is a popular practice with people I serve in recovery, as it can teach us how to rest and even relax deeply without chemical assistance.

Although yoga is ideal for stabilization and preparation, it also has the potential to bring up feelings and body sensations that can take a person by surprise. For instance, many people begin to cry or feel strong emotions when they learn a pose that stretches or extends the hips, one of the major areas affected by unhealed trauma. Thus, it is important to know that they are practicing yoga in a safe enough setting with an instructor who may be aware of their emotional concerns about yoga practice. I often encourage people who are going to try yoga for the first time to talk to an instructor by phone or email before attending a class.

Because yoga and other conscious movement are very important to my personal recovery and in my work as a professional, I maintain a wide variety of resources for teachers and people in recovery alike at www.traumamadesimple.com. You can check out my video series on that site in a practice I co-created with fellow yogini Jessica Sowers called Yoga Unchained, a trauma-focused approach to yoga. And in the spirit of the idea that *there's always a modification,* if yoga doesn't seem like a good fit for you, consider working with any movement practice that will help you to better pay attention to your internal world. You may find that gift in other Eastern practices like *T'ai Chi* and *Qi Gong*, in the expressive arts and dancing, in martial arts, or in any other exercise practice that you choose to approach with more meditative intention. I offer more on Eastern meditation practices and yoga in chapter 12 as we explore spiritual diversity.

THE EXPRESSIVE ARTS. Formal expressive arts therapy works with a fusion of the different ways individuals can express themselves—dance or movement, music, visual art, writing, filmmaking, and theater are some of the most popular examples of art forms. In *Process Not Perfection,* my book on using expressive arts therapy in trauma recovery, I extend the definition to include practices like gardening, cooking, clothing, and hair design. Any embodied channel that helps us express what we've been holding inside qualifies. We work with multiple art forms in the expressive arts because they offer people a buffet. There is one item in these expressive practices that you should at least be willing to try. As you progress further in the use of expressive arts, you may discover that the practice you most avoid is the one that best helps you step out of your comfort zone.

I can usually get my most resistant clients and people I know in recovery on board with first using music in some way. To quote the legendary Maya Angelou, "Music was my refuge. I could crawl into the space between the notes and curl my back to loneliness." Even Friedrich Nietzsche said, "Without music, life would be a mistake." The benefits of music on brain development are well documented in research literature. For many individuals in recovery, songs carry great significance. And music is a body-based intervention whether we are playing it or listening to it because of the vibrations it generates in our brains that can be felt in our bodies. Music incorporates the sense of sound vibration (which can even be experienced in a tactile sense by people with hearing loss). Music reaches parts of the brain that we cannot access if simply talking or thinking, and it can be applied in a variety of ways to enhance relaxation and promote empowerment in addicted survivors of trauma.

In this age of MP3 players and smartphones, the playlist has become very popular. I still remember the days when I listened to the radio and hit Play + Record on my Casio to make my own "mixtape," as we called them in the 1980s. We can leverage these new capacities for more easily making playlists and accessing music as we help people to build recovery capital. I encourage my clients to put together a playlist that they find significant to recovery—music that either helps them relax or helps them feel inspired. Sometimes, I encourage them to make multiple playlists along a variety of themes. One may help you to relax when you are struggling to fall asleep, another may help you feel more empowered or inspired. A client put together a playlist of music specifically for listening on the car ride home from therapy, knowing that she might need some extra help with grounding.

Another client struggled with being able to express certain feelings, like anger, that she was forbidden to express growing up in her home. She said to me one day in session, "I wouldn't even begin to know how to express anger, especially in a healthy way." An avid user of a certain online music service, I suggested that she type in the word "angry" into the search feature. Sure enough, that service featured a plethora of playlists specifically built around angry music. As a between-sessions assignment, she listened to these songs and used them as prompts to free-write in her journal. This experience opened up her capacity to feel and to express what she needed to in therapy.

People can benefit from music as part of their recovery whether they are using a simple playlist model or whether they choose to meditate on a specific piece of music when faced with a difficult situation. For instance, a person may need to listen to a relaxing or empowering song in the car before she feels stable enough to walk into a meeting. When I have encountered some difficult pitfalls in recovery related to standing up for myself, I listen and often dance to one of my empowering songs for that extra emotional lift. Some people use their musical talents to help with their recovery processes. Many recovery music websites feature the work of artists in recovery who use songwriting to help them work through issues. Although I have been a musician all my life, I did not start writing songs until I got sober.

Drum circles are growing in popularity. Drumming is an ancient art practiced by many indigenous cultures, both to promote community and to help people move energy through sound and action. Drumming is an outstanding body-based intervention to use as both a coping skill and later as a potential reprocessing strategy. Like with dancing, physical exercise, and other formal psychotherapies such as EMDR, drumming incorporates bilateral stimulation, the brain's inherent mechanism for promoting processing and restoring equilibrium. The nice thing about drumming is that a person can join a drum circle or perhaps attend a drumming workshop (yoga studios and performing arts centers often host such workshops), or a person can simply enhance sound and body release by creating his own percussion at home. Tabletops are ideal for improvisation, and people can even engage in foot-stomping or toe-tapping as a means of percussive, energy release.

The technique of imagery, sometimes called guided imagery or guided visualization, has many applications. We consider it to be one of the expressive art forms, especially since people can take what they learn from their imagery work and translate it into a visual creation. Most professional therapists use some form of guided imagery in their work with clients, with many focusing on guided imagery as their special modality in the treatment of trauma. Imagery is powerful, utilizing the potential of the human imagination for therapeutic benefit. Professionals often use imagery to allow their clients to tap into positive feelings by using a series of pictures or imagined experiences. Imagery is also beneficial for deeper trauma work as well as being a mechanism through which people can visualize the memory of the trauma, thus allowing them to encounter unresolved images, thoughts, experiences, or feelings, and hopefully reprocess these to some point of resolution.

I recommend that most people begin guided imagery work under the guidance of a professional, especially if the person has significant unresolved trauma. Although imagery may sound as simple as "picture yourself in your happy place," sometimes these happy or safe places can bring up some negative emotions as well. It helps to have that extra guidance of someone who is clinically trained. Once a counselor can help you discover a series of safe or calming images that work for you, you can apply these when emotional distress comes up as part of twelve-step meetings or in the completion of step work. Visit the Appendix for some recommendations on guided imagery, or the resources page at www.traumamadesimple.com for audio and video versions of guided visualizations and meditations you can experience.

In this chapter I've given you some of the basics that can form a solid foundation for riding the waves and emotions that come with being in early recovery as a survivor of trauma. As we often say in twelve-step culture, take what you like and leave the rest, although please be mindful of not holding a spirit of contempt prior to investigation. Many of the struggles that I've seen trauma survivors endure in attempting to work the steps and navigate their way through meetings can be solved by acquiring more body-based tools for coping. You may notice that by beginning to work some of the suggestions in this chapter you develop a real resonance to one of the practices. If so, consider exploring it further and deeper than the overviews I provide in this chapter. You may discover that one or more of these practices are just waiting to help you transform your experience with recovery!

TOOLKIT STRATEGY:
LEARNING BY DOING

In order to be truly effective in relaying these skills to your clients and those you work with in recovery, it is important that you experience them for yourself. As a way of building your own trauma toolkit for working with others, complete at least three of the activities described in this chapter. If you really want to expand your skill set, go ahead and give them all a try! Remember that you can use www.traumamadesimple.com as a guide any time.

It's the
Relationship That Heals

When I required addiction treatment in 2000, I didn't go to a fancy treatment center, nor did I seek out a twelve-step group in my own community. I moved to Bosnia and Herzegovina. As a twenty-one-year-old American expatriate vagabond seeking some kind of solution for the emptiness inside, I thought that working outside of the United States for a few years would help me "find myself." Yes, my move was a geographical cure at the time. And yet in the hills of Bosnia and Herzegovina, adjacent to my family's ancestral homeland of Croatia, I was led to an orange humanitarian aid trailer, formerly a priest's office, that would become my treatment center. In it, I learned one of the most valuable lessons in addressing addiction in a trauma-sensitive manner: it's the relationship that heals.

In this trailer I first revealed to Janet that I had a problem with chemicals. In this trailer she explained to me the disease of addiction and the implications for treating it. In this trailer we ended up meeting twice a week, engaging in the healing conversations that would become the basis of my own recovery. In this trailer she first delivered the line that would be pivotal in my recovery, later guiding the work I do with others: "Jamie, after everything you've been through, no wonder you became an alcoholic [validation] … what are you going to do about it now [challenge to action]?"

This was my "treatment center." Medjugorje, Bosnia and Herzegovina, 2001. For a full color photo, go to www.traumamadesimple.com/orangetrailer.

There is a misconception that to begin healing from the wounds of addiction and trauma, a person needs sophisticated treatment. While structured, trauma-informed treatment centers have helped countless addicted individuals get well, there is no inherent magic in the treatment centers that promotes healing. However, it is what these centers and programs have the potential to promote—the forging of healthy, recovery-oriented relationships—that we must consider as the most powerful healing mechanisms of action. This chapter imparts critical knowledge about the importance of the relationship in the healing process. This chapter also presents suggestions for promoting the highest levels of empathy and being effective in forging therapeutic or other healing relationships. What you are and how you deal with a person are typically more significant than anything you can say.

"The Gift" of a Healing Relationship

I get very concerned when professionals give Carl Rogers a bad rap. Although my graduate school professors requisitely covered client-centered therapy as we went through the many theories of counseling, they described Rogers as too "nondirective." His three central skills—unconditional positive regard, empathy, and congruence—although deemed important, seemed to be downplayed next to the cognitive-behavioral interventions that we learned. A message that I received in my early training was that if we really wanted to see changes in our patients, we needed to get in there and *do* something. When a friend of mine interviewed for her first job after graduate school, the program director asked which therapeutic theory best described her. Being an eclectic who believed in both direct intervention and the importance of forging a therapeutic alliance, she replied, "I guess I would consider myself a firm Carl Rogers."

Simply mentioning Rogers sank her.

The interviewer rolled his eyes and retorted, "Well, we're really very cognitive behavioral around here."

In this age of evidence-based treatment, the critical importance of the therapeutic relationship can be put on the back burner. Systems and providers can be so focused on a formulaic model of *doing*, that the necessary artistry of help regarding a person's *being* gets neglected. Let's consider for a moment what evidence-based practice really means. For over a decade, the American Psychological Association (APA), citing peer-reviewed literature, has described evidence-based practice as "the best available research with clinical expertise in the context of patient characteristics, culture, and preferences."[14] Thus, if we operate on straight intervention, no matter how much research support accompanies it, we are being ignorant providers if we dismiss what the client brings to the table.

Context matters.

And research supports that the therapeutic relationship rests at the heart of what we do as helpers. Honoring the therapeutic relationship and taking the necessary steps to build a high-quality working alliance between you and the person you serve are absolutely essential when you deliver any healing intervention for addiction. Respecting the therapeutic relationship is one simple factor that enhances our work with clients.

While working on my PhD, I attended a workshop led by the late Dr. David Powell, a senior addiction counselor who recommended that I read *The Gift of Therapy* by Irvin Yalom.

"Yalom?" I questioned. "Isn't he the guy who wrote the thousand-page text on group therapy?"

"Yes," said Dr. Powell. "*The Gift of Therapy* is different. It's written by a much older Yalom, who has learned from his mistakes, declaring that despite all of his years writing about techniques, it really is the relationship that matters most."

The book changed my life and my approach to clinical work.

In this 2001 classic, Yalom contends that therapy should be relationship driven, not theory driven. Paying attention to existential issues can deeply influence the nature of the therapeutic relationship and the therapy itself. In Yalom's view, a therapist has no place forcing solutions, a piece of guidance I first heard while attending meetings of Al-Anon Family Groups. When I began applying many of Yalom's principles to my own clinical work (principles he clearly traces back to Carl Rogers), I observed my own heightened effectiveness in working with clients. My client outcomes reflected the improvement.

Yalom highlights that as professionals, our perception of what went well in a therapy session may drastically differ from how the client viewed the session. The same phenomenon can play out in sponsor–sponsee interactions. In other words, we may think that we are relaying such directive wisdom to our clients or sponsees ... and it may be totally going over their heads. In contrast, a simple smile given to the people we serve as they share something might strike us as insignificant, but it could be powerfully healing to the client. Yalom expounds upon this phenomenon in his 1974 book, *Every Day Gets a Little Closer: A Twice-Told Therapy*. This book chronicled a year Yalom spent doing therapy with one particular client, Ginny Elkin. After each session, Yalom would write down his reflections of the session, and then Ginny would do the same. Yalom's reflections focused on technique and all of the "brilliant" things he said and did in the session. For the client, the impact of the session was all in the relationship.

If these relational ideas of Yalom's seem too flowery and passive for you, consider the research support. In the second edition (2009) of their book, *The Heart & Soul of Change: Delivering What Works in Therapy,* Barry

Duncan, Scott Miller, Bruce Wampold, and Mark Hubble concluded that the collaborative, therapeutic alliance between client and clinician is a primary factor in determining successful therapy outcomes and is more important than the specific execution of therapeutic protocols. My jaw dropped when I first read this book at the time of its release, amazed by just how much of what I believed in my heart about the relationship was supported through meta-analyses and rigorous literature reviews. They also stressed that obtaining continuous client feedback throughout the therapeutic process is a critical component in enhancing client care. If you are in a system that emphasizes use of evidence-based practice above everything else, consider that use of new measures developed by this team—the Partners for Change Outcome Management System (PCOMS) and Outcome Questionnaire Psychotherapy Quality Management System (OQ-Analyst)—now appear on the Substance Abuse and Mental Health Services Administration's National Registry of Evidence-Based Programs and Practices.

While I advocate the use of gaining feedback in such a way within systems that demand more quantitative evidence that something works, as a qualitative thinker I still find these measures a bit cold and technical. I am on board with the practice of getting continuous feedback from clients (and sponsees or other people we serve in our various recovery roles) throughout our engagement with them. Check in with the client to ensure that what you are working on and how you approach the recovery plan is truly working for them. This evaluation can be done through treatment plan review, formal outcome measures, or regularly asking (yes, every session), "How is the approach we're taking together working for you? Is there anything I or we can do differently?"

Asking these questions in a culture of feedback—letting the client know that they are free to ask questions and give feedback without getting punished or shamed in any way—is vital. The *culture of feedback* (a term I first learned from Scott Miller) runs contrary to some of the logic promoted in traditional recovery circles. If addicted people messed up their lives so badly, shouldn't they just sit back and take suggestions? Although taking new suggestions is an important part of lifestyle change, we must not ignore the fact that the people we serve really are the best experts on the subject of their lives.

The collective body of research, as originally presented in *The Heart & Soul of Change,* shows that little difference exists among the specific factors (e.g., techniques or interventions) of bona fide, researched methods intended to be therapeutic. Thus, assignment to a twelve-step facilitation group instead of a cognitive behavioral therapy group does not automatically determine a person's success in treatment. Rather, a series of four common factors, working in concert, contribute to a person's overall change. These common factors are: the clients and their extra-therapeutic factors (e.g., what they bring to the table in therapy and situations beyond the control of the clinician), models and techniques that work to engage and inspire the client, the therapeutic relationship or alliance, and therapist factors.

A New York psychiatrist named Saul Rosenzweig first proposed the common factors in 1936, predating the work of Rogers and Yalom. Rosenzweig was Carl Rogers's first clinical supervisor, and the impact he made on his young student was clear. Rosenzweig, even in his era, grew concerned with schools of therapy that zealously believed their approach was the "right way"—battles among philosophical approaches that continue to this day. Rosenzweig contended that by focusing on what is similar among approaches as we deliver services, we will be in the position to influence the most change. This idea is inherently trauma sensitive.

John Norcross drew similar conclusions in *Psychotherapy Relationships That Work: Therapist Contributions and Responsiveness to Patients* (2002), one of the formational texts I devoured in my early postgraduate years. Using a collection of empirical research studies, Norcross proved that the therapy relationship, together with discrete method, influences treatment outcomes. Norcross challenged therapists and helpers to hone these relational elements, noting that it is their responsibility to tailor these skills to the needs of individual patients. Throughout the years Norcross, one of the preeminent names associated with the art and science of change, has continued to edit collected volumes, steer task forces, and gather meta-analyses. The 2019 updates to *Psychotherapy Relationships That Work* (now published as two volumes) continue to articulate a concern that we spend too much time researching specific therapies and not enough resources on researching the people receiving these therapies and the contexts in which healing is being delivered. There is a direct contention that one-size-fits-all delivery of any method or approach is neither effective nor ethical.

None of this information means that we should just throw theory and technique out the window—they are clearly important. However, if we are adhering to technical elements or holding true to our chosen philosophy or paradigm out of principle at the expense of the relationship, that is problematic. Echoing the wisdom of Sir William Osler, the father of modern medicine, Norcross and Wampold offer: "It is much more important to know what sort of patient has a disease than what sort of disease a patient has."[15]

Consider this metaphor: If we put theory or philosophy in the driver's seat (e.g., twelve-step principles, cognitive behavioral therapy) and shove the relationship all the way back into the trunk of the car, the therapy isn't going to go anywhere. The therapeutic relationship needs to take the front seat. Carrying the metaphor one step further, let the client steer the course of the treatment and allow yourself as the counselor or helper to serve as the trusted front-seat navigator. At times, the client may need a rest, and you will need to take the wheel for a while. The technique is like having a navigating passenger in a car with a map or GPS system. It can give you good directions, especially when you're lost. Ultimately, the technique or philosophy should never be the entity actually doing the driving. Sometimes maps are hard to read and don't take into account the creative elements of a drive (e.g., point A to point B may look quicker, but if you've actually driven it before, you know there may be a better way to go). The driving–navigation metaphor becomes especially relevant in considering how to most effectively treat an addicted client with unresolved trauma. The literature in general traumatic stress studies indicates that the therapeutic alliance is an important mechanism in facilitating meaningful change for clients with complex PTSD, the most salient predictor of outcome success in treatment of such clients.

Enhancing Empathy: The Key
to a Strong Therapeutic Alliance

Forging a strong therapeutic alliance does not mean that you have to become your client's best friend. Releasing all boundaries and allowing that to happen can be countertherapeutic. A solid working alliance is when the people you are working with trust you, can relate to you, believe that you relate to them, and trust that the work you are doing together is helping them get well. In the discussion of best practices for working with addicted survivors of trauma in chapter 6, I concluded that being the best version of yourself is the most solid approach to take in working with addicted survivors of trauma. Genuineness is key with this population. Empathy must also be present.

Technical definitions abound in the psychotherapeutic professions to describe empathy. The origin of the word *empathy* draws us back to a German term that literally means "in feeling." Empathy, which calls for us to step into another's shoes and see life from their perspective, is a stronger degree of engagement with another than sympathy—which implies simple identification with the feelings of another.

In their best-selling book *Born for Love: Why Empathy Is Essential—and Endangered,* authors Bruce Perry (a noted trauma-focused physician) and journalist Maia Szalavitz make this useful distinction between empathy and sympathy:

> *When you empathize with someone, you try to see and feel the world from his or her perspective. Your primary feelings are more related to the other person's situation than your own. But when you sympathize, while you understand what others are going through, you don't necessarily feel it yourself right now, though you may be moved to help nonetheless.*[16]

It may be useful for you to consider these distinctions and ask yourself whether or not, as a helper, you have been more likely to display sympathy or empathy in working with others.

To truly practice empathy as therapists—which ultimately forges a clear path therapeutically as the APA definition suggests—we who work

154

with addicted survivors of trauma must be able to proverbially step into the shoes of the people we are helping. If we as helpers come across as ivory tower experts, we run an extremely high risk of alienating the people we serve. However, by approaching addicted survivors of trauma as empathetic collaborators, we will be able to more effectively foster therapeutic change.

Let's consider some of the ways that we as helpers can build upon the empathetic abilities we may already possess. There is an erroneous belief that people either have empathy or they don't. Building empathy is a skill that can be deliberately practiced, like many other skills in our counseling repertoire. Indeed, Scott Miller and many other individuals who worked on the original *Heart & Soul of Change* volumes are moving toward the promotion of deliberate practice in psychotherapists even more than emphasizing the importance of the common factors. This movement is based on more recent literature on what makes effective therapists with solid outcomes. Skills and approaches can and should be practiced.

One of the first steps in building our empathy potential is to approach what we do with an open heart and mind. No matter how accomplished we may be in our fields, how many degrees we have, or how many people we have sponsored or mentored over the years, stepping out of the expert role to really learn from our clients is a critical component. By first adopting this open mind, there is a variety of steps we can take to build our empathetic potential: attending open twelve-step meetings, volunteering at a homeless shelter or with another community project that serves the underprivileged, reading first-person accounts of addiction and/or trauma recovery, watching movies about those struggling with recovery, and simply viewing our patients or sponsees as teachers when they share with us. However, a professional can engage in all of these activities, and if they do so with a closed mind and a mighty ego, these exercises may be futile.

Working with your own mentor (it can be a colleague, not necessarily a clinical supervisor), is another way to cultivate deliberate practice of empathy. You can ask this mentor (or your own twelve-step sponsor) to help you role-play through several tricky or challenging scenarios in working with others. A helper without empathy is just as dangerous as a surgeon who can't keep a steady hand while making an incision. Empathy is such an important component of what defines the helping professions, yet too often I have observed that the further removed a helper is from suffering, the more potential they exhibit to lose their empathetic abilities.

I see this phenomenon play out in two ways. First, counselors and other helpers sometimes enter the professions without having experienced any major life suffering, or if they have, they have never taken active measures to do their own healing work. We can debate left and right with literature whether or not having personal psychotherapy impacts professional effectiveness. I obviously believe that it does, even if the sole gain from this experience is to help you cultivate a greater sense of empathy toward your clients or sponsees. Helpers who have not experienced a transformative healing process themselves are prone to falling into the role of expert without ever developing true empathy. Second, I have also encountered professionals and recovery sponsors who begin their vocations with a high degree of empathy. However, either through burnout or moving on with their lives so much they forget what it's like to be a newcomer struggling with sobriety, their potential for empathy can diminish.

If we find ourselves growing cold or bitter toward clients, we need to be able to find some way to step into their shoes and catch a glimpse of what it is like to suffer as they are suffering. For professionals in recovery or those of us who have dealt with major life traumas in the past, sometimes the simple act of allowing our minds to float back and tap into the memories can give us the necessary motivation. For counselors in recovery or recovery sponsors, sharing their personal stories at twelve-step meetings or in community forums, perhaps even self-disclosing appropriately in a group or individual treatment setting can serve as potent reminders.

Remember that at its origin, the word *trauma* means "wound." Go back to the physical image of a wound. How would you feel if a medical professional showed squeamishness at the sight of blood or injury? What would be the experience of hearing such a professional say, *This is too much for me to handle,* without securing the proper care? This is the same phenomenon that plays out when we do not practice trauma-informed empathy toward the people we serve. Even as an essentially empathetic person, if you show that you are overwhelmed or put off in the presence of another person sharing wounds with you, the quality of your relationship can suffer.

The best professionals, sponsors, and helpers to work with recovering individuals dealing with trauma are not necessarily those in recovery themselves. Rather, people who continue to work on themselves and the wounds that life brings their way are ideal mentors—professional or nonprofessional—for a trauma-informed journey through the recovery process. Life doesn't stop when we advance in our sobriety or in our professional careers. Willingness to continue our own healing quests will make us better at what we do.

TOOLKIT STRATEGY: SELF-EVALUATION

From 2008–2009, I had the privilege of conducting my dissertation research on the implementation of EMDR therapy and other trauma-focused modalities in a long-term addiction treatment facility. These women were not my clients, and I am grateful for what I learned from them in studying feedback about their treatment experience. Consider this list of characteristics that ten women, all of whom completed addiction treatment within a trauma-sensitive setting, identified as being reflective of their experiences with counselors:

POSITIVE EXPERIENCES	NEGATIVE EXPERIENCES
caring	rigid
trustworthy	scripted
intuitive	detached
natural	anxious
connected	unclear
comfortable with trauma work	uncomfortable with trauma
skilled	

(continues)

POSITIVE EXPERIENCES	NEGATIVE EXPERIENCES
accommodating	
magical	
wonderful	
commonsensical	
validating	
gentle	
nurturing	
facilitating	
smart	
consoling	
"the bomb"	

Examine each list. Which characteristics on the positive side do you generally exhibit? Which do you exhibit especially well? On the negative side, which characteristic(s) might you struggle with that you have the potential to address?

It Takes a Village:
Fostering Multi-Leveled Relationships

Relationships heal. However, in the spirit of growth and development as empathetic counselors, it is also important to realize that we, as helpers, are not solely responsible for helping a client get sober and well. Too often, professionals (and many recovery sponsors) feel so overly responsible for the success or failure of their clients or sponsees that they lose perspective on the idea that no singular factor helps a person, especially a traumatized person, obtain recovery. All relationships have the potential to heal, not just the relationship between therapist and client or between sponsor and sponsee. Thus, as facilitators of a person's recovery experience, one of the most trauma-proficient steps we can take is to help a person keep their eyes open to the potentially meaningful relationships around them and discover how these relationships can aid in recovery.

The term *support system* generally describes the people surrounding a person—people who literally support their recovery and have their best interests at heart. Interestingly, the term appears in many more contexts than just addiction recovery in our culture—those recovering from physical diseases like cancer often cite the importance of a support system. New parents can credit the importance of a support system in helping them adjust. The logic is simple: support systems consist of people who are on your side, people who are in a position to help you. They also love you enough to call you out if you are doing something destructive to your recovery. With the exception of a very few approaches to recovery that support self-sufficiency (most notably Rational Recovery), a hallmark of most recovery programs is the importance of building a solid support system. As professionals or sponsors, we are in a golden position to help people identify which people in their lives they can use as healthy supports, and to help them recognize the teachable moments with people and relationships that are all around them.

In addition to Janet, one of my wisest teachers during my time in Bosnia was a four-year-old girl named Anita. She came into my life at a time when I needed to learn from her noble example, and her influence on me proves that healing in relationships can come in all forms. Anita was one of the children living in Mother's Village, a foster home where I tutored young Croatian and Bosnian students in English and music. Mother's Village featured a fabulous swing set, and every day, Anita would watch the other children on the swings with curiosity. Although she wanted to partake in all the fun, Anita found herself too afraid to try. Eventually, I coaxed her into giving the swings a go with her sitting on my lap, and she soon felt brave enough to swing on her own. A few days later,

Anita began to push the boundaries of her curiosity, swinging higher and higher with each attempt.

Then, what I feared would happen struck. While attempting to swing and then jump off in midair for a graceful landing below (a maneuver that she saw many of the older kids try), Anita fell. Initially she cried, and I came over to hug her and see if she was okay. I thought, "Oh no, she's finally on the swings, and now this had to happen! She's not going to want to go near them again." The resilient Anita proved me wrong. After a minute or two of tears, she went back on the swing again, this time swinging higher than she ever had before. She even cried out joyously, "Look at me! I'm not afraid anymore! I'm not afraid anymore!"

All this happened at a time in my own life when I was trying to sort out my past wounds and embrace my own personal recovery. My experience of working with Anita, and seeing her resilient example, helped to quell my initial fears about recovery in a way that nothing else really has. This four-year-old child, riddled with her own trauma of being born into such a chaotic sociopolitical environment, helped me tap into my own sense of resilience. To this day, whenever I struggle with a fear issue, I think of Anita's smiling laughter as she played on the swing.

Relationships heal, sometimes in a way that we least expect them to. Helping clients and those new to recovery to see the healing potential in each relationship, even if that relationship just provides an opportunity to set a boundary and thus promote personal growth, is one of the most powerful tools in trauma-informed recovery. Recall the wisdom that my recovering friend Denise shared in chapter 5: Our relational lives can be the last and hardest part of our recovery to address because, for many of us, they were the first part of our life to get wounded. Remembering this, may we endeavor to create reparative, transformative experiences for people that we serve around these beautiful wounds.

TOOLKIT STRATEGY: STEP INTO THEIR SHOES—SKILLS FOR EMPATHY BUILDING

Think of someone you currently work with in your role as a helping professional, or recovery sponsor or leader. If you are not currently working with people in recovery, you can use a past case, or even bring a "celebrity" case to mind for this exercise.

Bring to mind a picture of that person. Notice what that individual looks like. Notice the identifying traits: gender, race, ethnicity, height, body type, any distinguishing physical features. Pay attention to what the person may be wearing upon walking into your facility, or maybe into a recovery meeting. Think about what brought that person there in the first place. Are they there because they want to be there? Are they there because someone told them that they had to be there? Think about how that person literally got there. If you're in a hospital setting, did the client come by ambulance or by car? If you're in an agency or office setting, did your client drive there or take the bus? Maybe the person walked or maybe someone gave them a lift.

If you are so willing, take a moment and try to "step into the shoes" of the person that you brought to mind. Now take a few moments and notice. Notice what is going through your mind as you walk into this facility or into this recovery meeting for the first time. Notice how you are feeling. Notice what is happening in your body. Take a few minutes and be with this experience.

When you are ready, step back into the role of yourself as the reader of this book, knowing that you can access this experience any time you need to step into the shoes of another.

You can find an extended audio version of this exercise on the audio resources section of www.traumamadesimple.com, or on Spotify (search "Trauma and the Twelve Steps: A Multi-Sensory Journey").

9

Best Practices for
Building Recovery Capital

In reflecting back on her treatment experience after four years in recovery from heroin addiction, Cindy noted, "I see the quality of work that I did here as a client, and it's incomparable to the other treatment centers that I have seen, because of the focus on trauma." As we examine Cindy's story in greater depth, we see how having her traumatic experiences and individual preferences respected as part of the treatment process was vital to her success.

Cindy's "taste for opiates," as she calls it, started at age fifteen when she developed a chronic kidney stone condition. Cindy's addiction progressed to polysubstance use, injecting combinations of cocaine and heroin just prior to entering treatment at the facility she referenced. From adolescence, Cindy acquired a variety of mental health diagnoses, including ADHD, depression, complex PTSD, bipolar disorder, obsessive-compulsive disorder, anxiety or social phobia, and borderline personality disorder. Cindy indicated that she first received the diagnosis of borderline personality disorder in her teens. The diagnosis was not surprising considering that by that age of fifteen, Cindy had already experienced a plethora of abandonment-related trauma, in addition to the alienation she felt due to identifying as lesbian at a Catholic school.

Prior to entering the trauma-focused program, a hospital-based treatment center detoxified Cindy and then sent her to treatment at a residential facility. However, after charting some time abstinent from chemicals, Cindy's mental health issues began to emerge in full force, especially dissociative symptoms. The residential treatment center did not know how to care for Cindy. Thus, they sent her to Amethyst, a facility whose story I tell in chapter 11, so that she could receive the holistic, trauma-sensitive help she needed. Cindy was able to stay involved with the program for a two-year period, accessing trauma-sensitive outpatient groups and EMDR therapy to help her work through her traumatic experiences and their impact on her mental health symptoms. For Cindy, this trauma-sensitive and trauma-focused approach was especially significant because she had problems accepting twelve-step recovery due to her struggles with religion and spirituality.

Amethyst also assisted Cindy in going back to school. She was able to complete an associate's degree in substance abuse counseling at a community college, and went on to receive a bachelor's degree in social work. Cindy was required to complete an internship at a drug and alcohol treatment center as part of her associate's degree. When she began her work at the traditional facility to which the school assigned her, she was horrified. Cindy shared, "Some of the women at this facility are able to stay up to six months, and the staff is doing nothing to address the trauma. And these women have layers and layers of it. Don't you think they would want to start addressing some of those layers?" After completing her internship, Cindy became even more grateful for the trauma-focused treatment she was able to receive.

Cindy's experience at the treatment center allowed her to acquire and foster recovery capital, the focus of this chapter. A term initially developed by Robert Granfield and William Cloud, *recovery capital* consists of the tangible and intangible resources that individuals can call upon to make recovery successful. Recovery capital can include a support group, twelve-step meetings, a sponsor, a church group, a job, hobbies, supportive family, motivation, and a place to live—essentially, whatever the people have going for them. Granfield and Cloud, two authors who fundamentally oppose twelve-step programming, coined this phrase in part to demonstrate that it's not necessarily the specific program or therapeutic approach that helps a person get sober. Rather, how a person acquires and uses the capital is paramount.

In trauma-informed addiction treatment, helping clients to identify and build upon their recovery capital is an essential function of initial preparation. Before a client can proceed with the cathartic activities traditionally associated with "trauma work," having a foundation of safety and coping skills is critical. Professionals, sponsors, and other members of the recovery community are in a position to help a client identify and build upon this recovery capital, thus beginning the process of lifestyle change required for meaningful, trauma-sensitive recovery. In this chapter, some necessary strategies are explored and explained.

Recovery Capital 101

To most effectively demonstrate the concept of recovery capital and its importance, take a minute and consider the recovery capital in your own life. Even if you do not identify as being in recovery, take a moment and consider what you have going for you. Do you have a place to live? Food to eat? A stable income? A supportive family? A strong work ethic? A moral compass? These are just some examples. If you are willing, take a few moments and identify everything you have that contributes to your living a functional life—this can include elements in your life that perhaps you are not currently accessing to their fullest potential. Write down your inventory if that feels appropriate.

In trauma-informed and trauma-focused care, it is important not to solely focus on the problems a person identifies. We must also help people identify what they have done that is right, healthy, or adaptive. Remember, a major guiding light of trauma-informed care is that it's not about what's wrong with you, it's about what happened to you. What strengths and resources have you been able to muster so far to survive these events?

This approach may be a bit of a paradigm shift for some twelve-step traditionalists who hang onto slogans like, "Your best thinking got you here," or to others who approach addiction as a moral or criminal problem. Remember, individuals struggling with addiction and trauma are likely coming for help with an already ingrained shame-based identity. It will be a radical new intervention for a professional or sponsor to be able to help them identify the positives.

For some of our clients, identifying the good can be a challenge. Most of us have had the experience of having clients come up empty when asked to name even one positive quality about themselves. Other clients come into treatment or a recovery program so weathered by life that helping them access the basic essentials of life such as safe and sober housing, food, and transportation can prove challenging. As the classic Abraham Maslow hierarchy approach would suggest, helping a person access these basic needs is a critical part of trauma-informed care. A client of mine once shared, "If I don't have a place to sleep tonight or food to eat, the last thing I want to think about is going to a [recovery] meeting." While traditionalists may argue with that logic, what my client shared is exactly what most traumatized individuals feel who present for treatment with little recovery capital.

Thus, as professional or recovery group leaders working in our community we must familiarize ourselves with the various resources available to the people we work with, and we must help them access these resources. I am not just talking about finding out which recovery meetings are out there and which ones are solid. When I first started working in community-based drug and alcohol treatment, I had to attend a two-day orientation on all the services available to residents of our county. We were literally required to get in our cars as part of the training and drive from site to site like a poker run. Although I initially felt this orientation would be a waste of time, to this day, the experience remains one of the most valuable trainings that I participated in as a professional. Basic resource linking *is* a part of trauma-informed care.

Case management (sometimes called different things depending on the state) is a vital yet often overlooked resource of early recovery. The Twelve Core Functions of Alcohol and Other Drug Treatment (not to be confused with the twelve steps) is a model incorporated by many state boards and other organizations to license or certify chemical dependency counselors. According to the Core Functions, case management encompasses activities that bring services, agencies, resources, or people together within a planned framework of action toward the achievement

TOOLKIT STRATEGY:
ACCESSING RESOURCES AND RECOVERY CAPITAL

For those of you who already excel at accessing community resources, this exercise may seem repetitive. However, you may be surprised at what else you might find out there by doing this exercise. Keep an open mind and give it a try.

Think about the last client or recovering person you worked with who had a major survival need, such as lack of adequate housing, inability to obtain furniture, or a need to acquire legal help in applying for Social Security Disability. Do an internet search or pick up the phone to call someone with whom you regularly network in your community, and find out what community resources may be available as well as how a person can access them. Feel free to repeat this exercise as many times as necessary. Always be willing to expand your knowledge base when it helps point a person toward resources.

of established goals. Case management may involve liaison activities and collateral contacts. These services fall outside the scope of psychotherapy yet are still indelibly vital to the healing process. Solid case management can promote enhanced therapy and treatment.

Many treatment centers have the resources to assign separate case managers to individuals in treatment, in addition to the primary counselors. Depending on resources available in the community or certain benefits allowed with state-appropriated services (e.g., Medicaid), many clients can access separate case management services as well as traditional therapy. Finding out if case management services are available is vital to developing a trauma-informed treatment plan. Some of the most successful episodes of treatment with very complicated clients happens when the clinician is able to work together with a separate case manager. Counseling sessions are freed up for therapy instead of activities that may fall under the realm of case management. Moreover, a solid case manager can provide a client with another outlet of caring support.

TOOLKIT STRATEGY:
ASSETS AND DEBITS

To help people evaluate the capital they have going for them in the service of their recovery, you as a professional, sponsor, or trusted friend can guide them through this simple inventory. I have included a clean copy of a worksheet you can use for this activity in the Appendix. A filled-out worksheet may look something like this:

Justin's Recovery: Assets and Debits

ASSETS	DEBITS
insurance to access treatment (VA)	lots of drinking or using friends
supportive family	some codependent family members
brother Tommy: calls me out on behavior	Mom enables me with money /excuse
place to live in good neighborhood (Mom's)	Mom keeps wine in house
supportive, effective twelve-step sponsor	lacks discipline about praying
access and transportation to meetings	afraid of driving car to bad neighborhood
believes in God	sexual relationship with girl who still drinks
military experience taught discipline	military-related PTSD (nightmares)
time to go to meetings	no job
loves nieces/nephews: wants to be there	lying, manipulation seem to be ingrained
desire to stop drinking or using	character traits

ASSETS	DEBITS
on probation for two years: required abstinence	
learning a new set of coping skills from therapist	
practices yoga and works out (runs)	
several friends, nonusers outside of meetings	
SSRI seems to help mood overall	

Some people are surprised by how many qualities are in the assets column, which can be an advantage of doing this as a formal inventory. Similarly, people may find themselves surprised by how many items are in the debits column, which can motivate them to begin working on building assets. Justin's sample list illustrates two important facets of recovery capital. First, just about anything a person can use to stay sober or meet their recovery goals qualifies as an asset, be it internal or external, tangible or intangible. Justin's list includes both external motivations (e.g., probation, relationship with nieces and nephews) and internal motivations (e.g., the desire to stay sober). Moreover, the list includes tangible resources (e.g., insurance, transportation) and intangible resources (e.g., family support). Take everything into consideration.

The second element is that no singular program, treatment center, or modality appears in the assets column of the list. For Justin, a twelve-step sponsor and meetings fit the bill. For others, it may be a church support group or another recovery program. The essential principle here is to call upon anything you can access to build the assets side of the list and make sure that, through your time working together, it becomes longer than the debits list. Moreover, meetings are not the only asset appearing in that column. This item is important to consider, as meetings alone will rarely suffice for someone in recovery—especially if unhealed trauma is part of the picture.

If people are willing, you can also take this exercise a step further by having them identify opportunities for turning the debits into assets. For instance, Justin has no job for the time being. There are several opportunities here. One, as a professional, you can work with him on identifying some of his vocational strengths as he searches for work. Two, you can emphasize that since he is not currently employed, that frees up time for him to go to more meetings and to schedule his therapy appointments without conflict. In looking at some of his issues with enabling or people who otherwise drink or use in his life, there are multiple opportunities there for Justin to build upon his skills in assertiveness and coping.

An anthem of this book is that teaching solid sets of coping skills has a clear place in helping a client build recovery capital, especially if a client comes to treatment with few items in the assets column. Little external recovery capital should not be an excuse for why a person cannot get sober or why trauma cannot be addressed. It simply means that you, as the helper, will need to assist your folks in *building* capital as part of their trauma-informed treatment plan, and teaching them a solid arsenal of coping skills can help with this task. While professionals may have the training to complete this task at a more clinical level with people, some of the most proactive sponsors and recovery community members I know are also equipped. As a nonprofessional, you can pass along your experience, strength, and hope about what has worked for you in acquiring and developing recovery capital.

How Recovery Capital Can Set the Stage for Deeper Work

Judy, a lower-income Caucasian woman in her late thirties, found herself in and out of community mental health facilities for the better part of her adult life. She suffered from both bipolar disorder and PTSD, resulting from a series of abuses at the hands of her alcoholic parents and sexual assaults in late adolescence. Judy reported periods of substance abuse throughout her adult life to cope with stress, usually when she was not compliant with her medications for the bipolar disorder. She struggled significantly with medication compliance. Although medication regulated her bipolar symptoms, she often complained about the side effects and cost of the medications.

Judy presented to a community treatment center that offered several therapeutic options for cathartic trauma work. As her therapist, I initially did not consider Judy a candidate for any of these therapies because she seemed "unstable." Working with cases like Judy's over the years has changed my relationship with that word. In reality, she just wasn't prepared and my job was to help her acquire resources to become prepared to change her life and meet her goals.

Judy was adamant that if she just got on the right medication, all her problems would go away. During the first two months of treatment, I was careful to meet her where she was in the stages of change and not use overt confrontation, even about behaviors that were clearly detrimental to her mental health progress (e.g., choosing certain friends, attempting to reason with her equally troubled ex-husband). As a result, a solid alliance formed. Through some trial and error, Judy's psychiatrist was able to find a medication that worked well in keeping the bipolar symptoms reasonably stabilized, and the level of Judy's day-to-day lability significantly decreased.

During these first couple of months, I worked with her on coping skills, including guided imagery and deep breathing. Judy responded well to these two exercises, so I suggested that she try adding some tactile coping skill elements, like pressure points and bilateral tapping (common in EMDR therapy). I explained the tapping as a process that might help to further deepen her sense of grounding and relaxation. Doing these exercises, Judy reported that she felt more relaxed than ever before. For the next few months, we engaged in a virtual boot camp of body-based coping skills training. Because Judy did not have much good going on in her life aside from having a government-subsidized housing apartment and having solid relationships with her case manager and therapist, building resources became incredibly important.

After seeing how well Judy responded to the coping skill exercises, I explained how she could use the bilateral stimulation in a different way to help process some of the traumatic memories. Judy was game. The first several sessions of trauma reprocessing with the EMDR modality went all over the place in terms of tangential disorganization. However, after these first several sessions, Judy was able to quickly reprocess a series of traumatic memories that were both recent (an accident) and deep seated (past abuse). We used EMDR therapy on and off over a nine-month period, which led to significant improvements in Judy's overall self-image and decision-making.

If the cathartic elements of trauma reprocessing began too quickly, especially if someone presented with as many complications as Judy did, more harm could have resulted. Many effective modalities ask a person to feel their feelings and sense into their body sensations in order to clear traumatic distress. While these tasks can ultimately be the source of their effectiveness, they can be both a trigger and a resource for people new to the recovery journey. It was important to introduce coping skills slowly and carefully, then add the bilateral stimulation, and then proceed with trauma reprocessing. Prepare for the journey, and the journey will go much more smoothly.

Readiness versus Preparation

When I first met one of my spiritual teachers, he told me that I wasn't ready. I asked him a series of challenging questions from the crossroads where I found myself in life. I struggled to make sense of deeper yoga teachings that would help me move from a place of doing to being. Ever the good student programmed to challenge what I was told at face value, I persisted with my questioning.

"You're not ready," he said.

On one hand, he had a point. I hadn't been ready for quite some time—yet I was there. Present. Doing the work. Asking the questions. Preparing myself in a manner that would allow me to become ready. On the other hand, I felt insulted to be told I wasn't ready when I was clearly willing and making preparations. It made me think of every time I'd told a client, "You're not ready yet," and I suddenly chided myself, realizing how demeaning and degrading that could have felt for them. Since that incident in the fall of 2015, I stopped using the word *ready* in clinical settings with my clients or in teaching with my students.

A visceral reaction overcomes me every time that I hear the word *ready*. Maybe because I realized how ugly it sounded when pelted at me. I also became attuned to how often people say, "I'm not ready." And I recognized how frequently my clinical consultees worry that their clients weren't ready to go further with their work. When they express this worry, the subtext suggests that they do not feel ready to take a client further. Folks that I mentor can doubt their ability to teach a class or accept a professional opportunity I present, claiming they are not ready. Why did I suddenly hate the word so much? In addition to it feeling like an insult, it felt like others were using "I'm not ready" as an excuse or an easy way to express distrust in their own abilities within the natural flow of process.

For years I taught the importance of client readiness in moving forward with deeper phases of twelve-step work or trauma therapy. My experience with my teacher caused me to reevaluate the word and everything I believed about it. Like I do at any crossroads in inquiry, I turned to word origin for some answers. The word *ready* traces back to thirteenth- and fourteenth-century Middle English, where it is largely conflated with the word *prepared* or *preparedness*. Additionally, there is an element of the original word usage that also implies promptness (i.e., not dragging out the process). Ready and prepared may seem like synonyms, yet there are subtle differences that may offer some solutions.

Most seem to associate *readiness* as a state of mind or a mental quality, whereas *preparedness* or being prepared is more logistical. There are plenty of examples out there of people believing they are ready for something (e.g., marriage, a hike on the Appalachian Trial), only to find out they are ill-prepared. For me, embracing the full meaning of the word *prepare* and all its forms (preparedness, preparation) is where we find our freedom to grow and to realize our intentions. The Latin root from which we draw the English word *prepare* draws from the same root as *to parent*.

To bring something to life! Taking the action to get ourselves prepared inevitably impacts our attitude of readiness. If we declare that we're not ready and do nothing to get ready (i.e., to prepare), we can find ourselves in an excuse-making loop for years. Moreover, consider that such a thing as perfect readiness may not even exist.

During a *Trauma and the 12 Steps* workshop, a participant posed a question about readiness to do the steps, especially the fourth and fifth step.

"Who is ever really *ready* to do a fourth step?" I replied.

Letting people off the hook from doing a fourth and eventually a fifth step is not the answer. Rather, how can we better prepare them for the challenges of these steps and guide them through the difficulty? I've heard too many sponsors tell people to "just do step four and don't come back until you're ready to do the fifth." With that lack of guidance, no wonder people don't feel ready and keep procrastinating. To be clear, forcing people to do the steps is not the answer. There is value to not rushing any process. Yet playing the "I'm not ready" card, even if it is out of legitimate fear, can keep us stuck in the rut of life behaviors and emotional states that cause us problems. I have found that doing these steps is less scary with proper preparation and guidance. Preparation and guidance can assuage the fear.

What if we could learn to replace the declaration "I'm not ready" with the question "What can I do to get myself prepared?" There are other helpful questions too: "What kind of support will I need to grow into readiness?" or "How will taking action and making necessary preparations help me to get ready?"

To simply say "I'm not ready," especially when you have a goal of getting better, is generally not helpful. True, some people need some time. Yet I encourage people to productively use that time by taking proactive steps, no matter how small, toward their own healing.

Perhaps the overachieving, good student tendencies I carried throughout childhood have carried over into how I approach the healing process. I recognize my privilege. Since I decided to get sober and well in 2001, I've had the ability to access healing resources in the form of counseling, psychiatry, twelve-step meetings, and other holistic practices. I also had seasons of my life where unhealed trauma rendered me paralyzed and unable to fully take advantage of them. Realizing what I do have and mustering enough willingness to prepare myself has long been the key that's opened the door to readiness. I've seen people without the resources I can access make up for it with willingness to prepare themselves in whatever way possible. Which leads to a final question: When we say, "I'm not ready," are we really declaring that we're not willing?

I've seen the answer to that question go both ways for people. And in both contexts, the lynchpin seems to be preparation. Taking action steps. Change will come as it is meant to when we put one foot in front of the other with a minimum of stalling. There's a recovery saying: *it's easier to act your way into better thinking than to think your way into better acting.* This approach is generally more trauma informed than the change the thinking, change the behavior mantra that can dominate cognitive-behavioral discourse. *Acting your way into better thinking* recognizes that our thoughts keep us stuck. Our thoughts tell us things like, "I'm not ready." Our actions move us toward a different reality and eventually a different attitude and outlook on life.

10

Strategies for Reprocessing and Reintegration

In working with addiction professionals as both colleagues and workshop students, there is a line I consistently hear that sums up their resistance to doing trauma work with clients: "I just don't want to go somewhere with them before they're ready to handle it. What if they relapse?"

The concern is legitimate. Opening up the Pandora's Box of past traumas may destabilize people, perhaps even leading them to relapse, if proper preparation is not in place. On the other hand, Pandora's Box may already be open. I still hear from friends and colleagues working in treatment centers that they are actually told to shut down trauma if clients start talking about it in group. Generally this directive comes from a place of fear—fear that other clients will get triggered and a domino effect will ensue, and fear that the staff running the groups is not properly trained to handle what might happen.

In reality, you can't shut down trauma. This attitude is part of the ignorant narrative that keeps people suffering and dying. Sure, there are measures that you can take to validate people, contain affect, and help them manage the trauma reaction until a more appropriate time arises in which to work on it deeply. When you shut down trauma it will come out some other way that, more likely than not, will lead people back into the addiction cycle.

So perhaps we can learn to replace the previous concern with better questions:

▶ How can I, as the professional, sponsor, or other helping guide assist in preparing people to handle what may come up as they move into doing the deeper, necessary work?

▶ When can clients, especially those with addiction issues, move from the preparation stages of treatment into the processing or reprocessing stages,[17] where they are more likely to do the cathartic work?

▶ What needs to be in place for people in order for this work to happen? Where or how can I support, depending on my role (e.g., sponsor, professional, etc.)?

There are no finite answers to these questions, and the answers may be different depending upon your role. As a treatment professional helping to set the stage and prepare someone, your role is largely foundational, where the trauma-focused psychotherapist who will see the person after treatment may be best set up to do more intensive care. As a sponsor, it may be outside of your ethical scope to do some of the practices explained in this chapter, yet you ought to still have an awareness of what is available to the people you serve. Also, as a sponsor or other non-clinician who is in a support role, your presence in the person's life as they go through an intensely trauma-focused psychotherapy can be invaluable.

From Stabilization to Processing: Further Evaluation Questions

In trauma-focused psychotherapy, we can ask a series of questions on a case-by-case basis to help evaluate whether or not a client is ready to move from preparation work to processing experiences. Pierre Janet's Stage Model for the Treatment of Traumatic Stress (sometimes called the consensus model), tracing back to the late nineteenth century, is largely used in the field today to explain this transition. The three stages originally proposed by Janet include:

- ▸ **Stage 1:** Stabilization, symptom-oriented treatment, and preparation for liquidation of traumatic memories.

- ▸ **Stage 2:** Identification, exploration, and modification of traumatic memories.

- ▸ **Stage 3:** Relapse prevention, relief of residual symptomatology, personality reintegration, and rehabilitation.[18]

The simplicity is clear: There needs to be a beginning, a middle, and an end (even if this "ending" is better conceptualized as maintenance) to the healing structure.

One of the great misconceptions about trauma work is that it's all about catharsis, or the second component of Janet's structure. However, if a patient or clinician jumps into catharsis without having a foundation of stabilization, which includes a therapeutic alliance and a set of coping or affect regulation skills, further damage can result. As a former research subject of mine once explained, stabilization or preparation work lessens the chance that a person is going to come unglued by what may come up in the identification and exploration of trauma.

Another great misconception about trauma work, especially with the savvy, quick-cure marketing around many of the newer approaches to trauma treatment, is that once something is processed or cleared, then it's gone—it's a nonissue. A healthier approach can be to look at trauma as something that can be healed. Even after a person has a major catharsis or breakthrough in counseling, there is still work to be done with their adjustment to life. Imagine if a person went into a hospital for major surgery, and the blockage or impediment was cleared but no postoperative follow-up was recommended.

Consider how the consensus model fits with the wound-healing metaphor introduced in chapter 3. Stabilization is like providing immediate attention to a wound. Using a simple scrape or cut as an example, stabilization might mean cleaning out the wound and disinfecting the area after it's had a chance to bleed for a while. Then, a dressing is generally applied to stop the bleeding and prevent infection or other impediments to healing. However, for a wound to truly heal, the dressing cannot stay on forever. The wound needs to be exposed to the light and air. Healing needs to happen from the inside out, a process that can take a great deal of time. This process is the middle stage. In trauma work the term *processing* or *reprocessing* can be simply defined as "healing." After a wound heals, it generally leaves a scar. In cases of relatively benign wounding, that scar may clear up altogether. With more significant injuries, a person may need to get used to living with a scar or whatever aftermath is left behind after the wound heals.

As "old" as the Janet stage model may seem, it is still in wide use and the standard of care for many major clinical organizations. The model is not without controversy since other scholars contend that there cannot be true stabilization of an individual until they've healed the traumatic underpinnings of what ails them. Like many models, it is meant to be a guide only, not a perfect flow. True stabilization cannot happen for many until the deeper wounds have healed, a major reason why I've long preferred the term *preparation* over *stabilization,* to describe the functions of Janet Stage One. The questions that follow can also help you navigate the delicate balance between preparation-level work and deeper healing. Yes, we want people to be able to reasonably handle what may come up and protect themselves. Yet we must also be realistic and realize that if we wait for a person to be perfectly stabilized before going deeper into the healing process, we may be waiting a long time. A variety of other consequences, including death, can happen if we wait too long.

Using these guidelines can also help us evaluate how well we are helping clients build their individualized recovery capital. They are not meant to be a perfect checklist, simply components that can help guide you in your clinical decision making. If you are a sponsor recommending that your sponsee seek outside help, you may also find these useful as you help the sponsee to get ready and/or seek out the best possible pathway for added help:

HAVE I ASSESSED FOR SECONDARY GAINS? Secondary gains are what a person "gets" out of staying stuck in his symptoms. These gains can be as tangible as a government disability check or as subtle as maintaining an excuse for irresponsible behavior because of the diagnosis (e.g.,

"Well, it's the PTSD acting up"). I usually approach this issue with clients as directly as possible. If they seem to be clinging to reasons for staying stuck in maladaptive behavior, I talk about it with them in the context of our therapeutic alliance. The technique of developing discrepancy used in motivational interviewing can be golden for this purpose, especially as an alternative to traditional confrontation.

In the discrepancy technique, we point out a behavior or attitude that seems to be causing a problem or prevents the person in question from reaching a stated goal. So it may play out as such: "On one hand, you say that you want to set better boundaries with your family and not let them run your life so much, yet on the other hand, you don't seem willing to let go of the financial support they are offering you. Help me understand." I use discrepancy when a person is showing resistance about doing a piece of therapeutic work, especially one that's related to trauma. Addressing that may play out in such a way: "So on one hand your goal is to be free of your past and the old ways of thinking that seem to be stuck there, and on the other hand every time we go to work on it in therapy you change the subject."

With discrepancy, you take the personality conflict out of traditional confrontation and simply point out what the people in question may need to arrive at their own conclusions. I find that sponsors can also take on the secondary gains issue with people they serve, sometimes even more effectively than professionals can. The imperative of the relationship is essential if secondary gains are going to be directly addressed. Sponsors can have the added value of sharing from their experience, strength, and hope about how they had to let go of a secondary gain in order to get well.

WHAT IS THE CLIENT'S MOTIVATION FOR WANTING TO DO TRAUMA PROCESSING OR REPROCESSING WORK? I am hesitant to do any trauma processing work with a client when the reason given for seeking treatment is "to find out why I am the way I am" or "to find out why I drink, use, or act this way." Why questions and the pursuits that follow are generally unproductive. I am especially hesitant to do this with people if they have made no effort to embrace lifestyle change, and they feel that a simple explanation for their problems lies in the past.

In the spirit of safety, I will not do trauma processing work unless I am reasonably convinced that a client bases their motivations for doing so on getting well and not ascribing blame to others or finding "magic" answers. All trauma reprocessing therapies may reveal some clues from the past. I make sure a client knows it's what they do with those clues that matters. Once more, even though the judgment call inherent in this task may fall largely on the shoulders of professionals, sponsors or members of a support group are certainly qualified to help someone they work with explore motive and discourage quick fixes.

DOES THE CLIENT UNDERSTAND WHAT MAY HAPPEN IF CHANGE RESULTS AND THE EFFECTS OF THE TRAUMA ON LIFE START TO SHIFT? If trauma reprocessing works for the client, they may genuinely change and resultantly adopt healthier lifestyle patterns. Discuss this with a client ahead of time to make sure they are aware of this potential, especially if people in their life are used to them being sick, stuck or otherwise unhealthy. This is often the case in dysfunctional or addictive family dynamics. Throughout my career I've had to work with many clients on handling the new stress they incur when others around them don't like this healthier version of themselves. The process may not be easy, yet it is one that trauma-focused recovery strategies can help a person address.

For many people, the fear that life might get better and that this may require additional changes is what keeps people stuck from moving forward in their work. This phenomenon is well-known among those of us who work in the business of change. A sponsor or support group member's sharing of experience, strength, and hope on this matter can be a tremendous benefit as a person navigates the change process in their own life.

DOES THE CLIENT HAVE EMOTIONAL SUPPORT RESOURCES, INCLUDING BUT NOT LIMITED TO A SPONSOR, HOME GROUP AND SUPPORT NETWORK, CHURCH GROUP, AND ACCESS TO HEALTHY FRIENDS AND FAMILY? Another way to ask this question could be: If the clients experience an emotionally draining counseling session and have some disturbance after they go home, is there someone healthy and supportive, besides you as the clinician, whom your client can call? I encourage clients to let at least one person in their life know they are going through intense counseling about traumatic issues in their past before we begin cathartic work. The absence of a support system does not necessarily rule out such therapy with a client. It does mean that you must spend more time preparing. If the client is genuinely without any positive social support, explore whether there are twenty-four-hour on-call services in your community or ask yourself whether you would be willing to be contacted more regularly via your answering service during this client's trauma processing.

If you are a sponsor or support group member and you are aware that someone you are working with may be going through some deeper trauma work, ask how you can best support. Something as simple as being there to call or text can make a world of difference. The person may even find it comforting to go to a meeting or spend some extra time with you in the days or weeks that follow such a clinical session.

IS THE CLIENT ABLE TO REASONABLY CALM, RELAX, OR OTHERWISE NEUTRALIZE THEIR AFFECT WHEN DISTRESSED? The clients do not have to be able to perfectly calm themselves when distressed. If they could, your services probably would not be necessary! Ask these simple questions in your evaluation: Can they use one or more coping skills to self-soothe in a healthy way? Do I have reasonable assurance that the person can and does use these skills outside of session? Has the client shown that they can entertain a difficult emotion or experience in life without totally unraveling (metaphorically speaking) and resorting to unhealthy behaviors?

I always have clients test out, on their own time, the coping skills and affect regulation exercises on which we have worked together before I proceed with trauma processing. Encouraging your clients to work with their sponsors or support group members on this process is vital. The clients who practice skills in between sessions generally stand the greatest chance of success when we transition into the deeper digging of trauma resolution work.

IS THERE A SUFFICIENT AMOUNT OF ADAPTIVE, HEALTHY MATERIAL IN THE CLIENT'S LIFE? This is the classic evaluation of recovery capital. Adaptive, healthy material can include everything from acquisition of basic needs (e.g., food, water, shelter) to work, hobbies, a supportive family, life goals, and healthy friends. The absence of such positive material does not rule out trauma processing or reprocessing work; it does necessitate more advanced preparation in the realm of recovery capital. Consider revisiting chapter 9 at any point if you, as the professional or a sponsor, feel stuck on how to help a person strengthen their resourcing in this area.

DOES THE PERSON UNDERSTAND THAT EMOTIONAL INTENSITY MAY HEIGHTEN, AT LEAST FOR A WHILE, AS THAT PERSON ENGAGES IN DEEPER TRAUMA WORK? Most of us are familiar with the axiom that things can get worse before they get better. Circling back to the trauma as wound metaphor introduced in chapter 3 and revisited throughout the book, sometimes the treatment of any injury (physical or emotional) may sting. If you've ever been through a process of physical therapy following an injury or required surgery for a physical condition, you are aware of this fact. Hopefully this treatment helped you heal in the long run.

The same applies for wound care of the emotional, spiritual, and recovery variety that is the focus of this book. The treatment itself can come with some pain and emotional intensity. We are asking people to feel things in their body and soul, which may be a completely new phenomenon to them. Alerting people to this intensity without scaring them away from it is vital. I explain that many of the treatments I offer in the modern era, like EMDR therapy and expressive arts therapy, do not require them to go into detailed narratives of what happened and that they are in control of how far we go during any given session. Yet I am pretty direct about my caution that to truly heal a wound, we must allow ourselves to feel (at least on some level) that which we buried or avoided at the time.

This process can sound intense, which is why I follow up my candid caution with a reminder about preparation. I tell my clients that I wouldn't encourage them to do work that I didn't feel they were prepared to handle. Generally, people take comfort in the thoroughness of the preparation and having a plan. Aligning a sponsor or recovery support circle into this process of preparation can be a tremendous asset in helping people deal with whatever may come up in between sessions, or to address the moving and shifting of emotion in their own lives.

Addressing Feelings Phobia

This area of discussion is so important, I dedicate a whole section to it instead of just a single question. You may be filled with questions yourself after reading the last evaluation question, flummoxed at the prospect of preparing a person to engage emotionally. When so much of a person's traumatic wounding may be wrapped up around terror in even feeling or experiencing things emotionally, doesn't the trauma work need to begin there? In many, if not most cases, it must.

When a friend recently talked about long-term struggles with anxiety, I mounted my usual soapbox about the importance of feeling your feelings fully and not stuffing them away. As a trauma-focused therapist and a yogi, my perspective is that most of the symptoms that trouble us are the result of unhealed emotional wounds that never got a chance to heal at earlier times in our lives. Until we permit ourselves to feel what we weren't able, willing, or allowed to feel at these earlier points, we'll remain in a loop of distress that manifests in a variety of symptoms.

"But I thought the idea was not to engage my feelings? To not let them get the best of me?" my friend asked.

My eyes rolled and my fury rose, knowing that the friend heard this from either a cognitively driven therapist or a psychiatrist. *Feelings phobia* is alive and well among mental health providers. Once, a student reported to me that his psychiatric medical director was so nervous about clients not being able to handle feelings, she forbade any treatments at their clinic that might make patients cry. I felt the Hulk rising up in my chest about to bust out as I heard this report, so infuriated that providers—either due to their own fear or restrictions that systemic forces placed upon them—are deliberately keeping people stuck in a rut when they offer such direction.

Our feelings are not the problem. Everything we do to keep from feeling our feelings and experiencing our emotions—even the dark and heavy ones—is the real problem. We engage in addictive behaviors, we isolate and cut off connection, and we begin to accept phenomena like panic attacks, nervousness, persistent body distress, and dissociative numbing as the norm. While I am not opposed to psychiatric medication responsibly prescribed within a larger context of care, I get concerned when people become so fixated on getting their medication type(s) and dosage just right. We believe that finding this medical solution will help us to survive the rigors of daily living, and for a time, it might. There are even some conditions and organic brain structures where psychiatric medication may be necessary for survival.

But are we meant only to survive?

Or by refusing to listen to what our feelings, experiences, and sensations have to share with us about what needs healing, are we cutting ourselves off from the deepest well of healing available to us?

So many of my early childhood memories center around being made to feel weird *because* I felt things so intensely. I am the girl who cried for days when the bad people painted Big Bird blue in the 1985 Sesame Street film *Follow That Bird*. I am the girl who was constantly told that she was too sensitive. I am also the girl who knew that if I expressed what I felt about many of the happenings of my childhood, my safety would be threatened. So I turned inward, first with eating. The arts eventually gave me an outlet that served as a bit of a release valve, yet when my perfectionistic tendencies shut those down in my life, drugs and alcohol became the natural way to temper my experiences of feeling things so damn *deeply*. Fortunately, my recovery path led me back to the expressive arts as a healthy outlet for expression. And I can now embrace my sensitivity as a character asset. Getting to this place required time spent in healing practices and learning to remove the scripts of judgment around my feelings.

My clients, friends, and my own lived experience teach me a great deal about what makes it so commonplace to block the feeling and expression of even the most natural of emotions. Reasons include fear that I won't be able to handle what comes up, fear of being judged, fear that I'm a bad person for feeling what I do, fear of being rejected, fear that the feelings will never go away and will end up destroying me, fear of hurting others, fear of people taking advantage of my vulnerability, fear of doing the hard work, fear that no one will understand or get me, fear that my sense of safety or connection to people I love will be taken away, fear of being seen, fear of making real changes in my life…. With all of these fears, of course medicating alone seems appealing!

Consider, however, that these fears do not develop in a vacuum. We generally learn them from somewhere—from our families of origin, from society, from the systems in which we get educated and eventually go to work. For many of us, it's literally the "systems" like foster care, incarceration, and yes, the medical and mental health fields that can teach us these horrid lessons. No wonder so many of us are afraid to feel when people in positions of power, even people who we are told are there to help us, can literally be the source of our feelings phobia.

It's not my place to analyze whether parents, guardians, teachers, or care providers had malicious intent back when they first said, "Don't cry." I do ask clients and sponsees to consider how this and other messages around feelings and emotions shaped early experiences. A common thread for many of us is that some of our earliest wounding was also paired with damaging messages about what it means to *express* feelings— let alone *have* them. So whether, as a young man, you were taught that boys don't cry; or whether you learned that crying only got you in more trouble, regardless of your gender expression, these source messages must be explored if it is your intention to overcome feelings phobia.

Consider that trying to stop yourself from feeling your feelings is as futile as trying to stop the flow of a river, the waves of the ocean, or yes— as futile as trying to stop yourself from doing your business when your body signals that it's time to find a toilet. Or at least somewhere to let it out, even if it's a roadside bush or a makeshift litter box (which I once had to create on an overnight bus through India with no toilet on board). All whimsy aside, think about the last time you had to "go to the bathroom." What if you were told, or even told yourself, I have to hold it in— indefinitely! Consider the level of pain and distress that would ensue, and how eventually what needs to come out will come out in an even messier, uncontained way.

As gross as it sounds, this is what we do when we do not allow ourselves the proper outlet to feel through our feelings, an experience of human living that is as natural as needing to do this physical business. Bringing this metaphor full circle, consider how most of us were toilet trained to be able to take care of these physical needs in a safe and sanitary way. And yet most of us never received the same level of patient training and instruction about the naturalness of feelings and how to express them healthfully. Every idea I am promoting in this book is to help both professionals and sponsors or other recovery support figures help the people they serve with this training ground.

Every time people let themselves feel a feeling is a victory in this healing process of experiencing the world, not just surviving it. It's difficult to take a person through this process unless we've been through it ourselves. When professionals and sponsors have not done this work at a personal level, that's where we hear comments like, *You've got to shut trauma down when patients bring it up,* or, *The point is not to engage with your feelings.* Once I hear fewer of these comments coming from professional circles, I will know that we are making real progress in fueling the paradigm shift forward.

Facilitating the Work of Trauma Processing

All professionals must make a personal judgment call—based on their training, experience, and comfort with emotional affect—about whether or not they feel qualified to take a person further with trauma work. As a trauma–addiction specialist, I often get questioned about what really qualifies a professional to work with trauma in addicted individuals. I assure clinicians that if they are considering the broadest possible definition of trauma, it is likely that they have already engaged in some pieces of processing work with a client, whether they realize it or not. That being said, in order to effectively do processing or reprocessing activities with an addicted survivor of trauma, you must be personally comfortable with trauma, affect, and the sheer horror of material that may surface. Have you addressed enough of your own issues to stay present and not destabi-lize yourself in the presence of clients' reactions?

You must also have a similar level of comfort with addiction and be will-ing to demonstrate the person-centered qualities discussed in chapter 9. If you have created an environment of safety and flexibility in your thera-peutic setting, and if you have also allowed for adequate preparation, you may be able to work with a client on processing or reprocessing trauma, implementing the skills and techniques you are comfortable using in practice. If these strategies seem insufficient to deal with the level of work that seems required among your clientele, you may be in the position of needing to seek further training. Or better yet, to do more of your own personal work that is trauma focused.

In this section of the chapter I discuss the general principles of help-ing people process trauma, and some of the time-honored strategies that some professionals and even well-suited sponsors may use to help guide people through the process. The scope of this book does not allow for a detailed explanation of each modality currently available to help people process or reprocess trauma. Many of these specialized modalities require advanced training, so I've dedicated a section in the Appendix to learning more about these specific modalities and where you can go for advanced training if you are qualified. If you are a sponsor or in another support role, looking up more information about these modalities on recommended websites may help you best support the people you serve.

One of the primary principles of effective trauma work is to find which approach will work best for the individual client. Some people need to tell the story in great detail to be able to connect the cognitive pieces of their trauma with the emotional and somatic aspects in order for full resolution to occur. For others, speaking the story in great detail simply generates too much distress, and writing may be a better option. Others may work out the distress on the yoga mat or out in nature for this integration to occur, and still others may utilize a combination of all of these elements. There is no one right way to help a client reprocess trauma. Effectiveness in this area is really a matter of offering people a variety of options or tasks that they can engage in to allow for resolution and integration.

Medical leaders in the field like Daniel Siegel and Bessel van der Kolk emphasize the importance of integration for the deepest levels of healing. You can think of this integration as the three brains of the triune brain (discussed in chapter 3) learning how to optimally communicate with each other. Unhealed trauma creates discord in the system and the brains need to learn to work together as they are designed. Like many trauma professionals, I've come to embrace Bessel van der Kolk's *The Body Keeps the Score* as a modern classic in the field of trauma-focused literature. Van der Kolk states, "For real change to take place, the body needs to learn that the danger has passed and to live in the reality of the present."[19] This is a useful overall definition of what it truly means to process or heal trauma. Revisiting the wound care metaphor, *processing* is analogous to healing. Just as a physical wound must heal properly, so must an emotional wound.

Van der Kolk offers a brilliant framework for healing in *The Body Keeps the Score* that aligns so well with the triune brain model. To help survivors feel alive in the present and move on with their lives, a combination of strategies is typically needed in each of these three areas:

- **Top-down methods** (accessing the neocortex), such as talking, connecting with others, self-knowledge. These methods typically access the neocortex.

- **Technology or outside strategies** (accessing the limbic brain), including medications to shut down inappropriate alarm reactions and other therapies/technologies. These change the way the brain organizes information.

- **Bottom-up methods** (accessing the brainstem, limbic brain, or both). These allow the body to have experiences that deeply and viscerally contradict the helplessness, rage, and collapse that typically result from trauma.

Returning to the wound metaphor, consider how top-down methods can be very important initially for stabilizing a wound, just as we might wash out a cut or put a dressing on an injury. Yet continuing to do this without allowing for healing at deeper levels means that the wound will never truly heal.

TOP-DOWN METHODS. The three primary examples that van der Kolk offers for top-down methods—talking, connecting with others, and self-knowledge—offer an ideal description of what happens in twelve-step meetings and in treatment settings fueled largely by a twelve-step paradigm. While the general argument in modern trauma-focused care is that these tasks can't provide people with a sufficiently holistic recovery experience, they are still important. Especially when we consider that as human beings we generally talk with each other to establish relationship and the beginning stages of rapport. Moreover, remember that the genesis of the recovery movement was one alcoholic helping another, so we cannot dismiss the relevance of a good, connecting conversation. In addition to using our verbal and cognitive capacity to begin sharing our stories (if possible) and connecting with others, the importance of psychoeducation or self-knowledge has long been embraced as important to the healing process.

Learning about addiction and the impact of trauma on the brain and on our behavior can be a game changer for individuals caught in the quagmire of shame and belief that they struggle simply because they are defective. As Eastern thought teaches, ignorance ends when knowledge begins. We empower people when we equip them with the knowledge they may need to see themselves and their struggles in a new light.

Some people would describe the healing practice of telling one's story as a top-down approach to healing. For some people it is, especially if the practice focuses on the cognitive and factual aspects of the narrative. We've likely encountered the types of clients or people in meetings who can talk freely about what happened to them, yet they still seem stuck or in some cases, not emotionally connected to the content of the story. In my clinical experience, when people only tell the story without connecting with it in more of a bottom-up way, processing or healing may be incomplete.

One of the popular healing methods defining much of addiction treatment in North America is cognitive behavioral therapy. While there seems to be a great backlash among cognitive behavioral approaches from holistic trauma therapists, I'd like to be clear that cognitive behavioral therapy is not the enemy. The problem is when cognitive behavioral therapy is the sole treatment people receive. As acknowledged, top-down treatments may be essential to get the proverbial ball rolling in the healing process. Moreover, in the forms of cognitive behavioral therapy where emphasis is placed on the *behavioral* elements and connecting with emotional content, some productive value can be gleaned.

This does not mean that we have to abandon cognitive-behavioral interventions as part of trauma-sensitive processing; it does mean that we need to modify them with simple, body-based approaches and sensitivity to the role that the past plays. Remember the slogan, "It is better to act your way into better thinking than to think your way into better acting." Learning to engage in healthier behaviors and embracing action-oriented coping skills may effectively and adaptively impact a person's thinking. Thus, if you are primarily a cognitive behavioral therapist, you can use many of your existing techniques to help clients reprocess their traumas, as long as you bring the body into the process and recognize the limitations of cognitions alone.

An entire approach called Mindfulness-Based Cognitive Therapy (MBCBT) is built on this principle of integrating mindfulness-informed interventions into time-honored cognitive strategies. The wildly popular dialectical behavior therapy (DBT), acceptance and commitment therapy (ACT), and Mindfulness-Based Relapse Prevention (MBRP) therapy are also considered to be a part of this new wave of cognitive therapies that recognize the limitations of cognitive work alone. Mindfulness and other embodied strategies are used to fortify the content of standard cognitive-behavioral work to help people better manage affect and distress.

Other approaches that have gained attention in recent years include Trauma-Focused CBT, Cognitive Processing Therapy, and the various forms of exposure therapy. While I personally do not find these very useful in my own practice because they are too narratively focused, I find them important to note here in the spirit of multiple paths to recovery that defines this book. If I work with a client who has primarily gone through one of these methods as part of treatment, I generally need to pick up where this other work left off in order to address places where the client may still be stuck in fully experiencing emotion and body sensation. Addressing these stuck points is best done by the following two categories of intervention.

TECHNOLOGY. Technology is any development designed to make a work or task easier. Consider that the wheel was once high technology. Notice that the Amish or groups of people without access to electricity still use technology by this definition. Technology is anything applied and received at the level of the limbic brain (the central processing unit of human experience) to make a process like healing or transforming trauma more efficient.

In his model, van der Kolk names medication as an example of technology. For many of us, using medication as part of our healing plan may be part of our process. As I stated earlier in this chapter, I am not opposed to medical solutions if they are properly and responsibly prescribed within the larger context of healing. This view is excessively liberal for some who may describe themselves as more old school or traditional in their view of recovery and very naïve to others in constant search of the medical solution. I'll leave you and your clients to decide what is right for you. Be aware that if medication is getting in the way of deeper healing of trauma while promoting symptom relief alone, there may be cause for concern. Which brings us to the second part of van der Kolk's description—other therapies or technologies that change the way the brain organizes information.

Examples of such therapies generating a great deal of attention in modern therapeutic circles include EMDR therapy, the closely related Somatic Experiencing (SE) and Sensorimotor Psychotherapy, Neurofeedback, and any variety of creative or expressive arts therapies. New twists and turns on these methods are continuing to be explored every day, with spin-offs of each (e.g., Brainspotting, which developed from EMDR therapy) gaining notoriety. Even older and more time-honored therapeutic methods like psychoanalysis, hypnotherapy, and Gestalt psychotherapy would meet this definition of technology. Through the systemic application of a therapeutic protocol, facilitators are helping people change the way their brains reorganize and store information.

Addiction treatment often incorporates two methods from the Gestalt tradition of psychotherapy: the *empty chair* technique and the *unsent letter* technique. When used properly within the context of adequate preparation and stabilization, both can be excellent for trauma processing. In the empty chair technique, clients may imagine a perpetrator of trauma or other dysfunctional figure sitting in an empty chair across from them. Then, the clients say everything to that figure that they have been holding in. Sometimes, empty chair sessions can be very emotional, eliciting the necessary screams, wails, and tears that clients may have suppressed for decades.

A similar technique—and one of my personal favorites to use both formally within therapy and informally with twelve-step recovering peers—is the unsent letter. There are numerous variations on the unsent letter technique. The key is to find which variation or combination of variations will work best for a specific person. The basic premise of the unsent letter is that people write out everything they would like to say to the person who wounded them. When I encourage people to do this, I emphasize that the intention is not to send this letter (at least the initial draft of it), rather, to get out everything that needs to be expressed. I encourage people to write uncensored—swear, curse, lash out—just get out all of the feelings that they have held back.

After a person writes the first letter, you can collaboratively decide what would be most healing. For instance, some people find comfort in taking the letter to a gravesite in the case of a deceased abuser or family member. Other people may take great joy in ripping the letter up, feeling the physical sensations as they tear the pages and throw them away. Very often, clients do this in my office and dump the torn pages in my wastebasket, symbolizing that they are letting the material go and leaving it behind in the office. One client even flushed hers down my toilet! Many people find great spiritual significance in going outside and burning the pages, watching the smoke rise to the sky as a symbol of ultimate release to some entity that is greater than the individual. When I wrote a profanity-laced unsent letter many years ago, I put it in the prayer intentions bin at a church, knowing that this church burns the intentions after a few weeks. For me, it symbolized turning my pain over to my Higher Power. The options and combinations are endless.

Some people like to write one letter to the same person each week or each month until they feel that the issue has resolved and they can try to embrace some semblance of forgiveness. Once, a client wrote one letter each week to her deceased mother. She found that with each week, the level of anger dissipated. At the end of six weeks, she had arrived at a place of loving acceptance about her mother's life and the pain that her mother caused her.

Another option involves the writers imagining what the response to the letters might be. After writing the unsent letter, the clients write two letters back to themselves from the point of view of the abuser—one letter represents the words that the clients would *like* to hear from the abuser, and the other letter contains the words with which the abuser would *likely* respond. Then, you can have the clients notice their reactions and feelings after reading each letter.

One question naturally arises as we explore empty chair and unsent letter: Should the client ever really confront the abuser face-to-face or should they ever actually send the letter? Opinions vary on this matter. I tend to embrace the recovery logic that we, as people, can make *ourselves* irrational when we try to reason with irrational people. Thus, I typically find that confronting the abuser or actually sending the letters to be fruitless efforts unless the client has the express understanding that the abuser will likely ignore, stonewall, or further demean them. Some people, knowing the risks, still feel that they need to engage in this confrontation for their own resolution. I generally support a client taking the risk if adequate preparation and recovery basics are in place. However, in most cases, I feel that the empty chair or unsent letter techniques provide elegant, safe alternatives that typically yield just as much, or even more good, than if people actually engaged in confrontation or sending the letter.

The various examples of emerging therapeutic technologies that I mentioned in this section come with varying degrees of evidence and support. EMDR therapy, for instance, is one of the two most researched therapies on the planet for the efficacious treatment of healing PTSD. Research specifically on its use with substance use and other addictive disorders is limited yet emerging. EMDR has been widely used with individuals at various levels of recovery since its introduction in 1989, primarily because of the high co-occurrence between untreated PTSD and addictive disorders. A primary finding in my own dissertation research from 2009 is that the EMDR clinician's adequate understanding of substance use and addictive disorders and knowing *how* to apply the EMDR in context is imperative. My colleague and collaborative partner Dr. Stephen Dansiger is currently launching the MET(T)A protocol, a curriculum for introducing EMDR therapy and mindfulness-informed strategies as primary treatment methods alongside twelve-step support in addiction treatment facilities. While specific research data on the success of this method is still being gathered, its logic makes good sense as a way to blend innovation about healing trauma from the bottom up while also respecting what tradition recovery teaches us about stabilizing from the top down.

As in many facets of society, the research is often slow to catch up with what we realize is working in practice. Most of us involved with the actual *doing* are not involved with academic institutions that can easily support research. You hear the term "evidence-based" tossed around conversations in the helping professions quite a bit these days, and I often get asked if a certain new therapy is evidence-based for addiction or trauma.

So what constitutes good evidence?

Some people want to see a rigorous standard of randomized controlled research studies that meet some organization's recipe for a gold standard, before they accept something as evidence-based. Others (like me), see these types of research studies and standards as out of touch with what goes on in the real world. My best guidance is to use your judgment, based on the setting in which you practice and on what you know in your gut to be true about human nature. Yes, some of these practices have more research basis than others. However, I am never one to dispute what a collection of clients and people in the community are reporting to be helpful.

Recall the definition of *evidence-based practice* covered in chapter 8, as described by the American Psychological Association: "the best available research with clinical expertise in the context of patient characteristics, culture, and preferences." Context matters, and the ultimate sign of whether or not something is working reflects in the specific changes a person is making in their lives. As a program, if you claim yourself to be evidence-based because you're working from a manual that bears such a stamp on its cover, yet people aren't engaged and retaining what they learn in treatment, is your program really operating at a high standard of excellence?

If, as a program administrator, you are worried about whether or not something is formally listed as evidence-based, check out the website of the Substance Abuse and Mental Health Services Administration (SAMHSA), at www.samhsa.gov. This site offers a complete listing of what the organization considers to be evidence-based practices, or emerging promising practices based on their research standards. Then again, if petting a horse or working with animals helped you overcome your trauma in a truly holistic manner, that may be all the evidence that you personally need, right? Like with so many things in this field and in discussions about recovery, defining *evidence* often depends on whom you ask.

BOTTOM-UP METHODS.   When I teach trauma-focused trainings, I offer van der Kolk's definition of bottom-up methods as allowing the body to have experiences that deeply and viscerally contradict the helplessness, rage, and collapse that result from the trauma. I ask people what has allowed them to experience this contradiction and I get responses as various as learning how to make love or have sex in a nurturing context to experiencing a good, solid cry in the presence of a supportive friend. Some people talk about the relationships they forge with their pets, others discuss an experience with expressive arts or spiritual practice, and others profess to the healing power of a specific psychotherapy. Once more, evidence of what works is subjective—which makes sense when we consider that how people experience the wounds of trauma is a subjective construct.

As a professional, I truly know that something has healed from the bottom up when people have shifted at a total level—when they know in both the head and the heart that they are *not* the horrible messages they received about themselves or their place in the world as a result of the trauma. As a person in long-term recovery, I know for myself and can see it in others that people are healing from the bottom up when they realize that what happened to them no longer has to control their lives. From both of my perspectives, I recognize that total, inside-out healing happens when we can embrace the story of what may have happened to us without getting too attached to it. Yogis call this *dis-identification*. From this place of detachment and release, we can discover new stories to embrace and new ways of being in our lives!

There are a variety of ways for people to embrace and release the stories of their trauma that can lead to resolution. As the case of Jeff demonstrated in chapter 4, for some, being able to share their stories over and over again at twelve-step meetings until the major emotional charge in the stories lessens is one way to use storytelling as a method of processing or healing. Others find similar healing in fourth- and fifth-step work. There are some who may never feel optimally comfortable sharing the story in front of a group of people, so writing it down, either literally or through the use of fiction and allegory, is an option. A client once wrote an entire novel about his traumatic experience, changing certain names and situations while exaggerating other elements for dramatic effect. As I read his work, it was clear to me that he used the story as a way of creating a new, more desired ending for himself that helped him move on from the trauma. In certain African cultures, speaking about the exact details of a trauma is taboo, yet using allegory—specifically animals as characters—is a more than acceptable manner of telling the story for the purpose of catharsis.

Songwriting and other expressive elements like dance, drama, and the visual arts are other outstanding ways to tell the story for the purposes of release and resolution. If you listen to the work of many singer-songwriters who have battled the demons of addiction and trauma in their lives, it is clear how they have used their songwriting craft to reprocess many of their experiences. Neil Young's "The Needle and the Damage Done" and Stevie Nicks's "Landslide" are two of my favorite examples of this art. For many people in recovery, music is vital. Whether it comes in the form of making playlists, learning to perform, or even discovering your own songwriting potential, these avenues create experiences for transformation of stifled energy and emotion.

Many dance forms exist that can help individuals use movement as a way to tell their story and experience emotional cleansing, whether they are more therapeutic in nature or designed as a form of meditative practice. I developed the Dancing Mindfulness community practice (which now can be used as an expressive arts therapy practice) in 2012. While I experienced therapeutic and meditative dance in several other forms, Dancing Mindfulness was born when I realized that I could use dance to be present with the rising tide of heavy emotions that resulted from the most significant loss of my life. The yogis have taught for millennia that every experience invites an opportunity for awareness and meditation, while dance has also been used as a healing art since the dawn of time by the first peoples to inhabit the planet. With my creation of the Dancing Mindfulness practice I did not discover anything that my ancestors didn't already know. Rather, I was able to use my pain to create a container to experience and eventually teach meditation in a way that is fun, challenging, and ultimately accessible for modern audiences.

In professional psychotherapy, we've long been attuned to the healing power of witness. Many of our clients report that having someone trustworthy and nurturing to witness the sharing and transformation of our stories is the game changer for healing. I ask my colleagues in the field to bear in mind that this may happen in ways other than talk. Consider how writing, dance, movement, music, drama, and more modern avenues like filmmaking and music mixing can offer people templates in which to work. There are as many ways to tell a story as there are stories in the world, and infinitely more ways to create a new ending.

From Reprocessing to Reintegration

The word *integration* best encapsulates the ultimate goal of reprocessing or healing trauma. Through integration, one brings together parts of an experience that were once disjointed and chaotic and helps them fit together in a way that makes sense. Engaging in such a process may finally bring recovering individuals to a place where they are able to live life *"one day at a time."* This saying moves beyond a placating slogan and becomes a way of life. Engaging in such a process and having an integrated sense of wholeness emerge from the debris of scattered emotional shards can help a person truly heal from and move past the wounds of the past, embracing a lifestyle of recovery and wellness.

In the consensus model of trauma treatment, the third stage, reintegration, implies that we as human beings are born with an innate sense of wholeness and an ability to contribute to society at large. Engaging in the healing work of preparation and trauma processing restores people to their birthright. It is important that we, as helpers, not just leave people to fend for themselves after reprocessing the trauma.

Professionals and recovery sponsors have a duty to help a person through the process of readjusting to life without the weight. In the trauma literature this process is sometimes referred to as post-traumatic growth. Post-traumatic growth has long implied that in the reintegration phase, armed with a new sense of resilience and self-efficacy, what we once saw as our greatest deficits can become our greatest assets. Following the language of an AA promise, we will not regret the past or wish to shut the door on it.[20] A research subject once expressed that before treatment and recovery, her thoughts, feelings and experiences were all tangled up like a ball of yarn—and she needed something to untangle them. After treatment and recovery facilitated this process of untangling, she was able to take that yarn and knit it into something beautiful, like a sweater or a blanket. This metaphor has long been one of my favorites for what is meant by post-traumatic growth.

Helping a person in addiction recovery heal from the aftereffects of trauma does not have to be rocket science. Simple knowledge of how trauma affects a person, awareness of our own issues connected to trauma and addiction, attention to relational imperatives, and willingness to incorporate the entire being—body, mind, and spirit—into treatment are the keys. Carrying these essential guidelines into the reintegration process is no different. Adjustment, even positive adjustment, can cause its own share of stressors. However, what you *do* to help a person in the stabilization or preparation stages, especially paying attention to the healing quality of a relationship, has just as much impact in the reintegration stage.

It all really does come full circle.

The twelve-step model is built for productive interpretation of reintegration because in the philosophy of the twelve steps, we are always works in progress. There is no such thing as perfect healing or arriving at some magical promised land. Every year of our recovery journey may come with a new challenge for us to address and a deeper level of healing to be obtained. What I worked on at ten years, twelve years, or sixteen years sober may have overwhelmed me if I tried to tackle it in the earliest days of getting well. I'm grateful that I had the support to get well enough to be open to what the rest of the journey revealed. Echoing the wisdom of my late friend Denise once more, with the disease of addiction, we can choose how well we want to get.

May we, as professionals, sponsors, and other members of the recovery community be there to continue supporting each other as this process of revelation unfolds. This ongoing support and care when needed is the heart of a trauma-focused approach to reintegration. There is a slogan (one that I happen to like) that says, "More will be revealed." New wounds that we were not aware of when we entered a path of recovery may finally reveal themselves as traumas we never addressed. For some of us, reading a book such as this can elicit such revelations. There may be a tendency to experience some shame if this happens. I hear so many folks say things like, "Why haven't I figured it out yet?" Please consider that progressive healing is a normal part of recovery. Moreover, if trauma was not specifically addressed in your early recovery, once you become aware of it, it's only natural for what you haven't healed yet to come to the surface. Especially when you become aware.

Awareness, like knowledge, is the end of ignorance.

TOOLKIT STRATEGY:
FINDING WHAT WORKS

In order to help your clients or sponsees identify which modalities will best help them reprocess their traumatic experiences, it is first helpful for you as the professional to reflect upon what has worked for you to process or heal in your journey. Think about something in your life, be it a significant life transition or a major trauma. In your reflection, what helped you work through it and obtain some sort of functional resolution? Was it one modality or activity, or a combination? Moreover, how has the healing you experienced led to your own resilience or post-traumatic growth? Consider how the information you obtained in your reflection above might give you some insight into the people you serve.

11

Respect for Change—
Trauma-Sensitive
Recovery in a Diverse World

At the end of my service in Bosnia and Herzegovina, I attended a small AA conference in eastern Croatia. Twelve-step programs were slow to emerge in much of Eastern Europe during the communist era, so the early 2000s were an exciting time to get sober in that part of the world. Initially I was very moved by the conference, especially as someone in early recovery. Not only were expats and workers like me from various parts of the world at the conference, there were Croats, Bosnians, and Serbs in attendance. For a few brief moments I sensed into the Utopian potential of recovery— how people on different sides of a war, still struggling to overcome centuries of ethnic conflict, could be united by a common goal: the need to get sober and well. I heard about such meetings that existed in Jerusalem, where Israelis and Palestinians were able to put aside their differences in recognition of the bigger problem. And here I was, sitting in a meeting in my ancestral homeland! Could recovery be the path to world peace?

Thud.

I quickly fell from my cloud when a new battle ensued: whether it was appropriate to let "addicts" attend the conference and have voice at the meeting. An American aid worker got very vocal in his displeasure that a young group of NA members doing good work in Zagreb, Croatia's capital city, was allowed to speak at one of the conference meetings. The locals didn't seem to care—they were just glad that recovery was taking off in a part of the world that so desperately needed it. I sat there, shocked and rather triggered. The fighting that ensued at the meeting felt like a replication of trauma dynamics from the religious conflict of my early childhood and made absolutely no sense to me. Janet encouraged me not to worry about too much about the distinction between drug addiction and alcoholism, because in her neurologically sound view, it was all the same and all would kill me. If she had been splitting hairs about the differences between the two conditions like the people at this conference were, I never would have given twelve-step recovery a chance.

What I experienced at that conference was my first major exposure to one of the ugly truths of recovery—people will have their own fundamentalist interpretations of certain guidelines like *singleness of purpose,* while also ignoring one of the other basic traditions of most twelve-step recovery fellowships. That tradition, at least in AA terms, states that the "only requirement for membership is a desire to stop drinking."[21] Truly, that ought to be the *only* guideline we set for letting people attend closed meetings, with the word drinking being open to change depending on the fellowship. As the name suggests, open meetings (where you do not have to meet the requirement of the tradition) ought to be open to all.

People in recovery like to proclaim a literature-inspired slogan: "patience and tolerance are our code." To be truly trauma informed in meeting culture and in professional treatment, we have to go beyond patience and tolerance—acceptance is imperative. Acceptance of others regardless of their background or how they personally identify. Acceptance of others, no matter which path or paths of recovery they chose. Acceptance of others who are different from us.

In this chapter I explore what I observe as twelve-step culture's major barriers to offering spaces both accepting and affirming of all who enter in search of help. First I will make a case for why being accepting (a trauma-informed minimum) and affirming (a trauma-focused ideal) is an issue in the modern world. Then, I will offer specific explorations of diversity as it relates to the path of recovery and how people personally identify in terms of race, ethnicity, gender, and sexuality. Spiritual and religious diversity is such a large issue, I dedicate the entire next chapter to it.

This chapter may be a challenge for you to read, especially if you are a person who is pretty set in your perspectives about how the world should work and how recovery should operate. I don't ask you to agree with everything I share in this chapter. Being open to diversity and change does not negate the good work you've already done as a professional or sponsor. In the spirit of honesty, open-mindedness, and willingness that we ask those new to recovery to consider about a way of life in recovery, I ask you to try on these qualities in a new way as you read this chapter. The world has changed a great deal since the founding of Alcoholics Anonymous and twelve-step recovery in the 1930s. I write this chapter accepting that reality, and offer solutions for how we can better respond to the needs of those seeking recovery in the twenty-first century. This entire book is a presentation of how we can meld tradition and innovation. If you have stayed with me this far, hopefully you're willing to go a little further....

Why Honoring Diversity Matters

When I teach courses of the "Trauma 101" variety, I give a standard talk that parallels the introduction to trauma content in chapter 3. I explain how not all traumas or unhealed wounds necessarily meet the criteria for a *DSM* diagnosis. After offering this expanded definition of trauma, I ask participants to name some examples of trauma that come to mind beyond the most obvious (e.g., war, sexual assault, natural disasters). Usually people will next mention examples like divorce, toxic work environments, and caring for an ill family member. Only about half the time will anyone call out something like "poverty," and then I encourage them to keep going with that. What about things we as a culture have so normalized, we may even fail to identify them as traumatic? In addition to poverty, I offer examples like being impacted by racism, oppression, or discrimination for any reason.

I either hear crickets or unleash a torrent of very lively discussion.

In 2016 I had the privilege to give an EMDR therapy overview at a conference for treatment providers of color. We didn't even get to the content on EMDR. I was not surprised, yet was still amazed at how healing the validation of an experience like racism as traumatic was to my students in attendance. I listened to the attendees' experience, strength, and hope on the traumatic impact of being a person of color in communities and systems that will likely invalidate their experience. The conference taught me that validating the suffering people experience, especially in contexts when it is likely to be ignored or dismissed, is a vital first step in healing trauma. And healing trauma can be a life or death matter to people seeking recovery from addiction.

Consider the concept of negative cognitions that accompany any traumatic experience. In EMDR therapy and various other modalities, we describe *negative cognitions* as the messages people receive about themselves (e.g., "I am a failure," "I am permanently damaged," "No one will ever love me") or the world ("No one can be trusted," "I am in danger") resulting from a traumatic experience. In the fifth edition updated in 2013, even the *DSM* added the presence of such cognitions as part of the negative alterations in cognitions and mood criterion under the PTSD diagnosis.

My colleague Rajani Venkatraman Levis and her writing partner Laura Siniego introduced the idea of *oppressive cognitions* in a 2016 book chapter on cultural diversity in EMDR therapy. This construct takes the idea of *negative cognitions* a step further by recognizing that some of these messages we internalize are rooted in what we learned from others about our race, ethnicity, gender, or sexual identity. Examples of oppressive cognitions can be very specific (e.g., "Dark-skinned women are not beautiful," "I am a freak for being this way," "Real men don't cry," "I am trash because of where I come from," "I am an abomination because Jesus says so") or more generalized ("The world is not a safe place for people like me"). In the words of Melita Travis Johnson, an African-American woman, long-time social worker, and one of my personal mentors, "Oppression complicates—*and aggravates*—the recovery process."

Nikki Myers, the founder of Yoga of 12-Step Recovery, graciously shared her story for my 2014 book *Trauma Made Simple: Competencies in Assessment, Treatment, and Working with Survivors.* A powerful African-American woman who is a force for healing and good in the world, Nikki offered a reflection about being a child during the Civil Rights movement of the 1960s that speaks to the impact of oppressive cognitions as a trauma recovery issue:

> *Something had to be wrong with me if these people who looked like me were being treated this way. Everything I'd learned in school taught me that government and authority was to be respected, so if government and authority was doing this to children like me, I must be flawed.*[22]

Nikki's work, which aligns with Somatic Experiencing and the teachings of Peter Levine, recognizes that unhealed trauma leaves an energetic imprint on the body.

These visceral imprints are very real and can be even more impacting when they fester day in and day out. Although many people who have experienced oppression can pinpoint one or two major events in their lives that might qualify for a PTSD diagnosis, it's the cumulative impact that can be more damaging. A student of color once described her experience of racism to me as "the trauma of a thousand paper cuts." This brings the wound metaphor introduced in chapter 3 into sobering perspective.

At this point, you may dismiss what I've presented thus far as irrelevant because these experiences were not so for you. Or you may fear that drawing attention to the dynamics of oppression plays into the idea of *terminal uniqueness,* or the inclination many folks in recovery have to prove that they had it worse than others. Remember that a core component of trauma-informed care is honoring that just because something was a certain way for you, doesn't mean it was that way for everyone else. I am not a politician, pundit, sociologist, or diversity specialist, and it's well beyond the scope of this book for me to get into any debates on the matter. Consider, if you're familiar with the Big Book of *Alcoholics Anonymous,* how we are even encouraged to resign from the debating society in order to get well. So I am no longer a debater.

And yet I am a trauma specialist and can testify to the reality of oppression and the various ways it manifests itself as a legitimate form of wounding that needs to be addressed. My hope is that people in recovery who have not been personally affected by oppressive cognitions in any way can honor the struggle of people who have. Even if you have been impacted by oppressive cognitions based on how you grew up, please don't transpose this wounding onto others by getting into shouting matches about who had it worse. I've seen this happen too often in the rooms of recovery, and that is not how we help each other heal.

Alcoholics Anonymous was founded by two well-educated white men of privilege. If you are a white person reading this you may already be getting nervous at the very mention of the word *privilege*. Privilege doesn't mean that you don't have problems or your life hasn't been hard. A simple way to look at it is that you have not experienced the extra stress of having to navigate life with the added weight of oppression due to race, ethnicity, gender, class, or sexual orientation. Recognizing your privilege means honoring that you may not have to worry about what others face as a daily struggle. This recognition and the personal work that goes along with it are important if you are going to work with others in recovery who are different from you.

Failure to honor the struggle of an individual seeking help pushes more people away from seeking or retaining help than any other factor I've observed in my career. Recognize and acknowledge how others experience life—this is the very definition of empathy. If your biases and misconceptions about how people other than you experience the world is getting in the way of your being empathetic, there is likely more work to be done on yourself if you wish to be of optimal service to others. In the brilliant words of Pastor Nadia Bolz-Weber, herself a person in long-term recovery, "Our drug of choice is knowing who we're better than."[23] This hit me like a ton of bricks when I heard her say it out loud. It felt like the answer to why we can get ourselves into a frantic mess as a society, and why we can alienate people in recovery contexts.

If you feel uncomfortable about anything you have read thus far, or anything you read in the sections that follow, remember that discomfort is required for meaningful change. Hopefully you first picked up this book because you *want* to do better. The sections that follow will go into more of the specifics on how you *can*. The quest to do better must always include constant inventory and evaluation of ourselves, our biases, and where our own wounds may need healing.

Inclusion and Responsiveness

Meetings and treatment centers ought to be places where everyone feels welcome, regardless of who they are or where they come from. Controversy naturally ensues when we make statements like this, since we can also advocate for special meetings or even specialized treatment programs to exist. There are, for instance, both gender-specific meetings and treatment programs, and LGBT+-specific meetings and treatment programs. In some areas, there are twelve-step meetings that specifically address the needs of Black/African-American or Latinx individuals in recovery. Meetings and treatment centers have the right to establish themselves with a focus that responds to the needs of individuals in question.

A way I reconcile what seems to be a paradox is by looking at the intention of the meeting and the treatment center. If the meeting or treatment center does not specify whom they serve, the meeting's mission should be to welcome all who attend. At meetings, for instance, special efforts can be made to ensure that pamphlets on diversity published by AA, NA, and other fellowships are available. There is a long history of literature, at least at the level of pamphlets and newsletters, on the special needs of the Black/African-American individual, the Native American individual, and LGBT+ persons in recovery. In treatment centers, recovery literature from twelve-step and other sources by a variety of authors from various backgrounds ought to be represented if the centers have libraries.

In twelve-step meetings, which are not subject to a strict leadership format, it is the role of what is called the group conscience and chosen trusted servants to perform tasks like writing opening statements for meetings and addressing concerns as they are raised in meetings. Although the World Services leaders of twelve-step fellowships themselves can stay notoriously silent on issues like predatory behaviors in meetings, a group conscience meeting can address such problems at the level of individual group. If members of a group are concerned about discriminatory, predatory, or otherwise unwelcome behaviors that they observe toward other members, they can bring this issue to group conscience for it to be addressed. In such circumstances, I've seen modifications made to the opening group statement about what will not be tolerated at meetings (e.g., racist or inflammatory language, boundary-violating behaviors toward others).

On the professional side, everything treatment centers or clinical venues can and will do to promote a greater sense of representation in your staff is imperative. If your clinical staff and leadership is populated exclusively by straight white people, think about the message that sends to clients and the community about who is welcome. Another facet of this issue to discuss is tokenism. This happens when professional leadership allows a "token" person of color or "token" sexual minority on staff without listening meaningfully to their contributions and perspectives. I've heard clinical leaders say things like, "We do LGBT-focused treatment, we have a gay person on staff," more times than I can count. Not only does this represent tokenism and its problems, it also demonstrates an easy-way-out attitude when it comes to fully looking at the unique needs of traditionally underrepresented people.

This leads us to the other side of the issue—is there a place for "specific" treatment programs and meetings that meet the unique needs of a special population, or is establishing a population as "special" a discriminatory practice? Clearly my answer is no. I've already mentioned the long history of specific meetings for certain populations in twelve-step groups if the needs of the community call for them and twelve-step group members are willing to start them. There is also a long precedent for specialized tracks within treatment programs for certain professionals (e.g., doctors, nurses, pilots), and in the 1980s we started to see more gender-specific treatment programs or tracks for women.

In twelve-step communities, accusations abound that these specialty tracks promote terminal uniqueness and exclusion. In reality, the specialized meetings and treatment tracks that have formed to address the unique needs of people based on race and ethnicity, gender, and sexual orientation began because such people felt their stories were not being heard by the mainstream members of meetings or clinical professionals at treatment centers.

One such story is that of Ginny O'Keefe, the original founder of Amethyst, Inc. in Columbus, Ohio. Now in her seventies, Ginny shares that in the early 1980s, she and many other women in the Columbus area found themselves in the minority at twelve-step meetings. They naturally gravitated toward each other, and a common thread in their stories was trauma. Trauma that they did not feel safe or welcome to talk about at meetings predominated by men. Ginny and her original group of women secured the funding to open and grow Amethyst, a facility that at the height of its ability to procure resources and funding was the premier trauma-focused facility for women in Ohio. Care was long term, women were allowed to come to treatment with their children, and specialty programming in both lifestyle needs and trauma interventions was offered.

The program that Ginny originally developed, and even in her advanced years would like to try to start again, was forged in the fire of responsiveness—responsiveness to the needs of women. This idea of *responsiveness* is the solution for addressing the needs of people whose needs do not seem to be met by the mainstream. For instance, in my early years as a therapist I steadily recommended gender-specific meetings for female clients especially, even though I advocated that males go to men's meetings when available. As I've evolved in the last two decades as a professional, I've realized some sticking points in the conventional recovery logic of *women with women, men with men*. The intention of such a suggestion was that it's important to form connections that are nonromantic, and perhaps even to eventually see other members of your sex as allies and not the enemy. However, this doesn't take into account how a woman who identifies as lesbian, bisexual, pansexual, or otherwise attracted romantically to women may feel in such settings. The same applies for men who have attractions to other men and how that may complicate their involvement in men's groups.

Moreover, there is a much greater sense of attunement now than in the 1980s to the idea that gender is not the binary, black-and-white construct that people once thought. Some people see themselves as gender-nonconforming and wouldn't neatly identify as belonging at one meeting or another. Some people identify as transgender and are in active transition. One such friend in transition used their long-term sponsor (a male) in addition to a new female sponsor for quite some time. This is an example of a responsive solution that helped the individual receive what they needed in recovery, in a way that was safe for them. As I mentioned in chapter 5, as a bisexual female I am currently sponsored by an older gay male. Together he and I cosponsor another young bisexual woman. There are a variety of solutions that can work in situations where simple black-and-white answers may not be practical.

I prefer the terminology and direction of gender-responsive instead of gender-specific treatment. Gender-responsive approaches take into consideration what messages an individual learned about gender and how these messages impacted their development or exacerbated their experience of trauma. One of the classics in the addiction literature is a 1994 book from pioneer Stephanie Covington called *A Woman's Way through the Twelve Steps,* a work that changed the lives of countless women. My friend Dan Griffin followed up with *A Man's Way through the Twelve Steps* in 2009. This made a great deal of sense to me when I saw it debut. After all, men's meetings exist in recovery communities, so it would make sense for men to have a similar resource.

In getting to know Dan as a personal friend and studying his work, I became more attuned to what it means to be gender responsive. We can easily write off men as the mainstream because recovery fellowships were founded by men and can still be predominated by men. A great myth in the field, often supported by data and statistics, is that men are not impacted by trauma as much as women. I've never taken these statistics very seriously. It is generally even more stigmatizing for men to disclose experiences like sexual abuse than it is to admit having a problem with addiction, and this withholding shows up in survey data. Trauma is an issue for all genders. As Dan has helped me to understand, the messages in which men are steeped via our cultural socialization can make it even harder for men to seek help.

As Dan explains, the Rules of Recovery that we generally lay out for people are that you have to ask for help, get vulnerable, and show emotions. Yet men are typically socialized to not ask for help, not be vulnerable, and not show emotions. You can see where the natural problem arises. In Dan's experience, a female clinician's willingness to acknowledge their understanding of this socialization to a male client can be a game changer in moving care forward. This act of validation can be very difficult for female survivors of trauma working with men, especially in the era of the #MeToo movement—as we can be quick to blame toxic masculinity for social problems. Yet have we stopped to consider the impact of unhealed trauma in the way that men may act out?

There are no simple answers to many of these questions. When one of my associates heard Dan's contention that it's more permissive culturally for women to be emotional, she responded, "Yeah, we're allowed to be emotional. But not too emotional. Or we get labeled as crazy." Dan recognizes these issues too. He and I have long believed that the way to productively move forward is to recognize that we're all in this together and have conversations where we feel safe enough to express our experiences freely. In the resources section of the Appendix, I provide a link to an episode of his podcast *The Man Rules,* where Dan and I take this idea out for a dance. I also include a link to some of his teaching videos.

Although there are many more specialty populations we can cover as part of this discussion, there is only so much that can be done in one book. Visit the Appendix so you can continue to explore on your own based on where the gaps may exist in your knowledge. I hope that the ideas of not making assumptions based on your way and worldview, and being responsive to the needs of individuals rings out as an imperative.

Because of horrible, hateful comments I've heard from people in twelve-step communities about folks who identify as gay, lesbian, bisexual, transgender, or as part of any other minority group based on sexuality or gender expression, I draw special attention to this community. We often use the abbreviation LGBT+ to include that there are many other "letters" that find a home in this community (e.g., queer—which is often used as a catchall identifier, questioning, intersex, asexual). A common thread for all of us using one of these letters is not feeling understood, validated, or welcomed by the mainstream of people who otherwise identify as straight.

I include a comprehensive list of resources where you can learn more in the Appendix. In a book of this nature, I cannot give you an entire primer on the fundamentals of understanding our community or working with LGBT+ folks. I can, however, invite you to look at your biases and misconceptions, many of which may be based on beliefs that are religious and culturally ingrained in nature. The way that LGBT+ people have been shamed and mocked—especially by religious influences like parents, clergy, or socialization that is religiously charged—is traumatic and leaves tremendous impact. Suicide rates and instances of addiction and mental health concerns are higher in our community, especially among bisexual and trans individuals, than any national average. My hope is that at some time in the not-too-distant future, people who identify as LGBT+ can walk into a twelve-step meeting or a treatment center and not be further exposed to shaming treatment. The ugliness of shame can make the path harder for people who have been made to feel less than for whom they love and how they identify.

Even though the twelve steps are described as a spiritual, not religious program and we are advised to leave religion out of it, in reality certain meetings and treatment centers are heavily influenced by conservative Christianity. Although I address this impact more fully in the next chapter, it must be mentioned here as it relates to trauma experienced by LGBT+ individuals. Even if you are a member of a twelve-step group or a professional who has no intention on budging from your interpretation of religious beliefs, at the very least, please make a commitment to do no harm. If you can't be fully welcoming, embracing, and affirming, please refrain from commentary—which often comes in the form of slurs like "faggot" or "tranny" made at meetings, or snide references to people's "lifestyles." In my personal experience, some of the most liberal people I've known through the years in twelve-step meetings can still vocalize some of the myths that exist about bisexual people (e.g., "Something's wrong with you if you can't pick a side"). If you are willing to take your commitment to a trauma-informed way of life even further, consider having a real conversation with someone who identifies as LGBT+ and listen with an open mind and heart.

With transgender and nonbinary individuals, using their correct pronouns and name without snarky inflections or disapprovals goes a long way. Only a few years ago I attended a large addiction studies conference in the Midwest and my head nearly exploded when I heard a professional ask a question about a trans client. In the context of the question, he referred to celebrity Caitlyn Jenner as a "he/she." There is no room for this behavior among professionals. If you are reading this as a professional, you are encouraged to examine the ethical codes of your own profession—most of which clearly state that it is your job to receive clinically sound training on working with LGBT+ clients. There are more resources in the Appendix. I've even included one of my favorite articles from Pastor Mark Sandlin responding to the biblical justifications that many people in society, even professionals, will use to justify disrespectful treatment of LGBT+ folks.

I believe that people can change. Even people who are set in their beliefs can make commitments to treat others kindly. Having grown up in a conservative, religious household, I once knew the arguments used to chastise LGBT+ folks, people who had abortions, and people who were perceived to be scrounging off of the system. I even professed (albeit halfheartedly) to believe many of these things myself, all the while knowing in my heart of hearts that I was attracted to both women and men. I did my work, I looked at my own issues, and I had deep conversations with people who are not like me. Today, I believe and behave differently, even though I still cherish some of the old-fashioned values with which I was raised. And I still love many people who conservatively practice their respective religions, even having close relationships with several of them. The reason I can still do this, which I share because it offers a solution, is that they genuinely make me feel accepted, appreciated, and not on some kind of path to hell. They respect my journey and I respect theirs.

Multiple Paths to Recovery Are Possible

Another area where I can admit my change is on the issue of medication-assisted treatment and the implementation of other practices like psychedelics and harm reduction paths to recovery. Ask any twelve-stepper and they will likely have a pretty adamant opinion. I'm most likely to hear that you're not *really* sober if you are on a pharmacotherapy like methadone or Suboxone, or if you are still smoking cannabis even if you no longer inject opioids (one of the many ways people may practice harm reduction). Of course I have my opinions and they are just that—opinions. As a twelve-step proponent who has chosen the path of abstinence for myself, I believe that the less you rely on things outside yourself to feel better on the inside, the greater your chances of long-term wellness. I get concerned when medication-assisted treatment programs seem to promote a sense of long-term dependence on that replacement therapy instead of working with people to taper off. Yet my opinions about those matters should never impact my ability to make a person who is on a medication-assisted treatment regimen or on a path of harm reduction feel any less welcome at a meeting.

I will be curious to see what research and practice continue to reveal about the impact of psychedelic experiences on recovery from both addiction and trauma-related disorders. At this point in my recovery, having such an experience is not an option for me, and I don't believe that it would have helped any more or less than the treatment experiences I received early on. Bill Wilson, the cofounder of AA, experimented with psychedelics and dealt with a whole host of other problems and character defects (e.g., infidelity) even as a person in recovery. So while those of us who are leaders in recovery communities can express our concerns through the lens of experience, strength, and hope, we must always treat people kindly. And even though twelve-step culture may be rigid about many things, we will only survive and grow in the modern era by recognizing that ours is not the only way.

In the vignette that opened this chapter I expressed my concern about rigidity that certain meetings in certain fellowships express about keeping their meetings solely about one thing (e.g., alcohol, narcotics, food, insert whatever). These *singleness of purpose* interpretations came from a well-intentioned place of not turning the meeting into something it's not intended to be (e.g., clinical group therapy, religious services). However, there must be more flexibility as the times change and young people's exposure to other drugs becomes even more commonplace than accessibility to alcohol.

One of the most troublesome defenses of *singleness of purpose* I've ever heard is, "What if someone who is only alcoholic comes into a meeting and hears someone from the podium talking about drugs? Then he'll compare himself out, thinks he doesn't belong here, and may never come back." I ask you to stop this biased thinking, which may be fueled by fear that a certain "undesirable" element will come to meetings and scare others away. It's some of the same bias I hear from people with clear drinking problems believing that "the junkies" are to blame for what ails society. When the comparison of our suffering turns into a game of finger-pointing that prevents us from seeing others' suffering, we block ourselves from the full realization of our own wholeness.

Remember Pastor Nadia's wisdom and ask yourself, is my drug of choice still believing that I'm better than other people? If your answer is yes, thank yourself for being honest, and ask yourself (in concert with your Higher Power if you have one) if more needs to be revealed. Not only will honest work on this process make twelve-step recovery contexts safer and more trauma-informed for people now and moving forward, it will take your recovery to the next level.

TOOLKIT STRATEGY:
OPPRESSIVE COGNITIONS
AND LEARNING FROM THEM

The intention of this exercise is not to compare suffering. It is, however, for you to take a look at or do an inventory on the messages you may carry about yourself that are oppressive in nature. When have others made you feel less than because of who you are, how you look, or where you come from? In addition to the major special population groups we covered in this chapter, you may carry oppressive cognitions based on things like weight or appearance, poverty or class, or level of education.

After doing some writing or reflection in this area, ask yourself, What has helped me transform these oppressive cognitions or horrible messages that I carry about myself because of who I am? Maybe you are still feeling stuck in this area. If so, what might you need to address going forward in your healing?

Taking this a step further, if you have ever worked with a person who comes from a different background or walk of life than you, what did you do that seemed to be successful? How could you have handled some part of that relationship or those interactions differently, knowing what you know now?

12

Embracing Spiritual Diversity

In 2018, I came out of retirement as a twelve-step sponsor. Due to the weight of my teaching and travel commitments, I decided many years back that taking on sponsees would not be practical for me or fair to my sponsees. Yet when I was able to find and begin working with my current sponsor at the beginning of 2016, my entire recovery got a reboot. For years I've criticized the lack of good, flexible, trauma-informed sponsorship in twelve-step communities and was grateful that Chintan (my current sponsor) came into my life. I struggled with being fully candid with my long-term sponsor before him. So when a woman in our community in long-term recovery asked me to sponsor her, because I knew she needed something beyond a traditional spoon-feeding of the twelve steps, everything inside me said yes. What I originally feared might turn into extra commitments burdensome to my schedule overtaxed by sponsoring and supporting so many folks, has actually revitalized my passion for recovery. That renewed passion fuels my drive for sharing this chapter.

There are many people still interested in learning from the twelve-step path who need other spiritual care beyond what the spirituality of twelve-step recovery can offer. Just as we must embrace the changing nature of the recovery community as discussed in the last chapter, we must also embrace a wider degree of spiritual diversity in meeting the needs of people we serve. While the twelve-step path has largely been described as spiritual and not religious, many meetings, treatment centers, and sponsors still infuse the program with a great deal of their own religious fervor. Sometimes this is regional or influenced by the ethic of a community, other times an individual's religious interpretation of God *as I understand Him* comes through and gets projected onto others. One of the largest criticisms I've fielded from other professionals in my work is that the twelve steps are too religious and try to push God on people. This criticism is valid in many contexts, and it breaks my heart because this was not intended by what many of the original founders or the flexible language allowed for in *Alcoholics Anonymous* and other texts.

In this chapter, I attempt to unravel some of the puzzles. I begin by defining spiritual abuse and explaining why many individuals coming into recovery are affected by it. The ultimate solution I propose is the embrace of spiritual diversity. In other words, to allow for the language of God *as I understand Him* (or Her, or Them, etc.) to be as flexible as is possible and healthy for people on a twelve-step path. For some people this may look like a traditional Christian, Jewish, or Muslim God. For others it may include embrace of Eastern religions and practices, Native and indigenous spiritual practices, and other mystical paths. I also make a case for how we in the twelve-step community can be more accepting and affirming of those who identify as atheist or agnostic.

Like chapter 11, this may be a difficult read because I am challenging you to reexamine your own beliefs and how you treat people. You've done this much work on learning to be more trauma informed, so congratulations on coming this far! This is the last piece that needs addressing in order to more fully and respectfully meet the needs of a changing recovery community in the years ahead. My intention in writing this chapter is not to get you to change your own beliefs. Rather, my hope is that you can be more embracing of how others may need to believe and practice differently. For them, your acceptance and affirmation of their right to do so might make all the difference in how they experience recovery.

The Reality of Spiritual Abuse

A simple, working definition of spiritual abuse is whenever a person or system in a position of power uses God or any other spiritual construct as a weapon to control, manipulate, or demean. The power differentials can take many forms including religious or spiritual leader to congregant or disciple, teacher to student, sponsor to sponsee, and parent to child. In the largest possible sense, the power that a theocratic political state exercises over its people can also be viewed as spiritually abusive, especially when the language of "God's will" or "God's plan" is used to justify discrimination or withdrawal of basic rights.

When I tell others that I teach about spiritual abuse, one of the first responses I receive is, "Oh, you mean things like cults? Or ritual Satanic abuse?" These associations exist largely because of the media attention they generate or the shock value they elicit when their rituals and practices are exposed. However, spiritual abuse is much more mainstream and more common. This truth is usually rather difficult for us to swallow, particularly if we practice a spiritual program, work in ministry, or raise children in spiritual traditions; and we may be challenged to look at our own behavior around these dynamics. The likes of Jim Jones and David Koresh do not have the market cornered on spiritually abusing the vulnerable. Indeed, the church, temple, or mosque down the street; the local, folksy yoga studio; political leadership structures; and yes—twelve-step meetings and sponsors—can all be guilty of using spiritually abusive tactics. Wherever religion or spirituality and a power differential exist, spiritual abuse can happen.

Please consider that many people who find themselves in need of a recovery program have experienced spiritual abuse on some level. Growing up in a religious context can make people susceptible, especially if the teachings of this religion were used to shame sexual orientation, gender identification, or any other behavioral expressions that were judged to be deviant. I have rarely worked with someone in the LGBT+ community who hasn't experienced spiritual abuse on some level. Moreover, many religious groups judge or shame having an addiction problem in the first place, using the language of sin and moral weakness. I grew up in such a context—which is why I found the disease model of addiction to be empowering, and the idea that I could choose a God *of my own understanding* as a breath of fresh air.

Therefore it saddens me when people in need of care can be spiritually abused in twelve-step environments. If you are currently working a twelve-step program and your sponsor, guide, or mentor is trying to force you to adopt a certain conception of God, that can be more about their own unhealed issues. That's not what the flexible structure of the program intends. If you are a sponsor or clinician who believes strongly that people need to develop a spiritual way of life to get sober, please be considerate of a person's history. Their exposure to spiritually abusive dynamics outside or inside of twelve-step contexts may make them justifiably more brittle to this notion.

Instead, consider asking what that person may need to help them heal the wounds of spiritual abuse. Like any other trauma, spiritual abuse is a wound in need of care. For some, having the religious and spiritual elements downplayed or not even used may be part of the solution. For others, truly feeling free to develop a new relationship with spirituality or even religion may be the key to freedom. Remember that the program does allow people to find their own conceptualization of God, Higher Power, or as one of my teachers offers as an alternative, Inner Power. This can mean a simple switching-up of pronouns. During an incident when some of my own spiritual trauma got triggered, I sensed into this dread about spirituality and the patriarchy being aligned. Dr. Steve, my dear friend and professional partner, said in support, "Jamie, I think you need to remove all use of masculine pronouns when referring to God." That made all the difference in my continued healing.

My question for you as a sponsor, professional, or guide is whether you are willing to allow for the same degree of flexibility as you help others.

Spiritual Diversity and Spiritual Fusion

Many people healing from previously wounding experiences with spirituality or religion find it vital to explore other avenues than those in which they were raised. Some get this fresh outlook from the twelve steps alone, whereas others need something more. In this section I offer some insights into what *something more* means not only for people who identify as having been spiritually wounded, but also for anyone seeking enrichment in their recovery journey. A major part of empowerment following trauma recovery is choice.

YOGA AND EASTERN MEDITATION PRACTICES.   To clump yoga and Eastern meditation into one simple section is a bit reductionist. Even though they were both born in the same crucible of ancient India, there are many varieties of study and practice. For people wanting to explore yoga as more than just a physical practice, there are philosophical teachings in the practice that line right up with recovery lifestyle or that help people to go deeper. There are many other yoga teachers in recovery that offer their experiences with the natural blending of these two paths. In the Appendix I share these and many other ideas for connecting with emerging yoga and recovery fellowships and programs throughout the world. A similar phenomenon is happening with Buddhist meditation approaches as complements to recovery, and I offer many of these resources as well.

Refuge Recovery, a path of Buddhist meditations and meetings originally founded by Noah Levine, has become a popular twelve-step alternative or complement. Although rocked by scandal just prior to this writing due to Levine's sexual misconduct, I still believe there is a great deal of merit in the ideas of Refuge Recovery and am glad to see that the enthusiasm it has generated for Buddhist approaches to recovery is not waning. Other groups such as Recovery Dharma have formed. My friend Darren Littlejohn's work *The 12-Step Buddhist* (now in its second edition) also offers insight for the power of fusion, and this has led to a new meeting form he developed called Compassionate Recovery (more information in the Appendix).

I've witnessed the power of combining the practices of yoga and meditation with twelve-step recovery principles, while taking an active role in facilitating such groups in my own community. Even in the small city of Warren, Ohio, we offer special meetings for women's yoga recovery, men's yoga recovery, and meditation in recovery. These are not aligned with any twelve-step fellowships and we use a combination of different recovery, yoga, and meditation approaches to guide us. Check around your local community about the existence of such groups. You may be surprised by what you find!

If you are a person in recovery or even a professional who finds these Eastern approaches to be weird or suspect, I invite you to check your biases and sources of misinformation. The amount of myths and untruths I've heard about Eastern approaches to spirituality from scared people in my Christian circles could fuel my writing another book for clarification. Instead of judging, ask someone in recovery who finds these paths appealing how they are helpful. For many of us wounded by the Abrahamic faiths (Christianity, Judaism, Islam) or even by previous exposure to rigid twelve-steppers, other practices that you may judge as weird give us a healthy dose of spiritual food without the trauma triggers or old shame-based reminders.

WELLBRIETY AND NATIVE APPROACHES TO RECOVERY. The spiritual traditions of Native Americans and other indigenous peoples on our planet are vast and nourishing. For people with Native roots, the simple power of claiming one's connection to those roots can open up a whole new world of possibilities in recovery. Even people without direct Native connections draw strength from the teachings of indigenous peoples on the art of healing. In the Four Fold Way described by Angeles Arrien, the four healing salves of indigenous healing include music, dance, storytelling, and silence. Visit the Appendix for more resources and ideas.

Perhaps the most well-known program that directly addresses recovery through a Native lens is the Wellbriety movement. Based in Colorado Springs although global in outreach, Wellbriety assumes a more circular and cyclical approach to healing, as opposed to linear steps. This approach reflects Native approaches to wellness and soul healing. I highly recommend their books, programs, and multitude of online resources to anyone that feels a connection to this path.

ATHEISTS AND AGNOSTICS IN RECOVERY. There is a long track record of atheists and agnostics being mistreated by people in twelve-step recovery. I've heard professionals and sponsors alike disparage the efforts of specialty groups being formed at treatment centers, and put down the existence of meetings for atheists and agnostics. In *Do Tell! Stories by Atheists and Agnostics in AA*, several people share their experiences of meetings they form through proper AA channels not getting listed in local meeting directories. Just about every agnostic person I've known in recovery finds the notorious "We Agnostics" chapter in the AA Big Book to be insulting, placating, and just another attempt to evangelize to the ways of a Divine God.

So why do I include this group in a chapter on spiritual diversity? Because treating people who do not believe in God with dignity is a trauma-informed issue. Although some atheists or agnostics do not like or use the word *spiritual*, for many atheists, it is possible to be spiritual without believing in God. Mike L., the husband of my sponsor Chintan, knew that he was atheist at the age of seven. For Mike, being spiritual means being moral, considerate, good to your fellow man, and living an upright life. I've heard similar beliefs from other beloved atheists and agnostics in my life. They believe that their power comes from within, yet can still draw inspiration and joy from the love and happiness of a group that surrounds them.

For Mike, following the Big Book suggestion, "we cease fighting everything and everyone,"[24] has been key for him to be able to work the steps and translate the "God" language of the program into something more neutral for him. He does not begrudge people their beliefs and often sponsors men who believe in God. Mike shares that some aspects of meetings can bother him; for instance, when chairpersons ask for prayers from the podium. He believes that this was not intended to be a part of meetings but that Christian influences on meetings were bound to happen. For Mike, who has been in recovery for over thirty years, having a sponsor who "couldn't care less" if he believed in God or not was very helpful to him. There's a great lesson to be learned here if you are a sponsor or a professional—let people be who they are and let people believe what they will (or won't) believe.

Even as a person who believes in God, I found reading *Do Tell! Stories by Atheists and Agnostics in AA* extremely helpful. A former client of mine has a story in that book and he sent it to me in gratitude, just as I was going through a bit of a dark night of the soul in my own life. What that book showed me is that even when I doubt that God cares or that any of this works, I still have the fundamentals of the recovery program to support me and that can make all the difference. You may be surprised how some of the ideas in this book or resources available from organizations like AA Agnostica or AA Beyond Belief (see Appendix) can be helpful to you, however you identify or describe your spirituality.

ENDLESS POSSIBILITIES FOR FUSION.   If there is a spiritual or religious path that resonates with you, go to your favorite internet search engine and type in that path plus "in recovery." There is likely some group or some resource that can be explored. I have friends, for instance, who have taken part in groups like Pagans in Recovery and Wiccans in Recovery. There is a growing movement called Church of the Latter-Day Dude, based on the spiritual path of Jeff Bridges's character, The Dude, in the 1998 film *The Big Lebowski*. The practicality of this path speaks to many people I meet in recovery. Even the religious paths that we may identify as more mainstream (e.g., Christianity, Judaism, Islam) have programs that specifically amplify the elements of those beliefs, either in concert with or as an alternative to twelve-step programming.

My caution with faith-based programming is to think critically about whether or not people are being *shamed* into recovery with tactics that resemble spiritual abuse. Although it's possible to get sober this way, I am concerned about whether or not their new path is the most trauma-informed way to heal. We must also be aware about the phenomenon of spiritual bypass. The term, originally coined in the 1970s by Buddhist teacher John Welwood, implies the use of our spiritual practices as a way to avoid feeling emotion or engaging in deeper healing. Religious people may do it when they say things like, "Jesus saved me and redeemed me, all is forgiven," without doing the underlying work. Pure twelve-steppers can be just as guilty of it when they use spiritual slogans like, "Let go and let God," without feeling the pain fully and addressing what needs to be healed. Such approaches may be sufficient to stabilize a wound. However, they will not heal the wound from the inside out, which is necessary for total healing.

Conclusion: We're All Just Walking Each Other Home

The Ram Dass teaching that *we're all just walking each other home* has now reached the level of prosaic social media meme, so popular has it become. I hope that in its mass dissemination, the message does not lose its power—for its wisdom offers the solution to the problems I address in this book. Like many people who grew up wounded by faith, and like many who identify as meaning-seekers in this modern world where disconnection abounds, I find that the teachings of Ram Dass are a balm for my soul.

Ram Dass was born Richard Alpert and (along with Timothy Leary) was fired from his role as a high-powered Harvard psychology professor in the 1960s. Their experimentations with psychedelics became a little too wild a party for the administration. After leaving Harvard he and Leary continued with their work, yet restlessness eventually led Alpert to India. One of his intentions was to talk with old yogis and meditators and determine the exact impact of LSD on the human experience, and explore its role in raising levels of consciousness. Alpert's quest led him to the Himalayas where he met his guru, Neem Karoli Baba. The saint who would become his guru was not impacted one bit by the LSD when Alpert gave it to him. Now a famous teaching among followers of this lineage, Neem Karoli Baba declared that this kind of "medicine" was good for beginners, although it would not keep you in the state of consciousness you desire. He taught that only love can do that.

Only love can do that.

The kind of love that does not judge, scorn, or require that you be a certain way. Love that embraces. Love that accepts. Love that is so powerful, it can dispel any fear that trauma creates. Love that knocks down walls and builds bridges in their wake.

Love is what will allow us as a recovery community, to be more tolerant, accepting, and affirming of each other. Love will help us to heal the wounds that keep us stuck inside, the wounds that may ultimately keep us from being of service to others. Love will help us to walk each other home.

TOOLKIT STRATEGY:
WHAT DOES IT MEAN TO WALK EACH OTHER HOME?

Spend a few moments in the practice of your choice—sitting medita-tion, walking meditation, writing, or some other expressive practice. Contemplate the Ram Dass teaching that we are all just walking each other home.

Notice what the word home means to you in that quote. Home to the love of God? Home to the true nature of your Self? Home to a life that you want to relish and not escape? As a person in recovery, what does home mean to you today?

Now ask yourself, who is helping to walk me home, wherever I may be on my journey? And how can I better be this servant of love for others?

Appendix:
Handouts and Resources

Use the tools in this section at your own discretion. They reflect skills, techniques, and strategies covered in this book. Feel free to copy them and use them as needed in your clinical settings, with sponsees, in community workshops, or with others you serve at meetings. Most of the handouts are self-explanatory, and you can refer back to the pertinent sections in the book for further explanation.

HANDOUT 1: *TRAUMA AND THE 12 STEPS* MEETING OR GROUP FORMAT— This is a copy of the Trauma and the 12 Steps meeting format that I debuted on In The Rooms in 2016. Although the individual who inherited the meeting from me has tweaked it slightly, it is still in use at the time of this writing. If you feel called to start a similar group or discussion in your community, please consider using some of the safety precautions in here as a guideline. As interest grows in trauma-informed recovery groups, you may be in a very powerful place to host such meetings or workshops in your homes and communities. Educating the general recovery community can start with you, and discussion of this nature can be a powerful way to do that. If you would like more support in this process or want to learn more about setting up a meeting or workshop in your community, please contact the Institute for Creative Mindfulness at support@instituteforcreativemindfulness.com.

HANDOUT 2: WOUND CARE 101: PLANNING YOUR TREATMENT— This worksheet gives people in recovery a visual overview of the three-stage consensus model of trauma treatment. This tool may help them better see the general layout of a trauma-sensitive treatment plan.

HANDOUT 3: ASSETS AND DEBITS COLUMN— Explained in chapter 9, this handout encourages people to list their assets (the tangible and intangible resources they have going for them in the service of their recovery) and debits (the roadblocks, tangible or intangible, standing in the way of overall wellness).

HANDOUT 4: FINDING WHERE I MOST BELONG— This worksheet can help people take inventory of the various recovery meetings they are exploring as part of their recovery. Encourage people to reflect on what they liked about the meeting, what they didn't like about the meeting, what trauma triggers may have been set off by the meeting or group, and what, if anything, they did to help them get through any problems at the meeting. This handout can be used as a method of inventory review in clinical sessions or in work with sponsees.

HELPFUL RESOURCES FOR LEARNING MORE ABOUT OPTIONS FOR TRAUMA-FOCUSED WORK— This list gives you a general overview of where to find more information about some of the modalities for trauma therapy covered in chapter 10. Many other approaches and modalities not covered in chapter 10 due to space constraints are also listed here.

HELPFUL RESOURCES FOR LEARNING MORE ABOUT OTHER RECOVERY SUPPORT— Throughout the book I mention many resources that people in twelve-step recovery have found helpful either as a complement to twelve-step recovery or in place of twelve-step recovery. I've done my best to list my recommendations in one place.

FURTHER READING— Any of the books that I reference in the main part of this book for expanding your knowledge are catalogued here for your convenience. I also give recommendations for where to get more information on topics that could only be covered in a brief manner due to space constraints (e.g., supplementary holistic modalities, working with the LGBT+ community).

Trauma and the 12 Steps Meeting Format

Welcome to the Trauma and the 12 Steps Meeting, inspired by the book *Trauma and the 12 Steps* by Dr. Jamie Marich. Trauma and the 12 Steps is an all-paths meeting that is not affiliated with any particular twelve-step group. We welcome anyone to this meeting who believes that healing unaddressed trauma is vital to their growth in recovery. We also welcome those interested in learning more about trauma, and about how unhealed trauma can keep us stuck in our recovery journey. Our definition of trauma is very broad—the word *trauma* comes from the Greek word meaning "wound." The metaphor of the wound can be incredibly useful. If wounds remain unhealed and unaddressed, they can fester and affect us in many areas of our daily living. You are not required to have any specific clinical diagnosis to be affected by unhealed trauma, and we welcome anyone who feels called to this meeting.

To keep the meeting as safe as possible for all in attendance, let's establish some meeting ground rules to keep our sharing orderly:

1. Please limit your comments to three to four minutes so that all people who want to can share.

2. This meeting is not group therapy and is not meant to be a replacement for group therapy or professional treatment. It is a place where we can share our experience, strength, and hope about what works in recovery. We ask that you refrain from going into any specific details of your traumatic experience out of respect to those in the group who may be particularly sensitive to being triggered at this point in their journey. If you believe you are experiencing a mental health crisis, we ask that you please send the chairperson a private message and we will do our best to suggest a course of action outside of the meeting.

3. When there are ten minutes left in the meeting, the guest chairperson will wrap up the open sharing and will lead us in a breathing, grounding, or other coping skill exercise so that we can leave our meeting in the solution.

231

Wound Care 101: Planning Your Treatment

STEP 1: BANDAGING THE WOUNDS

Useful Coping Skills	When to Use the Skill(s)

STEP 2: LOOKING BENEATH THE SURFACE

Issues I Will Need to Work on to Reach My Goals or Intentions

STEP 3: TOTAL HEALING

What My Life Will Look Like after I've Done the Healing Work

Recovery Capital: Assets and Debits

ASSETS:	DEBITS:
What I Have Going for Me In Recovery	What's Working against Me in Recovery

Finding Where I Most Belong:
A Log of My Recovery Meeting Experiences

MEETING AND DATE	LIKES	DISLIKES	TRIGGERS	WHAT HELPED TO ADDRESS ANY TRIGGERS

Helpful Resources for Learning More about Options for Trauma-Focused Work

APPROACH	RECOMMENDED WEBSITES
Accelerated Experiential Dynamic Psychotherapy (AEDP)	www.aedpinstitute.org
Acceptance and Commitment Therapy (ACT)	www.contextualpsychology.org/act
Art Therapy	https://arttherapy.org
Body-Centered Psychotherapy and Somatic Psychology	https://usabp.org
Brainspotting	https://brainspotting.com
Cognitive Processing Therapy	https://cptforptsd.com
Coherence Therapy	www.coherencetherapy.org
Dance/Movement Therapy	www.adta.org
Developmental Needs Meeting Strategy	www.dnmsinstitute.com
Dialectical Behavior Therapy (DBT)	https://linehaninstitute.org
Drama Therapy	www.nadta.org
Emotional Freedom Techniques (EFT)	www.emofree.com
Energy Psychology	www.energypsych.org
Equine Assisted Therapy	www.eagala.org
Exposure Therapy	www.apa.org/ptsd-guideline /patients-and-families/exposure-therapy
Expressive Arts Therapy	www.ieata.org
Eye Movement Desensitization and Reprocessing (EMDR)	www.emdria.org
Focusing	www.focusing.org
Gestalt Therapy	https://aagt.org
Hakomi Mindful Somatic Psychoherapy	www.hakomiinstitute.com
Hypnosis and Hypnotherapy	www.asch.net

APPROACH	RECOMMENDED WEBSITES
Internal Family Systems Therapy (IFS)	www.selfleadership.org
Music Therapy	www.musictherapy.org
Narrative Therapy	https://narrativetherapycentre.com
Neuro Emotional Technique (NET)	www.netmindbody.com
Neurofeedback	www.isnr.org
Neuro-Linguistic Programming (NLP)	www.neurolinguisticprogramming.com
Play Therapy	www.a4pt.org
Progressive Counting (PC)	www.childtrauma.com/treatment/pc
Psychoanalysis	www.apsa.org
Psychomotor Therapeutic System	https://pbsp.com
The Sanctuary Model	www.sanctuaryweb.com
Sensorimotor Psychotherapy	www.sensorimotorpsychotherapy.org
Somatic Experiencing	www.somaticexperiencing.com
Trauma-Focused Cognitive Behavioral Therapy (TF-CBT)	https://tfcbt.org
Trauma Incident Reduction (TIR)	www.tira.org
Trauma Resiliency Model and Community Resiliency Model	www.traumaresourceinstitute.com/home
Yoga Therapy	www.iayt.org

Helpful Resources for Learning More about Other Recovery Support

This is a list of the resources mentioned in the body of this book, as well as a few others that may be helpful as you look to widen the net of your support. If you are a Facebook user, please consider looking up our closed group, *Trauma and the 12 Steps Networking Group*, to connect with others.

ORGANIZATION	RECOMMENDED WEBSITE
AA Agnostica	https://aaagnostica.org
AA Beyond Belief	https://aabeyondbelief.org
ACEs Too High	https://acestoohigh.com
The Breathe Network: Healing Sexual Trauma	www.thebreathenetwork.org
Coming Out: UCLA Resource Center	www.lgbt.ucla.edu/Resources /Coming-Out
Compassionate Recovery	https://compassionaterecovery.net
Dan Griffin: The Man Rules Podcast and Other Resources	www.dangriffin.com
Dancing Mindfulness	www.dancingmindfulness.com
The Fix: Addiction and Recovery, Straight Up	www.thefix.com
Gender Spectrum (Free Online Resources)	www.genderspectrum.org
HealingTREE: Trauma Resources, Education & Empowerment	https://healingtreenonprofit.org
In The Rooms: Online Recovery Meetings and Support	www.intherooms.com
Liv's Recovery Kitchen	www.livsrecoverykitchen.com
Medication-Assisted Recovery Anonymous	www.mara-international.org

ORGANIZATION	RECOMMENDED WEBSITE
NALGAP: The Association of Lesbian, Gay, Bisexual, Transgender Addiction Professionals and Their Allies	www.nalgap.org
Recovery 2.0: Life Beyond Addiction	https://r20.com
Recovery Dharma	https://recoverydharma.org
Refuge Recovery	https://refugerecovery.org
Secular AA	https://secularaa.org
She Recovers: Self-Identified Women in Recovery	https://sherecovers.co
Trauma and Dissociative Disorders Explained	http://traumadissociation.com
Trauma Made Simple/Trauma & the 12 Steps: The Official Resources Site of Dr. Jamie Marich	www.traumamadesimple.com
The Trauma Therapist Project	www.thetraumatherapistproject.com
Wellbriety Movement	https://wellbriety.com
Yoga for Clinicians	www.yogaforclinicians.com
Yoga of Recovery	www.yogaofrecovery.com
Yoga of Twelve Step Recovery (Y12SR)	https://y12sr.com
Yoga Unchained	www.yogaunchained.com

Further Reading

I've elected not to list individual texts from the various twelve-step fellowships in this section since, when you count all the groups that have spun
off of Alcoholics Anonymous, Narcotics Anonymous, and Al-Anon, the
numbers are in the hundreds! If a certain fellowship interests you, look it
up and explore their literature. I am focusing here on resources that are
not directly published by the fellowships, yet still can help enhance your
ability to trauma-inform your recovery work.

Please also be on the lookout for the forthcoming companion meditation reader and step guide that will accompany the content of *Trauma and
the 12 Steps*, prepared by myself and Dr. Stephen Dansiger.

Addiction and Recovery Resources

Adams, A. J. *Undrunk: A Skeptic's Guide to AA*. Center City, MN: Hazelden, 2009.

Black, Claudia. *Unspoken Legacy: Addressing the Impact of Trauma and Addiction
within the Family*. Las Vegas, NV: Central Recovery Press, 2018.

Brown, Brené. *Daring Greatly: How the Courage to Be Vulnerable Transforms the Way We
Live, Love, Parent, and Lead*. New York: Avery, 2012.

C., Roger. *Do Tell! Stories by Atheists and Agnostics in AA*. Canada: AA Agnostica,
2015.

David, Anna. *How to Get Successful by F*cking Up Your Life: Essays on Addiction and
Recovery*. Bowker, 2019.

Elrod, Hal, Anna David, and Joe Polish. *The Miracle Morning for Addiction Recovery:
Letting Go of Who You've Been for Who You Can Become*. Vol. 12. Austin, TX: Hal
Elrod International, Inc., 2018.

Fletcher, Anne M. *Sober for Good: New Solutions for Drinking Problems—Advice from Those Who Have Succeeded.* New York: Houghton Mifflin, 2001.

Granfield, Robert, and William Cloud. *Coming Clean: Overcoming Addiction without Treatment.* New York: New York University Press, 1999.

Kurtz, Ernest. *Not-God: A History of Alcoholics Anonymous.* Center City, MN: Hazelden, 1991.

Levine, Noah. *Refuge Recovery: A Buddhist Path to Recovering from Addiction.* New York: HarperOne, 2014.

Mager, Dan. *Roots and Wings: A Guide to Mindful Parenting in Recovery.* Las Vegas, NV: Central Recovery Press, 2018.

Mager, Dan. *Some Assembly Required: A Balanced Approach to Recovery from Addiction and Chronic Pain.* Las Vegas, NV: Central Recovery Press, 2013.

Marshall, Shelley. *Young, Sober, and Free: Experience, Strength, and Hope for Young Adults.* 2nd ed. Center City, MN: Hazelden, 2003.

Maté, Gabor. *In the Realm of Hungry Ghosts: Close Encounters with Addiction.* Berkeley, CA: North Atlantic Books, 2010.

Nowinski, Joseph, and Stuart Baker. *The Twelve-Step Facilitation Handbook: A Systematic Approach to Early Recovery from Alcoholism and Addiction.* 2nd ed. Center City, MN: Hazelden, 2006.

Prochaska, James O., John C. Norcross, and Carlo C. DiClemente. *Changing for Good: A Revolutionary Six-Stage Program for Overcoming Bad Habits and Moving Your Life Positively Forward.* New York: Morrow, 1994.

Rosen, Tommy. *RECOVERY 2.0: Move Beyond Addiction and Upgrade Your Life.* Carlsbad, CA: Hay House Inc., 2014.

Solomon, Melanie. *AA: Not the Only Way—Your One Stop Resource Guide to Twelve-Step Alternatives.* 2nd ed. Venice, CA: Capalo Press, 2008.

Szalavitz, Maia. *Unbroken Brain: A Revolutionary New Way of Understanding Addiction.* London: Picador, 2017.

Twerski, Abraham J. *Waking up Just in Time: A Therapist Shows How to Use the Twelve Steps Approach to Life's Ups and Downs.* New York: St. Martin's Griffin, 1995.

Volpicelli, Joseph, and Maia Szalavitz. *Recovery Options: The Complete Guide.* New York: John Wiley & Sons, 2000.

Weiss, Robert. *Prodependence: Moving Beyond Codependency.* Deerfield Beach, FL: Health Communications, Inc., 2018.

White, William. *Slaying the Dragon: The History of Addiction Treatment and Recovery in America.* 2nd ed. Bloomington, IL: Chestnut Health Systems, 2014.

Yalom, Irvin. *The Gift of Therapy: An Open Letter to a New Generation of Therapists and Their Patients.* New York: Harper Perennial, 2017.

Cultural Competency

Anderson, Carol. *White Rage: The Unspoken Truth of Our Racial Divide.* New York: Bloomsbury, 2017.

Arrien, Angeles. *The Four Fold Way: Walking the Paths of the Warrior, Teacher, Healer, and Visionary.* San Francisco: HarperSanFrancisco, 1993.

Bell, Derrick. *Faces at the Bottom of the Well: The Permanence of Racism.* New York: Basic Books, 1992.

Bennett, Jr., Lerone. *Before the Mayflower: A History of the Negro in America, 1619–1962.* BN Publishing, 2019.

Degruy, Joy. *Post Traumatic Slave Syndrome: America's Legacy of Enduring Injury and Healing.* rev. ed. Joy Degruy Publications, Inc., 2017.

DiAngelo, Robin. *White Fragility: Why It's So Hard for White People to Talk About Racism.* Boston: Beacon Press, 2018.

Fanon, Frantz. *Black Skin, White Masks.* Translated by Richard Philcox. New York: Grove Press, 2008.

hooks, bell. *Where We Stand: Class Matters.* New York: Routledge, 2000.

Johnson, Allan G. *Privilege, Power, and Difference.* 3rd ed. New York: McGraw-Hill Education, 2017.

Roberts, Dorothy. *Killing the Black Body: Race, Reproduction, and the Meaning of Liberty.* New York: Vintage Books, 1998.

Rothenberg, Paula S. *Race, Class, and Gender in the United States: An Integrated Study.* 7th ed. New York: Worth Publishers, 2006.

Thandeka. *Learning to Be White: Money, Race and God in America.* New York: Continuum, 2000.

Gender Responsive

Ackerman, Robert. *Perfect Daughters: Adult Daughters of Alcoholics.* Deerfield Beach, FL: Health Communications Inc., 2002.

Ackerman, Robert. *Silent Sons: A Book for and About Men.* New York: Touchstone, 1994.

Covington, Stephanie, Dan Griffin, and Rick Dauer. *A Man's Workbook: A Program for Treating Addiction.* San Francisco: Jossey-Bass, 2011.

Covington, Stephanie. *A Woman's Way through the Twelve Steps.* Center City, MN: Hazelden, 1994.

Griffin, Dan. *A Man's Way through Relationships: Learning to Love and Be Loved.* Las Vegas, NV: Central Recovery Press, 2014.

Griffin, Dan. *A Man's Way through the Twelve Steps.* Center City, MN: Hazelden, 2009.

Hien, Denise, Lisa Caren Litt, Lisa R. Cohen, Gloria M. Miele, and Aimee Camp-bell. *Trauma Services for Women in Substance Abuse Treatment: An Integrated Approach.* Washington, DC: American Psychological Association Press, 2009.

Roth, Geneen. *Women Food and God: An Unexpected Path to Almost Everything.* New York: Scribner, 2010.

Valters Paintner, Christine. *The Wisdom of the Body: A Contemplative Journey to Whole-ness for Women.* Notre Dame, IN: Sorin Books, 2017.

General Trauma and Psychotherapy Resources

Banitt, Susan Pease. *The Trauma Tool Kit: Healing PTSD from the Inside Out.* Whea-ton, IL: Quest Books, 2012.

Banitt, Susan Pease. *Wisdom, Attachment, and Love in Trauma Therapy: Beyond Evidence-Based Practice.* New York: Routledge, 2018.

Briere, John, and Catherine Scott. *Principles of Trauma Therapy: A Guide to Symp-toms, Evaluation, and Treatment (DSM-5 Update).* 2nd ed. Los Angeles: SAGE Publishing, 2015.

Burana, Lily. *I Love a Man in Uniform: A Memoir of Love, War, and Other Battles.* New York: Weinstein Books, 2009.

Burke Harris, Nadine. *The Deepest Well: Healing the Long-Term Effects of Childhood Adversity.* New York: Houghton Mifflin Harcourt, 2018.

Caldwell, Christine. *Bodyfulness: Somatic Practices for Presence, Empowerment, and Waking Up in This Life.* Boulder, CO: Shambhala Publications, 2018.

Courtois, Christine A., and Julian D. Ford. *Treating Complex Traumatic Stress Disor-ders: An Evidence-Based Guide.* New York: The Guilford Press, 2009.

Crane, Judy. *The Trauma Heart: We Are Not Bad People Trying to Be Good, We Are Wounded People Trying to Heal.* Deerfield Beach, FL: Health Communications, Inc., 2017.

Curran, Linda. *101 Trauma-Informed Interventions: Activities, Exercises and Assignments to Move the Client and Therapy Forward.* Eau Claire, WI: PESI Publishing, 2013.

Curran, Linda. *Trauma Competency: A Clinician's Guide.* Eau Claire, WI: PESI Pub-lishing, 2010.

Dayton, Tian. *Trauma and Addiction: Ending the Cycle of Pain through Emotional Lit-eracy.* Deerfield Beach, FL: Health Communications, Inc, 2000.

Duncan, Barry L., Scott D. Miller, Bruce E. Wampold, and Mark A. Hubble, eds. *The Heart & Soul of Change: Delivering What Works in Therapy.* 2nd ed. Washing-ton, DC: American Psychological Association, 2010.

Evans, Katie, and J. Michael Sullivan. *Treating Addicted Survivors of Trauma.* New York: The Guilford Press, 1994.

Fisher, Janina. *Healing the Fragmented Selves of Trauma Survivors: Overcoming Internal Self-Alienation.* New York: Routledge, 2017.

Herman, Judith L. *Trauma and Recovery: The Aftermath of Violence—From Domestic Abuse to Political Terror.* New York: Basic Books, 1992.

Howell, Elizabeth F. *The Dissociative Mind.* New York: Routledge, 2005.

Levine, Peter A. *In an Unspoken Voice: How the Body Releases Trauma and Restores Goodness.* Berkeley, CA: North Atlantic Books, 2010.

Levine, Peter A., and Ann Frederick. *Waking the Tiger: Healing Trauma.* Berkeley, CA: North Atlantic Books, 1997.

MacLean, Paul D. *The Triune Brain in Evolution: Role in Paleocerebral Functions.* New York: Plenum Press, 1990.

Marich, Jamie. *Process Not Perfection: Expressive Arts Solutions for Trauma Recovery.* Warren, OH: Creative Mindfulness Media, 2019.

Marich, Jamie. *Trauma Made Simple: Competencies in Assessment, Treatment and Working with Survivors.* Eau Claire, WI: PESI Publishing & Media, 2014.

Miller, Dusty, and Laurie Guidry. *Addictions and Trauma Recovery: Healing the Body, Mind, & Spirit.* New York: W. W. Norton & Company, 2001.

Najavits, Lisa. *Finding Your Best Self: Recovery from Addiction, Trauma, or Both.* rev. ed. New York: The Guilford Press, 2019.

Najavits, Lisa. *Seeking Safety: A Treatment Manual for PTSD and Substance Abuse.* New York: The Guilford Press, 2001.

Ouimette, Paige, and Pamela J. Brown. *Trauma and Substance Abuse: Causes, Consequences, and Treatment of Comorbid Disorders.* Washington, DC: American Psychological Association Press, 2004.

Perry, Bruce D., and Maia Szalavitz. *Born for Love: Why Empathy is Essential—and Endangered.* New York: HarperCollins, 2010.

Rothschild, Babette. *The Body Remembers: The Psychophysiology of Trauma and Trauma Treatment.* New York: W. W. Norton & Company, 2000.

Scaer, Robert. *The Trauma Spectrum: Hidden Wounds and Human Resiliency.* New York: W. W. Norton & Company, 2005.

Schwartz, Arielle. *The Complex PTSD Workbook: A Mind–Body Approach to Regaining Emotional Control and Becoming Whole.* Berkeley, CA: Althea Press, 2017.

Shapiro, Francine. *Getting Past Your Past: Take Control of Your Life with Self-Help Techniques from EMDR Therapy.* New York: Rodale, 2012.

Shapiro, Francine, and Margot Silk Forrest. *EMDR: The Breakthrough Therapy for Overcoming Anxiety, Stress, and Trauma.* 2nd ed. New York: Basic Books, 2016.

Solomon, Marion Fried, and Daniel J. Siegel, eds. *Healing Trauma: Attachment, Mind, Body, and Brain.* New York: W. W. Norton & Company, 2003.

van der Kolk, Bessel. *The Body Keeps the Score: Brain, Mind, and Body in the Healing of Trauma.* New York: Penguin Books, 2015.

Holistic Healing and Health

Grof, Stanislav. *The Holotropic Mind: The Three Levels of Consciousness and How They Shape Our Lives.* New York: HarperCollins, 1992.

Lusk, Julie, ed. *30 Scripts for Relaxation, Imagery & Inner Healing.* Duluth, MN: Whole Person Associates, 1993.

Naparstek, Belleruth. *Invisible Heroes: Survivors of Trauma and How They Heal.* New York: Bantam Books, 2004.

Naparstek, Belleruth. *Staying Well with Guided Imagery.* New York: Warner Books/ Grand Central Publishing, 1994.

Parnell, Laurel. *Tapping In: A Step-by-Step Guide to Activating Your Healing Resources through Bilateral Stimulation.* Boulder, CO: Sounds True Books, 2008.

Petrone, Elaine. *The Miracle Ball Method: Relieve Your Pain, Reshape Your Body, Reduce Your Stress.* New York: Workman Publishing Company, 2003.

Waldeck, Felicitas. *Jin Shin Jyutsu: Guide to Quick Aid and Healing From A–Z through the Laying On of Hands.* Munich: Creative-Story, 2011.

LGBT+

Downs, Alan. *The Velvet Rage: Overcoming the Pain of Growing Up Gay in a Straight Man's World,* 2nd ed. Philadelphia, PA: Da Capo Press, 2012.

Sandlin, Mark. "Clobbering 'Biblical' Gay Bashing." Patheos.com. October 11, 2011. www.patheos.com/blogs/thegodarticle/2011/10/clobbering-biblical -gay-bashing (accessed September 5, 2019).

Shelton, Michael. *Fundamentals of LGBT Substance Use Disorders: Multiple Identities, Multiple Challenges.* New York: Harrington Park Press, 2017.

Weiss, Robert. *Cruise Control: Understanding Sex Addiction in Gay Men.* Carefree, AZ: Gentle Path Press, 2013.

Meditation, Spirituality and Yoga

Brown, Brené. *The Gifts of Imperfection: Let Go of Who You Think You're Supposed to Be and Embrace Who You Are.* Center City, MN: Hazelden, 2010.

Clayton, Ingrid Mathieu. *Recovering Spirituality: Achieving Emotional Sobriety in Your Spiritual Practice.* Center City, MN: Hazelden, 2011.

Cunningham, Annalisa. *Healing Addiction with Yoga: A Yoga Program for People in 12-Step Recovery.* 3rd ed. Forres, Scotland, UK: Findhorn Press, 2010.

Dansiger, Stephen. *Mindfulness for Anger Management: Transformative Skills for Overcoming Anger and Managing Powerful Emotions.* Emeryville, CA: Althea Press, 2018.

Danylchuk, Lisa. *Embodied Healing: Using Yoga to Recover from Trauma and Extreme Stress.* McLean, VA: Difference Press, 2015.

Danylchuk, Lisa. *Yoga for Trauma Recovery.* New York: Routledge, 2019.

Desai, Kamini. *Yoga Nidra: The Art of Transformational Sleep.* Twin Lakes, WI: Lotus Press, 2017.

Emerson, David. *Trauma-Sensitive Yoga in Therapy: Bringing the Body into Treatment.* New York: W. W. Norton & Company, 2015.

Emerson, David, and Elizabeth Hopper. *Overcoming Trauma through Yoga: Reclaiming Your Body.* Berkeley, CA: North Atlantic Books, 2011.

Gunaratana, Bhante Henepola. *Mindfulness in Plain English.* 20th Anniversary Edition. Somerville, MA: Wisdom Press, 2011.

Hanh, Thich Nhat. *The Miracle of Mindfulness: An Introduction to the Practice of Meditation.* Boston: The Beacon Press, 1999.

Hawk, Kyczy. *Yoga and the Twelve-Step Path.* Las Vegas, NV: Central Recovery Press, 2012.

Hawk, Kyczy. *Yogic Tools for Recovery: A Guide for Working the Twelve Steps.* Las Vegas, NV: Central Recovery Press, 2017.

Kabat-Zinn, Jon. *Full Catastrophe Living: Using the Wisdom of Your Body and Mind to Face Stress, Pain, and Illness.* New York: Bantam Books, 1990/2013.

Kabat-Zinn, Jon. *Mindfulness for Beginners: Reclaiming the Present Moment and Your Life.* Boulder, CO: Sounds True, Inc., 2012.

Keating, Thomas. *Divine Therapy and Addiction: Centering Prayer and the Twelve Steps.* New York: Lantern Books, 2009.

Littlejohn, Darren. *The 12-Step Buddhist: Enhance Recovery from Any Addiction.* 10th Anniversary Edition. New York: Atria Books, 2019.

Marich, Jamie. *Dancing Mindfulness: A Creative Path to Healing & Transformation.* Woodstock, VT: SkyLight Paths, 2015.

Nouwen, Henri. *The Inner Voice of Love: A Journey through Anguish to Freedom.* New York: Doubleday, 1996.

Nouwen, Henri. *Out of Solitude: Three Meditations on the Christian Life.* rev. ed. Notre Dame, IN: Ave Maria Press, 2004.

Rohr, Richard. *Breathing Under Water: Spirituality and the Twelve Steps.* Cincinnati, OH: Franciscan Media, 2011.

Shapiro, Rami. *Recovery—The Sacred Art: The Twelve Steps as Spiritual Practice.* Woodstock, VT: SkyLight Paths, 2009.

Siegel, Ronald D. *The Mindfulness Solution: Everyday Practices for Everyday Problems.* New York: The Guilford Press, 2009.

Twerski, Abraham. *Happiness and the Human Spirit: The Spirituality of Becoming the Best You Can Be.* Woodstock, VT: Jewish Lights Publishing, 2007.

Van Gelder, Kiera. *The Buddha and the Borderline: My Recovery from Borderline Personality Disorder through Dialectical Behavior Therapy, Buddhism, and Online Dating.* Oakland, CA: New Harbinger Publications, 2010.

Weintraub, Amy. *Yoga for Depression: A Compassionate Guide to Relieve Suffering through Yoga.* New York: Broadway Books, 2004.

Weintraub, Amy. *Yoga Skills for Therapists: Effective Practices for Mood Management.* New York: W. W. Norton & Co., 2012.

Spiritual Abuse Recovery

Bolz-Weber, Nadia. *Shameless: A Sexual Reformation.* New York: Convergent Books, 2019.

Johnson, David, and Jeff VanVonderen. *The Subtle Power of Spiritual Abuse.* Minneapolis, MN: Bethany House Publishers, 1991.

Pasquale, Teresa B. *Sacred Wounds: A Path to Healing from Spiritual Trauma.* Chalice Press, 2015.

Riley, Reba. *Post-Traumatic Church Syndrome: A Memoir of Humor and Healing.* New York: Howard Books, 2015.

Notes

Chapter 2: There Is a Solution

1 Katie Evans and J. Michael Sullivan, *Treating Addicted Survivors of Trauma* (New York: The Guilford Press, 1994), 1–2.

2 Jamie Marich, "EMDR in Addiction Continuing Care: Case Study of a Cross-Addicted Female's Treatment and Recovery," *Journal of EMDR Practice and Research* 3, no. 2 (2009): 103.

Chapter 3: Trauma and Dissociation 101

3 Lily Burana, *I Love a Man in Uniform: A Memoir of Love, War, and Other Battles* (New York: Weinstein Books, 2009), 226–227.

4 Christine Courtois and Julian Ford, *Treating Complex Traumatic Stress Disorders: An Evidence-Based Guide* (New York: The Guilford Press, 2009), 1.

5 Adam O'Brien and Jamie Marich, "Addiction as Dissociation Model," Institute for Creative Mindfulness: *Redefine Therapy* (blog), October 15, 2019, www.instituteforcreativemindfulness.com/icm-blog-redefine-therapy/addiction-as-dissociation-model-by-adam-obrien-dr-jamie-marich.

6 Henri Nouwen, *Out of Solitude: Three Meditations on the Christian Life* (Notre Dame, IN: Ave Maria Press, 1974), 38.

Chapter 4: What Twelve-Step Recovery Can Offer Traumatized Individuals

7 Alcoholics Anonymous World Services, *Alcoholics Anonymous*, 4th ed. (New York: Author, 2001), 417.

8 Alcoholics Anonymous World Services, *Alcoholics Anonymous*, 552.

Chapter 5: Where Twelve-Step Recovery Can (and Often Does) Go Wrong

9   Alcoholics Anonymous World Services, *Alcoholics Anonymous*, 32.

Chapter 6: Working with Others in a Trauma-Sensitive Manner

10 John N. Briere and Catherine Scott, *Principles of Trauma Therapy: A Guide to Symptoms, Evaluation, and Treatment (DSM-5 Update)* (Los Angeles, CA: Sage, 2015), 104.

11 Briere and Scott, *Principles of Trauma Therapy*, 105.

12 Kiera Van Gelder, *The Buddha and the Borderline: My Recovery from Borderline Personality Disorder through Dialectical Behavior Therapy, Buddhism, and Online Dating* (Oakland, CA: New Harbinger Publications, 2010), 34.

Chapter 7: Bring Your Butt, the Rest Will Follow—The Importance of Honoring the Body in Addiction Recovery

13 Jon Kabat-Zinn, *Full Catastrophe Living: Using the Wisdom of Your Body and Mind to Face Stress, Pain, and Illness* (New York: Bantam, 1990/2013).

Chapter 8: It's the Relationship that Heals

14 American Psychological Association Presidential Task Force on Evidence-Based Practice, "Evidence-Based Practice in Psychology," *American Psychologist* 61, no. 4 (2005), 271–285.

15 John C. Norcross and Bruce E. Wampold, *Psychotherapy Relationships that Work, Volume 2: Evidence-Based Therapist Responsiveness*, 3rd ed. (New York: Oxford University Press, 2019), 2.

16 Bruce D. Perry and Maia Szalavitz, *Born for Love: Why Empathy is Essential—and Endangered* (New York: HarperCollins, 2010), 12–13.

Chapter 10: Strategies for Reprocessing and Reintegration

17 In the field of trauma-focused counseling, the word *processing* is generally synonymous with healing. Often defined as "working something through" so

that how a memory or issue is stored in the brain shifts to a more adaptive place, the term *processing* is in common use. However, the term can be used interchangeably with *reprocessing*, a term coined by Dr. Francine Shapiro in her 1989 development of eye movement desensitization and reprocessing (EMDR) therapy. She uses the word *reprocessing* to suggest that the memory or issue never got processed at the time it happened, so in practice, all processing work is *reprocessing*.

18   Otto van der Hart, Paul Brown, and Bessel van der Kolk, "Pierre Janet's Treatment of Post-Traumatic Stress," *Journal of Traumatic Stress* 2, no. 4 (1989), 1–11.

19   Bessel van der Kolk, *The Body Keeps the Score: Brain, Mind, and Body in the Healing of Trauma* (New York: Penguin Books, 2015), 21.

20   Alcoholics Anonymous World Services, *Alcoholics Anonymous*, 84.

Chapter 11: Respect for Change—Trauma-Sensitive Recovery in a Diverse World

21   Alcoholics Anonymous World Services, *Twelve Steps and Twelve Traditions*, 3rd ed. (New York: Author, 1981), 139.

22   Jamie Marich, *Trauma Made Simple: Competencies in Assessment, Treatment and Working with Survivors* (Eau Claire, WI: PESI Publishing & Media, 2014), 61.

23   Panel discussion at Wild Goose Festival, Hot Springs, NC, July 12, 2019.

Chapter 12: Embracing Spiritual Diversity

24   Alcoholics Anonymous World Services, *Alcoholics Anonymous*, 44.

Index

"With this expanded edition of *Trauma and the 12 Steps,* Jamie Marich extends and updates her compassionate, meaningful work for survivors of adverse childhood experiences (trauma). In her deeply compassionate voice, she reminds us that the wisdom found in twelve-step recovery is not simply a sobriety path for the addicted, but that it can also become a universal road-map to connection and healing from the inside out. I highly recommended this book for trauma survivors, their loved ones, and the clinicians who serve them."

—ROBERT WEISS, PhD, LCSW, CCO, founder and executive director at Seeking Integrity Treatment Centers and author of *Prodependence: Moving Beyond Codependency; Out of the Doghouse: A Step-by-Step Relationship-Saving Guide for Men Caught Cheating,* and *Sex Addiction 101: A Basic Guide to Healing from Sex, Porn, and Love Addiction*

"Every person in recovery, working in the field of recovery, or advocating for people in recovery should read this timely and thoughtful book. Beyond updating her earlier work on trauma, dissociation, and the body, Dr. Jamie Marich elegantly introduces and expands on the importance of concepts that are often left untreated in recovery literature. This includes an analysis of the traumatic impact of oppression, and exploring the impact of spiritual abuse as a form of trauma. Jamie's deft handling and honoring of cultural and spiritual diversity is a high point of this new work, but so too is her con-tinuation of what she has been doing for over a decade—which is to attempt to bridge the harmful divide between those who attack twelve-step ideology and practice and those who espouse it. Given the current addiction crisis in our world, surely the only right answer to the question 'what is the right pathway to recovery?' is all of them."

—DAWN NICKEL, PhD, founder of SHE RECOVERS

"In our never-ending quest for self-aggrandizement, we demonize addiction, obsess about trauma, and romanticize recovery. This makes ordinary living, which includes trauma, addiction, and recovery, all the more difficult. Yet, as Jamie Marich tells us in this wonderful new edition of *Trauma and the 12 Steps,* recovery is coming home: coming home to trauma, coming home to addiction, and making peace with reality as it is rather than as we insist it must be. Dr. Marich is a wise guide to homecoming and I encourage you to read this book and follow her advice."

—RABBI RAMI SHAPIRO, author of *Recovery–The Sacred Art: The Twelve Steps as Spiritual Practice*

"*Trauma and the 12 Steps* is an extraordinary state-of-the-art integration of psychological theory, psychotherapy practice, and twelve-step recovery. In this updated and revised edition, Dr. Jamie Marich skillfully weaves together her personal history, deep hard-won insights, and vast professional experience, with client anecdotes and extensive research to articulate the art and science of multimodal trauma-informed care and how it can be actualized in the context of both addiction treatment and twelve-step-oriented recovery. The result is a must-read volume that will be of great benefit to clinicians and other addiction treatment professionals, trauma survivors in twelve-step recovery, and anyone that struggles with co-occurring substance use and trauma. This is a work that embodies the essence of Step Twelve as well as one of the foundational spiritual principles of twelve-step recovery—service to others."

—DAN MAGER, MSW, executive director at Vance Johnson Recovery Center and author of *Roots and Wings: A Guide to Mindful Parenting in Recovery* and *Some Assembly Required: A Balanced Approach to Recovery from Addiction and Chronic Pain*

"By including the most current research and thinking on trauma, Dr. Jamie Marich supports in practical terms what we are now learning about the long-term deleterious effects of avoiding trauma in our recovery work. Without losing any of the passion and immediacy of the earlier edition, Marich continues in her wonderful style of interweaving actual stories into the development of a deep understanding of the pains and problems of undiagnosed and unaddressed trauma in the recovery journey."

—KYCZY HAWK, E-RYT 500, founder of S.O.A.R.™ (Success Over Addiction and Relapse) and author of *Yoga and The Twelve Step Path* and *Yogic Tools for Recovery: A Guide for Working the Twelve Steps*

"As clinicians, we can't strictly work with 'this part' or 'that part' of a person, we can only work with the whole person. In this regard, Dr. Marich's commitment to inclusivity is like a balm. She sensitively weaves her personal and professional expertise through the worlds of addiction and trauma, making vibrant and necessary connections for clinicians and clients alike. I highly recommend this book."

—INGRID CLAYTON, PhD, author of *Recovering Spirituality: Achieving Emotional Sobriety in Your Spiritual Practice*

"In this new edition of *Trauma and the 12 Steps*, Dr. Jamie Marich expands upon her groundbreaking work in trauma-informed addiction treatment. Jamie is a well-known voice for holistic care, challenging the entire field and the related recovery communities to examine their existing biases and indeed 'do better' to help people heal. I appreciate her candidness and willingness to share her own story in the context of such a professional book."

—SHERRY GABA, MSW, author of *Infinite Recovery: 6 Steps of Mindfulness, Positive Thinking, and the Law of Attraction to Break Free from Addiction*

"This book is powerful. *Trauma and the 12 Steps* is a must-read for everyone in the recovery process. Trauma has been much overlooked in the past and rarely mentioned in twelve-step recovery. Jamie brings this issue to the forefront again in this most needed revised edition. She has a wonderful way of weaving the twelve steps, yoga, meditation, and trauma therapy together to help heal our souls. As a man with thirty-six years of long-term twelve-step recovery, I applaud her for being a pioneer in addressing this very important topic of trauma to one's recovery."

—RON (RT) TANNEBAUM, cofounder of InTheRooms.com

"Through her expertise and dedication to the fields of trauma and addiction, Jamie illustrates quite wonderfully that substance-use disorders—while made up of similar symptoms—are experienced highly individually, and that clinicians and peers need to be sensitive to the individual's own experience in seeking and facilitating healing. I am hopeful that this book provides the opportunity to change the trajectory of people's recovery within twelve-step fellowships so they can experience the full benefits of a trauma-sensitive recovery."

—OLIVIA PENNELLE, recovery journalist and founder of *Liv's Recovery Kitchen*

"Dr. Jamie Marich does it again. Changing not only the conversation, but ultimately how we address addiction and substance abuse in our communities by including the role trauma plays. She challenges us in a nonconfrontational but informative way to start exploring how each of us can play a role in shifting toward a more trauma-focused approach when helping those in recovery. Whether you're a mental health or addiction professional, a sponsor, or in your own recovery, this book is a must-read to start fully understanding the underlying issues regarding addiction and substance abuse."

—SHANNON ORTIZ, LPCC-S, CCTP, founder and president of Light After Loss

"*Trauma and the 12 Steps* is the modern Big Book for those who know that trauma and dissociation are the roots of all addictions. Dr. Marich blends the essential addiction discussions with real clinical situations and helps deepen our understanding of human nature. This edition continues her straightforward and sensible approach to educating on this urgent topic. Anyone who reads this will benefit from its content."

> —ADAM O'BRIEN, LMHC, CASAC, Mutual Arising Counseling,
> Chatham, New York, and team member at the Institute for
> Creative Mindfulness

"Having worked professionally and personally in the recovery field for over thirty-five years, I can attest to the need for trauma-informed approaches to healing. For many, this approach is the transformative piece for sustainable, high quality, and resilient recovery. *Trauma and the 12 Steps* is a wealth of information. Dr. Marich's research is expansive, useful, and personal. Her approach is hopeful and inclusive. Dr. Marich's belief in the transformational power of the Twelve Steps to heal is enhanced by research and new science. In fact, *Trauma and the 12 Steps* is one of the finest examples of twelve-step work—to carry this message to others and to practice these principles in all our affairs—that I have ever seen."

> —CAROL ACKLEY, LADC, owner of Ackley Consulting and
> Training and certified trainer for Dr. Stephanie Covington and
> the Center for Gender and Justice

TRAUMA
AND THE
12 STEPS

**AN INCLUSIVE GUIDE TO
ENHANCING RECOVERY**

REVISED AND EXPANDED

JAMIE MARICH, PHD

North Atlantic Books
Berkeley, California

Published by
North Atlantic Books
Huichin, unceded Ohlone land
Berkeley, California

Cover art © gettyimages.com/dzubanovska
Cover design by Rob Johnson
Interior photos by Ellen DeCarlo
Triune brain model illustration by Michelle Tompkins
Book design Happenstance Type-O-Rama

Printed in the United States of America

Trauma and the 12 Steps, Revised and Expanded: An Inclusive Guide to Enhancing Recovery is sponsored and published by North Atlantic Books, an educational nonprofit based in the unceded Ohlone land Huichin (Berkeley, CA) that collaborates with partners to develop cross-cultural perspectives; nurture holistic views of art, science, the humanities, and healing; and seed personal and global transformation by publishing work on the relationship of body, spirit, and nature.

North Atlantic Books's publications are distributed to the US trade and internationally by Penguin Random House Publisher Services. For further information, visit our website at www.north atlanticbooks.com.

Library of Congress Cataloging-in-Publication Data

Names: Marich, Jamie, author.
Title: Trauma and the 12 steps, Revised and Expanded: an inclusive guide to enhancing recovery /
    Jaime Marich.
Other titles: Trauma and the twelve steps
Description: Revised and expanded. | Berkeley, California : North Atlantic
    Books, [2020] | Includes bibliographical references and index.
Identifiers: LCCN 2019052830 | ISBN 9781623174682 (trade paperback) | ISBN
    9781623174699 (ebook)
Subjects: LCSH: Twelve-step programs. | Psychic trauma–Treatment. |
    Post-traumatic stress disorder–Treatment.
Classification: LCC RC564 .M295 2020 | DDC 616.85/21—dc23
LC record available at https://lccn.loc.gov/2019052830

5 6 7 8 9 KPC 26 25 24 23

For Janet Leff (1941–2017)

*Because you worked your eleventh and twelfth steps,
I cherish the life I have today.*

I am eternally grateful …

And for Jason Fair (1978–2019)

Thank you for walking me home, you precious soul.

Contents

Foreword

Here is a long story told in a few words.

In 1889, Pierre Janet, a French psychiatrist, proposed a Three Stage Model of trauma treatment that is now viewed as the consensus model here in the twenty-first century. The resurrection of Janet and his work has brought about several theories, therapies, and modalities of healing that allow us to directly and effectively care for wounds caused by trauma and adverse life events.

In 1935, Bill Wilson and Dr. Bob Smith met for the first time at the Sieberling Gate Lodge in Akron, Ohio. They did not know it, but their mutually helpful overnight conversation changed the world. They posited together that connection and action were the answer to their alcohol problems, and the twelve steps were born. It was not long before the twelve steps were applied to many other difficulties and dilemmas.

Less than ten years ago, I found Jamie by conducting one of those daily random internet searches where I was looking for trauma resources. The search revealed an earlier edition of this book you hold in your hands, *Trauma and the 12 Steps*. Having been on my own twelve-step journey since 1989, I couldn't believe that someone out there had made this important and critical connection. Then I read the book and found that she did not just make the connection, she revealed the future—the possibility that we could leverage our knowledge of trauma and trauma treatment to help others develop a trauma-informed approach to the twelve-step program.

I reached out to Jamie and asked her to train the staff at an addictions rehab where we were utilizing EMDR therapy and mindfulness to provide a trauma-focused approach to the treatment. Jamie and I have been friends, colleagues, and collaborators ever since.

The original *Trauma and the 12 Steps* has already helped countless people. This book helps professionals understand the twelve steps and what it means to apply them in a trauma-informed fashion. It helps twelve-step–based and non-twelve-step–based treatment programs to more effectively utilize the principles and the tasks of the twelve steps to assist in their protocols. It helps sponsors and friends in twelve-step programs to speak to each other more mindfully and create more inclusive communities. It helps people who struggle with certain elements of the program— whether they be written in the literature or interpreted by members—that are not trauma informed and impact that person's ability to participate in recovery. It helps those who have found themselves relapsing at some point in their recovery to reduce shame and avoid a shame spiral, and to proceed in their recovery with the help of trauma-informed others.

Jamie's passion for the twelve steps and for trauma treatment is what this world needs right now. I truly believe that this revised and expanded edition will help launch the next phase in the life of twelve-step programs, and help the twelve steps to grow and sustain for years to come.

—*STEPHEN DANSIGER, PsyD, MFT,*
Los Angeles, CA

Acknowledgments

Recovery is the process of coming home. Coming home to sanity. Coming home to a new way of life. Coming home to myself. Today I live a life where I am at peace with myself on more days than not as a result of this transformation. In this edition, I am able to present a vision of wellness and hope for the future of what recovery can look like. I can offer this vision because others have helped walk me home. And these same people help me to live from the fullest fusion of my human and divine selves. I am honored to thank several of my guides for their role in this process.

A heartfelt thanks goes out to Shayna Keyles and the team at North Atlantic Books for taking a chance on this iteration of *Trauma and the 12 Steps* and allowing me such a powerful platform to share my voice. The earlier edition of *Trauma and the 12 Steps* had a difficult time finding a publishing home that accepted her just the way she was. Not only did Shayna and the team accept and trust my vision, they empowered me to write an even better book. Gratitude!

I also thank the fabulous new friends and colleagues I met through the earlier edition of *Trauma and the 12 Steps*, published in 2012. Your kindness and encouragement helped to affirm that there is value to this work and motivated me in this new edition. Special mentions are in order to Doug Edwards, Gary Enos, Phil McCabe, Jeff Zacharias, Carol Ackley, Rick Dauer, Eric Belsterling, Colette Carroll, Dan Mager, Kyczy Hawk, Colleen McKernan, Jeff Emerson, Darren Littlejohn, Rob Weiss, and Dan Griffin. The biggest hug of all is for my friend, "ice dance partner," and professional collaborator, Dr. Stephen Dansiger. We've gone on to teach, to write, and to support each other in our shared mission. And it all started because he "stalked me" (his words) after reading *Trauma and the 12 Steps.* I am honored that Steve gave me valuable input and support in this new incarnation of the work.

To my recovery family—Chintan, Mike, Joey, Jason, Julia, Gabby, Christina, Demi, Allie, Mary, James, and Holly—all of you make my life a special place and your influence is with me daily. To the Dancing Mindfulness and Institute for Creative Mindfulness communities—thank you for drying my tears and helping me transform them into gold. Special thanks must go out to my friend, chief operations officer, pirate-human, lady's maid, all-around life manager, and truly my everything, Mary Riley. Additional gratitude extended to Peyton Cram, (Ma) Melita Travis Johnson, and Kamala Tahyi for their invaluable feedback provided. To others in my family of choice—Amber S., Amber P., Cornelius, Erin, Malika, Mama Sharon, Mama Denise, Lori, Ethan, Brendan—thank you for being you; for accepting me, for loving me. To my village of healers—Elizabeth Davis, Melissa Layer, Erica Matthews, Satyavani Gayatri, Ramdas Ormond, Nirali Lauren McCrea, Kalindi Edwina Hoffman, and Yogeshwari Kamini Desai—*Jai Bhagwan* ("victory to the spirit"). To Adam—often through gritted teeth, I thank you for being my endless source of creative inspiration, much of it showing up in this book. Love and gratitude to my blood brother and the first to walk me home, Br. Paul Marich, OP.

Introduction

To heal the suffering connected to the crisis of addiction, we must learn to build bridges, not walls. We build walls when we promote our own preferred pathway as the best or most ideal way to get clean, sober, or well. Die-hard twelve-steppers do it just as fervently as those people and programs who oppose the twelve steps. It's a sad state of affairs when conversations on how to ease suffering feel like an antagonistic political battle blaring on cable news. Clinicians, policy makers, community advocates, clergy, twelve-step sponsors, members of twelve-step fellowships, and those walking other paths of recovery are all invited to respond to this challenge of bridge building together. This book is for all of you.

To build bridges, we must recognize that certain components of tradition are not all bad while acknowledging that it is harmful to stay stuck in the mentality of *this is the way we've always done it*. I wrote *Trauma and the 12 Steps* in 2012 out of my commitment to promote a both/and paradigm for healing addiction. I am still a proud member of a twelve-step fellowship, working the principles of twelve-step recovery in my daily life. I've also benefitted from massive amounts of outside help (e.g., trauma-focused psychotherapy, energy medicine) and diverse spiritual practices (e.g., yoga, meditation, trauma-informed martial arts). As a professional, I live with a foot in both worlds: actively involved with the mental health community specializing in the treatment of trauma while simultaneously training and consulting in the arena of addiction treatment. My client base is composed of individuals who are dealing with the entire spectrum of issues related to trauma, grief, dissociation, and addiction.

Some of the same challenges I experienced in 2012 remain. My approach seemed too trauma-focused for the addiction community and many twelve-steppers. I still take criticism from people in mental health and trauma circles for backing a program that they see as too antiquated, "old-school," or even harmful. I've also had the pleasure of meeting other folks who share similar struggles within recovery circles, which has helped me realize with even more certainty that I am not alone in my experiences or perspectives. Writing the book opened up the floodgates of communication between myself and many other professionals and individuals on a path of recovery (both twelve-step and non–twelve-step). I've been invited to give numerous trainings, retreats, and keynotes on the *Trauma and the 12 Steps* idea in the years since the original publication. These have all provided opportunities to create connections and have discussions about how a "one way or the other" approach to healing is not helping anyone. With the enthusiasm that comes from shared experience, strength, and a hope to do things better, I am even more excited to present you with this revised and expanded edition of *Trauma and the 12 Steps.*

This expanded edition honors the same original structure and ideas presented in the earlier edition. Exciting updates from the fields of trauma, dissociation, mindfulness, and addiction from 2012 to 2020 are included. Chapter 1 explains the problem with treating addiction as a stand-alone problem without considering the impact of unhealed trauma, with chapter 2 exploring how trauma-sensitive avenues for healing provide us with a solution for enhancing care. Chapter 3 offers a necessary primer on the fundamentals of trauma that lay a foundation for chapter 4 (how twelve-step recovery can be helpful to survivors of trauma) and chapter 5 (highlighting the areas where certain applications of twelve-step recovery can be harmful). Chapters 6 through 10 offer detailed presentations of how we can blend the approaches of twelve-step recovery with principles of trauma-informed helping strategies. These chapters examine relational elements, the importance of body-centered coping skills, trauma-focused preparation, and innovations in trauma-focused practices in psychotherapy and other healing arts.

Two new chapters appear in this edition. Chapter 11 focuses on honoring diversity and recognizing how the traumatic impact of oppression can further complicate the recovery process. Chapter 12 explores the importance of embracing various spiritual paths and includes the perspectives of atheists and agnostics. This final chapter explores the impact of spiritual abuse as a legitimate form of trauma that can make accepting any spiritual approach to recovery very difficult. A new appendix includes a format that groups can use to run an independent *Trauma and the 12 Steps*-inspired peer support meeting or workshop, based on an online group that I started on the virtual platform In The Rooms in 2016. All of these resources hold potential for inspiring fresh outlooks on recovery as we approach the century mark of the twelve-step era.

A great deal has changed in the world since Alcoholics Anonymous originated in 1935. We've learned much more about trauma and its impact on the brain since that time. This book, while fundamentally pro–twelve-step, continues the call made in the earlier edition to encompass what we have learned about trauma to help even more people. I welcome skeptics and critics, as many of the criticisms of twelve-step recovery are completely legitimate, based in true and valid experiences. There are certain treatment centers to which I would not refer clients because they employ a harmful rigidity that does not take the impact of unhealed trauma into account. Moreover, many twelve-step meetings that exist in the community are toxic. They can create an atmosphere of authoritarianism by the trusted servants (program-speak for the leadership), or turn a blind eye to behaviors that are unsafe to many (e.g., open sexual advances made at newer, vulnerable members; sponsors or meeting leadership putting down practices like psychotherapy or psychiatric care).

And yet I do not believe that we should throw the proverbial baby out with the bathwater when it comes to twelve-step recovery. There is still something supremely useful in this path of recovery that has done so much to change the global conversation around addiction. I believe this now even more than I did when I wrote the earlier edition.

When I gave a podcast interview for *Trauma and the 12 Steps* after the release of its earlier edition, the host asked me what I hoped to achieve by getting this work out into the world. Although I hadn't thought about it before, the answer flowed immediately: My hope is that every individual seeking recovery will be treated as my original sponsor, Janet Leff, treated me. Janet was trauma informed before the phrase was even cool in the clinical professions. While she worked the steps with the spirit of an old-timer, her life was one of attraction rather than promotion, to quote a well-known saying in the rooms of twelve-step recovery. She practiced instead of preached. She validated me and then challenged me, honoring my dignity every step of the way.

May we all draw inspiration from her example.

1

The Problem with the "They're Just Addicts" Mentality

It takes a special person to work with alcoholics and addicts, whether you serve in some professional capacity, or whether you serve as a member of a twelve-step or other fellowship program. Before you read another word of this book, allow me to thank you for your service. Working with those who suffer from addiction is more than just a job—it's a vocation. I say "it takes a special person" because the joy of helping someone recover often comes with frustration. There are those who don't want recovery and make your job seem like a living hell. Perhaps the most heartbreak can result when you work with someone who seems to want recovery, and they may even be giving it their all. And then ... relapse. Relapse is a mystifying phenomenon to understand. I want to share a story with you that opened my eyes to what we may be missing.

My Professional Journey Begins

I entered the field of addiction treatment as a novice counselor in 2004, eager and excited to bring the gift of recovery to others. One of my first jobs was in a reputable treatment facility near my hometown. The high rate of relapse that I observed quickly disillusioned me. The number of readmissions was troubling, and when clients complained that the treatment they received was very "one size fits all," I found myself agreeing with them. When I talked to my senior colleagues about these phenomena, they placated me with responses like, "They're just addicts. Until they come to terms with their addiction and realize that they want to treat their disease, they'll always be coming back." They addressed the one-size-fits-all complaint with, "Come on, Jamie, you know it's just their terminal uniqueness talking."

One day, I found occasion to consult with my clinical director about the high level of trauma-related problems I saw our clients struggling to address: sexual abuse, combat memories, horrific accidents, scars from growing up with alcoholic parents, and assaults. My clinical director warned me that I was getting sidetracked from the real problem (i.e., the addiction) by paying so much attention to these issues. "They're here because they're addicts," he insisted. Ever the devil's advocate, I asked if he believed that the trauma had anything to do with it. He immediately cut me off for complicating matters too much. Something inside me signaled danger. Not only did I disagree with what he told me, but I also felt his position was detrimental to our mission of helping others recover. I decided to get personal in trying to state my case to this clinical director.

"Do you mean to tell me," I said, "that I picked up opiates at the age of twelve because things were good in my life?"

"You picked up opiates at the age of twelve because you are an addict," he quipped back. I was very saddened to hear his position, especially since, in my early recovery, I was blessed with a series of trauma-sensitive professionals. Janet Leff, my first sponsor, honored my history and my struggles with trauma. She also knew the competent balance of not letting me turn them into excuses for prolonging my addiction progression. She once told me, "Jamie, after everything you've been through, no wonder you turned out to be an addict. The question is, what are you going to do about it now?" This guidance is the beating heart and living soul of the trauma-informed approach to the twelve steps that I advocate in this book.

Clearly, I did not last very long working at this treatment center. I saw so many patients—who had initially taken to recovery like ducks to water—relapse, leave, and return when the hard issues surfaced in their recovery. From my perspective, so much of it was about trauma. Major news-making events like war and natural disasters, ones we associate with post-traumatic stress disorder (PTSD), were certainly an issue. However, the life-changing events like verbal torment and unresolved disruptions to family systems also came with their share of destruction. All these adverse life experiences that keep us stuck in our shame seemed to be even more insidious. The emphasis on "Don't drink and go to meetings" and "Challenge your faulty thinking" that dominated this treatment center's culture seemed to ignore many of the issues that blocked the attainment of recovery.

The problems I encountered at this treatment center exist in many treatment centers throughout North America. Rigid acceptance of the disease model of addiction and near-fundamentalist adherence to twelve-step philosophies can hurt more clients than they can help. I am not opposed to the disease model of addiction, and I am a believer in the benefits of twelve-step programming for most people. The harm comes when we apply these philosophies at the exclusion of everything else that the fields of psychology, counseling, social work, and medicine have shed light on during the past several decades about the reality of trauma and its impact on the human experience.

Trauma-Informing the Twelve-Step Approach

Professionals, sponsors, and recovering individuals can continue using traditional twelve-step recovery philosophies in a manner that honors what the psychotherapeutic professions have learned about trauma. There is nothing wrong with using twelve-step recovery principles in treatment or in continuing care with individuals affected by trauma-related issues. This book explains how rigid application of twelve-step principles can do more harm than good for a traumatized person. In the spirit of "both/and" that defines my work, I will teach you some simple accommodations based on the latest knowledge of traumatic stress that can enhance the twelve-step recovery experience for trauma survivors.

Not all twelve-step fellowship meetings and twelve-step–oriented treatment programs are created equally. Even though the twelve steps were published as a suggested plan of action by Alcoholics Anonymous (AA) in 1939 in the volume that came to be called the Big Book, several hundred other fellowships have spun off from Alcoholics Anonymous. The traditions of Alcoholics Anonymous allow for group autonomy, except on those issues that affect Alcoholics Anonymous as a whole. Thus, you may have one twelve-step recovery group that interprets the twelve steps in an orthodox fashion. One group may have guidelines such as, "We only talk about alcohol here," setting the tone for the meeting. A meeting happening across town on the same night may be more embracing of its members talking about other addictions or conditions, such as mental health concerns and trauma.

Even though a great number of treatment centers in North America base themselves on the twelve-step philosophy, it is important to remember that these treatment programs are not the voice of Alcoholics Anonymous, Narcotics Anonymous, or any of the other twelve-step groups. These fellowships are not run by professionals, but rather by other group members elected as trusted servants. The fellowships offer community support. I am saddened to hear about individuals who have demeaning, negative experiences at twelve-step–based treatment centers and become scared away from attending twelve-step meetings in the community as a result. I have also seen a person in need of professional treatment be scared away because of one bad experience with a nonprofessional twelve-step group in the community (or even just one person in that group).

There is no such thing as perfect uniformity related to application of twelve-step recovery principles. There can be great beauty in that lack of uniformity, especially when this diversity promotes more openness in dialogue and understanding. Professionals, twelve-step sponsors, recovering individuals, families, and community members can more competently apply twelve-step ideas to working with recovering people by understanding trauma. I do not represent any particular twelve-step fellowship, and when I reference twelve-step recovery, I do so in a general manner. For the purposes of this book, the term *twelve-step recovery* refers to the general philosophy of the twelve steps and some of the other slogans and ideas that are typically associated with twelve-step groups (see inset on page 12, "The Twelve Steps of Alcoholics Anonymous").

Before moving ahead, let's consider what the phrase *trauma-sensitive* really means. I tend to use this phrase interchangeably with the phrase *trauma-informed* throughout the book. I also reference a newer construct, *trauma-focused,* in places. While the first two ideas are more about awareness of trauma and acting in a way to minimize harming others, being trauma-focused suggests that we must take more directive action in helping people to heal from the legacy of trauma. This book, and the strategies suggested within it for building your own personal "trauma toolkits," will teach you how to put these approaches into action.

There are numerous reasons for recovery communities to embrace these trauma-sensitive approaches. The most obvious is that many individuals in recovery affected by trauma return to their addiction of choice. If you have spent any time at all working in a treatment center or around twelve-step meetings, the unhealed trauma-addiction connection is obvious. These individuals often find it difficult not to be overwhelmed by the shame-based ideologies they acquired due to unhealed trauma, while trying to address the past and take appropriate responsibility for their actions.

This trauma can warrant a formal, *DSM-5* (*Diagnostic and Statistical Manual of Mental Disorders,* Fifth Edition) diagnosis of PTSD, or it can be what Francine Shapiro, founder of Eye Movement Desensitization and Reprocessing (EMDR) therapy, originally referred to as "small-t" trauma. Small-t traumas or adverse life experiences are disturbances that appear to be at the root of presenting clinical concerns. However, small-t traumas are generally not substantial enough to qualify for a diagnosis of PTSD in the current diagnostic systems. In chapter 3, I explore more fully the distinctions between the various types of trauma and how trauma may show up in addiction and other diagnoses. Regardless of the specific trauma, its effects can lead to or exacerbate an addictive disorder and ultimately hinder the recovery process if the trauma is not properly addressed.

Relapse is prevalent in many behavioral disorders, especially addiction. Although various models can explain relapse, the common theme is that poor self-efficacy and high volumes of negative emotion, coupled with poor coping skills, put an individual at greatest risk for relapsing on alcohol or other drugs following a period of sobriety. In simpler terms, if you don't like yourself and you deal with mostly troubling emotions, you are going to have a hard time staying sober—especially if you haven't learned any meaningful, effective ways to cope and to manage emotions.

The first model I encountered in my training to truly address the impact of unhealed trauma on relapse is called the Addictions and Trauma Recovery Integration Model (ATRIUM), developed by Dusty Miller and Lori Guidry. ATRIUM contends that traditional models of addiction recovery and relapse prevention fail to appropriately consider the significant role that unresolved trauma plays in an addicted individual's attempt at recovery. Though Miller and Guidry do not discredit the merit of traditional models such as the Minnesota model of treatment (based largely on twelve-step ideas) or cognitive behavioral therapy (CBT), they suggest that these approaches do not sufficiently address the role that trauma has played. This omission can set up individuals to fail in their recovery processes. Historically, Miller and Guidry were some of the first people in the addiction treatment community to declare that a more holistic approach to treating addiction is needed to promote long-term recovery and prevent potentially debilitating relapses. This holistic approach must include interventions that work with the emotions and the somatic or embodied experience of those seeking help. Resources developed by many other pioneers in the field of addiction who saw the need to more directly address trauma are listed in the Appendix.

An Invitation

Whatever your psychotherapeutic orientation or your personal beliefs about recovery, you can benefit from this book. I use the language of twelve-step recovery extensively in the text because I recognize the continued benefit of twelve-step programming, and make suggestions for how it can be taught in a more trauma-sensitive manner. I do believe that there are many paths to attaining addiction recovery, as long as the program or selected approach promotes a healthy lifestyle change for the individual. Regardless of the path chosen to attain recovery, we must take into account the realities of trauma and how to address them as an imperative if we are treating or otherwise mentoring people in this process.

There is an old, often-repeated Chinese proverb to describe trauma and its effects: "Once you've been bitten by a snake, you're afraid even of a piece of coiled rope." Let us remember this wisdom in our work with addicted people who are affected by trauma. May we endeavor to be a healing balm rather than a coiled rope. I attempt to give you the necessary tools to be that healing balm for yourself and for others you may serve. My challenge for you is to become even more open-minded to the trauma-sensitive perspective in your application of recovery principles when working with others, especially in the twelve-step paradigm.

I set out to accomplish this task in as candid a manner as possible, blending my own stories and ideas as a woman in long-term recovery with findings from clinical studies and the helping professions. Unless otherwise indicated, I have changed the names of all cases used in the book to protect anonymity. In many instances, the cases you are reading are composites (the details of two or more cases are combined) to further guard anonymity. My hope is that these series of stories, ideas, insights, and reflections will challenge you to think beyond the way you've always done recovery, whether that be as a twelve-step advocate, a twelve-step critic, or someone who lands in the middle. Please open your heart and your mind to the invitation to help build bridges and hopefully solve the crisis of suffering that is unhealed addiction.

THE TWELVE STEPS OF ALCOHOLICS ANONYMOUS

1. We admitted we were powerless over alcohol—that our lives had become unmanageable.

2. Came to believe that a Power greater than ourselves could restore us to sanity.

3. Made a decision to turn our will and our lives over to the care of God as we understood Him.

4. Made a searching and fearless moral inventory of ourselves.

5. Admitted to God, to ourselves, and to another human being the exact nature of our wrongs.

6. Were entirely ready to have God remove all these defects of character.

7. Humbly asked Him to remove our shortcomings.

8. Made a list of all persons we had harmed, and became willing to make amends to them all.

9. Made direct amends to such people wherever possible, except when to do so would injure them or others.

10. Continued to take personal inventory and when we were wrong promptly admitted it.

11. Sought through prayer and meditation to improve our conscious contact with God as we understood Him, praying only for knowledge of His will for us and the power to carry that out.

12. Having had a spiritual awakening as the result of these steps, we tried to carry this message to alcoholics and to practice these principles in all our affairs.

TOOLKIT STRATEGY: SELF-INQUIRY

Self-inquiry—taking a look at yourself, your tendencies, and your biases—is a skill. Knowing where you currently stand on your approach to working with people affected by addiction is critical. This knowledge includes self-inquiry about your thoughts, feelings, and experiences with developing a trauma-sensitive approach to this healing work.

- *Take a few minutes to write down how you would describe your approach to working with people in recovery. You can use the language of psychotherapeutic theory (e.g., twelve-step model, cognitive behavioral therapy, somatic psychotherapy), or you can keep your language informal, especially if you are not a treatment professional (e.g., "working a twelve-step program"). If writing is not feasible to you, simply spend three to five minutes in silent reflection or with a trusted person in conversation.*

- *Consider if there is room in your current approach to take on new, trauma-informed skills. If you have reservations about considering the role of trauma and how it can affect treatment, spend a few moments and jot down what your reservations may be about learning these new approaches. This is intended to be an exercise in self-inquiry, not shaming or judgment. If you are willing, perhaps consider sharing some of these reservations with a person (e.g., colleague, another member of a recovery program) and notice what you notice about yourself.*

- *What might you need in the way of support to take a more open view of this material? As a hint, you may find it more useful to replace the phrase "open-minded" with "open-hearted." Being open-hearted invites us into a greater sense of empathy in connecting with our fellow human beings. When we can connect with each other at the heart level, the sense of separateness and division can vanish. Bridges are more likely to be built.*

2

There Is a Solution

One evening, Nancy showed up at the community drug and alcohol facility in her county with an all-too-familiar feeling: I've been here before. In the previous twelve years, Nancy had gone through twelve or thirteen treatment facilities. She lost count somewhere around five. Additionally, she participated in AA during and after each treatment episode at the suggestion of each facility, yet she was never able to piece together any more than four months of sobriety. The funny thing was that Nancy never really minded going to AA; she always knew she belonged there. Something just never quite clicked for her.

Nancy sat down with the assessment counselor, still dressed up from an exhausting day of work at a job she hated. There was weariness in her eyes as she explained that the municipal court sent her for treatment after her third driving under the influence (DUI) charge. Nancy knew the lingo of twelve-step recovery and treatment. She did not need any convincing that she was an alcoholic or an addict.

"Oh, you don't have to diagnose me, I know," she said candidly. "But I can never seem to stay sober, even when I try my hardest."

The assessment counselor, pretty sure that she had established enough rapport with Nancy, began to ask some very tough questions about her history. What emerged from the rest of the interview was the picture of a woman with a complex case of post-traumatic stress disorder due to multiple sexual assaults accompanied by life-threatening violence. Sadly, the perpetrator in many of these assaults was her onetime husband.

"I know that all of this is an issue," Nancy told the counselor, "I just can't seem to get it all out. And when it comes time for me to do a fourth and fifth step in AA, I just run. I can't look at myself. All I see is garbage—it's too painful, and I run."

Chronic Relapsers or Chronically Unhealed Trauma?

Nancy's story is a real-life example of the problem presented in chapter 1. Too often, people labeled as "chronic relapsers" are really just struggling with the aftereffects of unresolved trauma. The legacy of this wounding can last for years, even decades, making tasks like doing fourth and fifth steps paralyzing impossibilities for the traumatized. This is not to say that a person with unresolved trauma can never do fourth and fifth steps. On the contrary, working all twelve steps can actually be beneficial for a traumatized person. When worked within a safe context that honors the wounds and scars left by trauma, the individual's chances of success in working the steps and staying sober are optimized.

Honor the struggle. Sounds simple, no? This idea is a major part of the solution to the dilemma that I outlined in chapter 1. Yet every time a treatment provider dismisses the impact of a client's history in favor of the "they're just addicts" mentality, they reject this simple solution. I first heard the phrase, "honor the struggle," from one of the best bosses I ever worked for, Ken Lloyd. The CEO of the community facility where I was on staff when I first met Nancy, Mr. Lloyd always stressed the importance of honoring the struggle that our clients experienced before coming to us. He asked us to continue honoring their struggle as they attempted to learn a new way of life in sobriety.

There are those who argue that placing too much emphasis on a client's history before entering recovery is the kiss of death. A major aspect of twelve-step recovery is to teach an addict to *live in today*. Several major psychotherapeutic schools of thought like reality therapy or choice theory and rational-emotive (RE) behavioral therapy also emphasize the importance of living in the now and not dwelling on the past. We must consider that our histories shape the people we are today. So, is there a balance? Can we teach recovering addicts to live one day at a time while honoring the struggle of their past, present, and future?

A Balanced Approach

This balance is a key part of the solution. Throughout the 1990s, many books emerged on the market about trauma and addiction interaction. Katie Evans and J. Michael Sullivan proposed a model in their book, *Treating Addicted Survivors of Trauma,* that I continue to find especially useful:

- ▶ Respecting client's history of trauma, especially childhood trauma, is a trauma-informed intervention in and of itself and enhances treatment quality.

- ▶ Treatment must include working on traumatic memories experientially, *after* foundational skills for safety and coping are established.

- ▶ Twelve-step approaches, including the disease model of addiction, still have value in trauma-informed treatment of addiction.

- ▶ Treatment models must be *integrated* and address the *synergism* of trauma and addiction. Separate tracks are generally ineffective.[1]

The components of the Evans–Sullivan approach to treatment are just as relevant today as when they first published them in 1994.

Trauma and the 12 Steps echoes that nothing is inherently wrong with the disease model of addiction, the twelve-step approach to recovery, or other avenues that lead an addicted individual to healthful lifestyle change that promotes recovery. To continue supporting the relevance of the disease model and twelve-step approaches in the modern era, we must respect a person's history of trauma. Respecting the trauma is honoring the struggle.

The second and third tenets of the Evans–Sullivan model offer a blueprint for conducting treatment in a balanced way. The solution is *not* to take people in need of medical detoxification and make them confront the demons of trauma through some radical trauma resolution method, thinking that they then will be free of the addiction! While there are some professionals who believe it is possible to cure a person of their addiction by resolving the core trauma that led to the addiction, this approach is far from what I am advocating. Resolving the trauma will not make the addiction go away instantly, just as treating the addiction will not make the effects of the trauma immediately disappear. As Evans and Sullivan contend, the trauma must be worked through after a foundation of safety and coping skills has been established. Establishing a modicum of functional sobriety can be a part of this safety. However, people working the twelve steps routinely go into steps four and five—the moral, inventory steps that can actually help them with trauma resolution—without having that safe enough foundation and solid, holistic coping established first. A recovering person (especially one with trauma issues) needs to be able to regulate and manage intense affect or emotional output, before attempting something as daunting as steps four and five.

The fifth element of the Evans–Sullivan model parallels my general approach to clinical work: the synergism of the trauma and the addiction must be addressed in a manner of treatment that is integrated. Treatment planning logic often leads to rather heated philosophical debates among professionals along the lines of, *which came first, the chicken or the egg?* In essence, did the trauma lead to the addiction, or did the addiction generate independently of the trauma? Some addiction professionals may be averse to integrated treatment on principle, fearing that it will play into an addict's sense of terminal uniqueness; that is, making excuses for problematic behaviors based on their perceived singularity. Other professionals may fear that addressing trauma is stretching the bounds of their job descriptions.

"But trauma is out of my league," you may be saying. "I have no experience working with trauma!"

Although you are not alone in your concerns, I must issue a challenge: If you are working with an addicted population, trauma competency is not an option. Trauma competency is a necessity. It doesn't matter which came first. What matters is that they are *both* present and they *both* must be addressed.

As Evans and Sullivan state, a large portion of clients presenting for treatment in any setting have a history of childhood trauma. Add to that equation traumas experienced in adulthood, or trauma that addicted individuals may have experienced while they were in active addiction. If a person was shot while scoping out a neighborhood for drugs, this still qualifies as a trauma. The last statement may puzzle you, especially if you see this shooting as a consequence of the person's addiction. Chapter 3 will more fully explain why a trauma is a trauma is a trauma.

That might sound like a familiar anthem that rings throughout many treatment centers across the globe: Addiction is addiction is addiction.

A Closer Look

Let's take a closer look at how an integrated approach, as initially described by Evans and Sullivan, worked for Nancy, the woman introduced at the beginning of this chapter. In a follow-up interview with Nancy that was published as part of a 2009 research project on trauma-focused addiction treatment, she shared that simply having the relevance of her trauma acknowledged during the assessment set a positive tone for her treatment. This positive tone helped her to feel safe with her counselor. Fortunately, Nancy was able to stay with the same assessing counselor as her primary counselor for treatment. Nancy was clearly part of the large portion of those who present for treatment with a history of childhood trauma, and her counselor respected this history from the initial assessment.

During treatment planning, Nancy and her counselor decided together that they should directly confront the trauma issues only after Nancy established enough of a foundation in her recovery. Thus, the first part of her treatment plan was to complete an eight-week outpatient Twelve-Step Facilitation treatment group (based on the work of Nowinski and Baker), attend three to four AA meetings a week, and begin working the first three steps with a sponsor.

After Nancy completed the Twelve-Step Facilitation treatment group with flying colors—during which time she developed relationships with a sponsor and support group—she began working with her counselor to deepen coping and relaxation skills. Deep breathing and guided imagery proved effective for Nancy. Once all of these skills were in place, Nancy agreed that she was ready to directly work on resolving the trauma issues during weekly individual sessions with her counselor at the community treatment center. Nancy's counselor presented her with two possible options: cognitive behavioral therapy (CBT) and eye movement desensitization and reprocessing (EMDR) therapy. Because she had heard good things about EMDR at a previous treatment center, Nancy opted to use this therapy to begin the cathartic journey of addressing the multiple abuses that began in preadolescence. Nancy had about three months of continuous sobriety when this journey began, and her counselor felt good about proceeding with the work because the foundation of safety and coping skills was in place.

After approximately ten weeks of individual sessions, during which time Nancy continued active AA involvement and work with her sponsor on the first three steps, Nancy began writing out a fourth step. Nancy decided that she wanted her counselor to hear her fifth step. For her, it was important to do a fifth step in an arena where she felt optimally safe. Not only did her counselor create a safe environment in their sessions, Nancy also felt an extra element of safety because of the counselor's legally binding commitment to confidentiality. Nowhere does it say that the fifth step needs to be heard by a sponsor or a minister; it just needs to be heard by *another human being*. Having a fifth step plan that honored her safety gave her some assurance during her fourth-step process, and after resolving a great deal of toxic shame during her EMDR sessions, Nancy was finally able to do a fourth and fifth step.

Nancy continued to work closely with her sponsor, and she continued sessions every other week with her counselor while she worked the rest of the steps. In total, Nancy was involved with the same treatment provider for about a year, staying sober the entire time. Nancy gave her first AA lead (public talk) upon celebrating eighteen months of sobriety, a remarkable feat considering that previously she had not been able to stay sober any longer than four months. Shortly after this first lead, I interviewed Nancy as part of a follow-up research project, and she shared some amazing insights about her recovery. Nancy credited the combination of EMDR, twelve-step work, opening up to a sponsor, seeing addiction as a life-or-death matter, her willingness to change, and deepening her spirituality as factors that worked *together* to get her sober and well. She also acknowledged that her trauma history made it difficult for her to work the twelve steps of AA during her prior attempts at recovery:

> *You can't put anything in the proper perspective. And you can't really get a heads-up on what really happened because you were so traumatized and you had such bad experiences and, like in my case, I had the trauma then I had the—I call it the aftereffect of my ex-husband— pounding over and over and over and over it for like fourteen years after that. I took so much responsibility for it. It was almost like I victimized myself all over again in my mind.*[2]

Nancy shared that all of these factors working together helped her achieve a perspective shift that led to her restoration as a sane human being.

Nancy is one of the many profiles in courage who have come through the doors of community treatment. Her story is a classic example of someone who benefited from the solution proposed by those of us who advocate an integrated approach to treatment and healing. Consider that this solution began when her counselor honored her struggle during the initial assessment.

One of the "old-school" twelve-step teachers who left a mark on me was the late Fr. Joseph Martin. Although I rolled my eyes at some of the preachy tone in his famous Chalk Talks that Janet made me watch, I remember an aha moment that happened as I listened to one of them. Fr. Martin boldly declared that there is no place for the "hot seat" in treatment. The point of treatment should be to build up the alcoholic or addict, not tear them down. Although we explore throughout *Trauma and the 12 Steps* how this does not mean condoning illegal, unethical, or immoral behavior, it is important to honor the humanity of those we work with at all times. Such a simple approach is one of the first steps that we can take to *living in the solution* in working with traumatized individuals suffering from addiction.

TOOLKIT STRATEGY: CONTINUED SELF-INQUIRY

Many professionals have trepidations about working with alcoholics and addicts. However, just as many professionals—even those comfortable with treating addiction—seem to have reservations when it comes to addressing trauma as part of an addiction treatment plan.

- *What are your fears or concerns about treating addiction or treating trauma? What about treating the two of them together? Common fears I hear expressed by people I teach are, "I just don't feel qualified to address the trauma," or, "If I get into the trauma stuff too soon, my patient may relapse." Take a few moments to inventory your concerns or potential concerns.*

- *Then, take a look back at the Evans and Sullivan model presented in this chapter. What solutions can you derive from that model that can address your concerns about treating addiction and trauma simultaneously?*

Trauma and Dissociation 101

I sometimes feel like a misfit in the world of social science research and practice. At conferences, my fellow attendees are transfixed by presentations about the latest brain research or the newest meta-analyses with the most elaborate research methodologies. This is all well and good, and the field needs all of these things. And yet I remain an English teacher at heart. My first major job after I graduated was working for a Catholic parish in postwar Bosnia and Herzegovina—primarily as an English teacher, music teacher, and language editor. While serving in this capacity, I became blazingly aware of trauma's impact on human development. My students were primarily children and young adults who lived at a parish-run children's home. The region was transitioning from decades of communist-era living and experiencing the aftermath of a major civil war. Many of these students were orphans, while others had parents who couldn't take care of them simply because of the deplorable social conditions in the country.

My students had difficulty focusing, and my sponsor Janet explained how this can be a symptom of traumatic stress. While I witnessed amazing displays of resilience in these children and young adults, I also observed an array of behaviors indicating that many had given up on life. My experiences during the two and a half years I spent in the country impacted me so much that I left my English teaching days behind me, returned to the United States, and began a master's degree program in counseling.

Trauma as Wound

Being an English teacher and a humanitarian is still at the core of my professional identity. I am best able to understand complicated clinical phenomena by looking at a word's origin. *Trauma* is no exception. The English word *trauma* comes from the Greek word meaning "wound." That word, *traumatikos,* implies that the wound can be healed.

Think for a moment about the word *wound* in a physical sense. What do we know about wounds and how they heal? When I present live trainings on trauma, I ask participants this question because discussing what we know about wounds in the physical sense helps us better understand trauma in the emotional sense. Let's examine some elementary knowledge.

Wounds come in many shapes and sizes. There are open wounds, which include incisions (such as those from knives), lacerations (tears), abrasions (grazes), punctures, penetration wounds, and gunshot wounds. Then you have closed wounds, such as contusions (bruises), hematomas (blood tumors), crushing injuries, or the slowly forming chronic wounds that can develop from conditions like diabetic ulcers. Each wound has its own distinct character, and various causes can lead to the respective wounding. More importantly, different wounds can affect different people in different ways.

Even as I look at the scars from old injuries that are still apparent on my skin, I am amazed at how no two of my wounds look alike. Sure, there are some similar patterns, especially with certain blisters—not to mention scratches from my pets. However, each one has left its distinct imprint on my body. Many of my past wounds have healed quickly, leaving no sign of physical scarring at all, whereas others have healed without complication and have left a mark, a reminder.

One of the miracles of creation is that no two people are alike. Consider this idea in our discussion of wounding, and we see that even if I experience an injury similar to yours, it is quite unlikely that we will wound in exactly the same way. Even though wound healing follows a similar process in all human beings, a myriad of other variables complicates

the process. For example, if one person experiences a laceration resulting from a sporting accident but her white blood cell production is poor
and her overall vitamin C levels are low, she likely will take longer to heal
than her peer with better white blood cell production and higher vitamin C levels who experiences the same injury. Think about other factors
like age, health conditions, overall skin plasticity, genetic disorders (e.g.,
hemophilia), location of the wound, and how soon the patient receives
appropriate treatment.

Most will agree that failure to receive the proper treatment after a
wounding can complicate the healing process. Sure, some wounds—
especially minor ones—often clear up on their own with little or no treatment. Consider the difference between a healthy person experiencing
a minor scrape and a hemophiliac getting that same scrape. Treatment
could be a life-or-death matter for the hemophiliac because of his condition. Most wounds require some level of treatment, even if that treatment
is as simple as cleaning the wound and putting a bandage or antibacterial
cream on it. Significant wounds may need sutures or stitches accompanied by a dose of precautionary antibiotics. The most severe wounds—
stab or gunshot wounds—require immediate medical attention, or the
sufferer risks loss of a limb in the long term (especially if infection sets
in). Death can result in the worst cases. In sum, if the injured neglects
requisite treatment, the wound can get worse, and this worsening can
lead to other debilitating physical symptoms.

Like physical wounds, emotional traumas come in various shapes
and sizes for people, resulting from a variety of causes. For some people,
simple traumas can clear up on their own. For others with more complicated emotional variables (many of which can be biologically based), the
healing process may take longer. If an individual who has experienced
a major emotional trauma doesn't obtain the proper conditions to heal
(which can include formal mental health treatment), it likely will take
longer for the trauma to heal. Other symptoms may develop in the process. A major factor when drawing parallels between physical and emotional trauma is the notion of re-wounding. It's bad enough for a person
to experience a traumatic event and not have the optimal conditions in

which to heal. Imagine if other people in that person's life keep picking at the wound with their insensitive comments and potentially retraumatizing behaviors. Of course, the wound is never going to get better. In all likelihood, it will worsen.

Let's look at a specific example here using a classic teaching from the addiction treatment field: *The three unwritten rules of an alcoholic home are: don't talk, don't trust, and don't feel.* These three conditions, as we will examine throughout the book, create the perfect environmental storm for emotional wounds to fester. It's like putting a person with an open physical sore in a tank of bacteria. So imagine that a child in an alcoholic home gets teased mercilessly by bullies at school, perhaps in situations where the child genuinely feels their life is endangered. That situation in and of itself would qualify as a trauma. Then, the child comes home and their father tells them to just put up and shut up. The child receives no help or consolation for the emotional wounding they've been experiencing at school. Moreover, the names that the child's father calls them, especially when he is drunk, simply reinforce what the bullies make them feel about themselves. The wound never gets a chance to heal. Not only that, the wound worsens because the child receives no support at home.

Emotional wounding can take on an even greater degree of pain than physical wounding, because physical wounds can leave outward evidence of their impact. People can be more likely to show us sympathy in the wake of physical injury, yet fail to validate us when the wounds are unseen. I am still saddened when I hear stories of professionals minimizing a person's trauma because they may not have had it "as bad" as someone else in the same treatment group, at least in the opinion of that insensitive professional. *If an experience is traumatic for the client, then it is traumatic; it is worthy of addressing clinically.* I have embraced this axiom since the very beginning of my career, and I believe that it has helped to promote positive, healing relationships with my clients. I am glad that my helpers took this approach with me, or I may have denied myself the treatment and wound care that I needed. All too often, I hear clients say, "Well, that really wasn't a trauma, it's not like I went to war or I was raped or anything...."

Sound like something you may have heard before?

Yes, it is a common tactic for abusers to say things like, "You don't know how good you have it," as a way to justify their own abusive treatment. Yet it breaks my heart when people I serve don't believe that they have "real trauma" because of a minimizing comment they heard from a treatment professional, twelve-step sponsor, or clergy. There is a genuine need to debunk the abundant myths and outdated ideas that still exist about the nature of trauma.

The *DSM* and the PTSD Diagnosis

Let's examine the ways in which some old ideas about trauma being synonymous with a PTSD diagnosis are outdated and do not serve people in recovery. The PTSD diagnosis first appeared in *DSM-III (Diagnostic and Statistical Manual of Mental Disorders,* Third Edition) in 1980, following the Vietnam War. The psychotherapeutic professions became more aware of the profound impact of war. Although the PTSD diagnosis was developed with combat veterans in mind, it was obvious that survivors of other life-threatening events (e.g., violent crimes, civilian experiences during war, natural disasters, and major accidents) exhibited similar symptoms. According to the most current version *(DSM-5)* published by the American Psychiatric Association, for PTSD to be officially diagnosed, the individual must have experienced a Criterion A trauma.

There are three categories of trauma that make up Criterion A: actual or threatened (a) death, (b) physical injury, or (c) sexual violation. This is more specific than the description used in earlier versions of the *DSM.* In the newer breakdown, all forms of sexual violation, regardless of threat of death or physical injury, can qualify for a PTSD diagnosis if the other symptomatic criteria are met. These criteria also include experiences such as vicarious traumatization, witnessing a trauma, and losing someone to a violent or accidental death.

Many clinicians do not think to look further; and in doing assessments, if they do not hear that a "major trauma" has taken place, they do not pursue the issue of trauma further. Although the newest version of the *DSM* still feels incomplete in addressing trauma, some steps have been made in the right direction. Broadening the scope of Criterion A is one of them. If you still believe that PTSD is just about war or a "threat to life and limb" in a physical sense, you are operating from an outdated understanding of trauma.

I challenge those I train to look deeper, even within the PTSD diagnosis. You may be surprised at what you find. Remember, a Criterion A trauma can be life *threatening* and still qualify. In other words, if your body, mind, and soul perceived that your life could have been in danger—even if it technically never was—the experience can still register under Criterion A. Honoring this component of the diagnosis allows us to honor the subjective nature of trauma. Think about a five-year-old child growing up in an alcoholic home, routinely watching their alcoholic parent beating their other parent. If that child perceives that their parent's life is in danger and their life may be next, it can qualify as a Criterion A trauma. The experience is subjective in nature. Another child in the same family may not perceive these events as life threatening, just very stressful. This is why, in conducting assessments, it is important that we get a sense of what these traumatic or wounding experiences *meant* to a client.

If you look a little further into the PTSD diagnosis as it appears in *DSM-5*, there is even more compelling evidence that many professionals do not even realize is there. I call this quick list the "nutshell" definition of PTSD:

- *Exposure* to actual or threatened a) death, b) serious injury, or c) sexual violation: either by direct experience or witnessing (Criterion A)

- *Intrusion* symptoms (Criterion B)

- *Avoidance* of stimuli associated with the trauma (Criterion C)

- *Cognitions and Mood* affected by negative alterations (Criterion D)

- *Arousal and reactivity* symptoms (Criterion E)

- *Duration* of symptoms longer than one month

- *Functional impairment* due to disturbances

28

Taking a closer look at criteria B, C, and D, I share with you my thoughts on what clinicians tend to overlook when it comes to trauma. Although the *DSM* has its limitations, starting here is vital, since many professionals are required to use this document in their clinical settings. Moreover, many individuals go through the mental health and addiction systems for years or even decades being slapped with other diagnoses without ever once having their experiences validated in the framework of trauma. I have seen clients and friends alike weep when they learn that the PTSD diagnosis exists, and that its descriptive elements apply to them.

Criterion B covers those symptoms that mark a reexperiencing of the trauma. The classic examples of reexperiencing symptoms are flashbacks, vivid dreams, and nightmares. Many people do not realize that other psychological symptoms like hallucinations or panic attacks can also be a part of Criterion B experiences. I remember a case that a colleague of mine once worked on in community treatment. This man (Jim) was a severe cocaine addict with a wide spectrum of mental health symptoms, including hallucinations. Jim, who had intermittent sobriety over the years, was nonresponsive to any medication he took for his hallucinatory symptoms. My colleague was wise enough to explore the content of his auditory hallucinations further, and it turns out that the "voice" telling him to kill himself was his abusive father. I truly believe that my colleague's ability to identify the root cause of his voices helped to enhance Jim's overall treatment experience. When I last heard about his progress, he had over four years of sobriety, more time than he had ever achieved in his adult life. My main message here is this: when a client talks about hearing or seeing things, don't automatically wash your hands of it, label it psychosis, and let the psychiatrist do all of the heavy lifting.

Ask.

Ask about the content of the voices and how they may be a part of the client's larger history. You may find out that getting these issues out on the table will enhance the treatment experience.

Criterion C refers to avoidance of stimuli associated with the trauma. The major symptoms that clinicians associate with this criterion include the person steering away from reminders of the trauma, such as not driving near the site of a crime or not wanting to talk about anything connected to the trauma. However, there are many more potential manifestations of Criterion C, including isolation, withdrawal from activities that used to be important, having a sense of a foreshortened future, restrictive range of affect, and fear of feelings. There are some clear parallels here to substance-abuse disorders. As many trauma specialists note, when an individual has a sense of a foreshortened future, instant gratification becomes more appealing. This lack of future orientation is especially common in complex or developmental trauma. Second, if a person is afraid of feeling or showing emotion related to traumatic etiology, drugs, alcohol, and other process addictions may become very appealing aids in keeping those feelings suppressed.

Consider the case of a girl we'll call Rachel. An uncle sexually abused her during her elementary school years, and she was never able to tell anybody. Although the abuse stopped by the time she was eight, during her teenage years and early adulthood, her family required her to go to holiday gatherings at her grandmother's house, where she had to see her uncle. Sometimes, she felt forced into the position of making small talk with him. After Rachel tried cannabis for the first time at the age of fourteen, she surmised that if she had to go to these family gatherings, smoking a joint before she went (and after she returned) helped her curb the overwhelming sense of anxiety that emerged from having contact with her abuser. These pleasurable experiences of smoking a joint to avoid the pain crystallized within her. She adopted this strategy into her adult life for dealing with uncomfortable emotions.

Criterion D is a new addition to *DSM-5*, although certainly not new to the experiences of trauma survivors—negative alterations to cognitions and mood. This new criterion describes the presence of unresolved trauma as significantly capable of altering a person's mood and the way that they see themselves in the world. To formally meet this criterion, you need at least two of seven potential symptoms: blocking out or not remembering important aspects of trauma; negative beliefs about oneself, others, or the world; distorted blame of self or others (related to trauma); persistent negative emotional state; diminished interest or participation in activities; feeling detached or estranged from others; and persistent inability to experience positive emotions.

Unhealed trauma can significantly alter your mood and how you show up in life. It can impact how you engage with other people. These realities are captured in the spirit of the newer Criterion D. Negative beliefs about oneself or others imprinted by the traumatic event, such as "I'm bad," and "My nervous system is permanently ruined," commonly expressed by survivors as "I am permanently damaged," are powerful indicators of how unhealed trauma can affect us. Drugs, alcohol, and other reinforcing behaviors that may show up as process addictions can introduce some level of initial relief to survivors of these internal states of dread.

Many traumatized individuals have also called upon pleasurable substances and behaviors for dealing with symptoms associated with Criterion E (formerly Criterion D), heightened arousal symptoms. The two major symptoms people tend to associate with this category are hypervigilance (always being on guard for something bad to happen) and an exaggerated startle response (where a person is more "jumpy" than what would be considered normal). However, clinicians tend to overlook four other major avoidance symptoms that often get lumped into other diagnostic categories without ever examining the trauma. One of the listed symptoms in *DSM-5* that meets Criterion E is problems focusing or paying attention. However, when people come into treatment (either addiction or mental health), clinicians can and often do attribute such a symptom to attention deficit hyperactivity disorder (ADHD). Sleep disturbance, which includes problems falling or staying asleep (without nightmares), is a valid symptom under Criterion E. Yet how many times are people with sleeping difficulties simply put on a medication without clinicians exploring the root issues? Other possible symptoms listed under Criterion D are increased irritability and outbursts of anger, and reckless and self-destructive behavior. When clients present with these symptoms, I often see one of two things happen. Mental health and psychiatric professionals can lump these symptoms into the bipolar spectrum, and addiction traditionalists write off these symptoms as part of the addiction.

Does unhealed trauma better explain these symptoms?

I'm not discounting the existence of diagnoses like attention deficit or bipolar disorders, nor am I refuting the notion that a person's anger difficulties can be a part of their addiction manifestation. I simply challenge professionals to look deeper because doing so can enhance the treatment process. It's important to explore whether trauma better explains the symptoms people demonstrate at our treatment centers, be it diagnosable PTSD per *DSM-5* or other clinically significant trauma.

Beyond PTSD

Jane entered treatment for crack cocaine addiction in her early forties. Even though she had a series of Criterion A traumas throughout her childhood, she reported that the first time she ever remembered feeling like she was worthless was during the first grade. Jane indicated that she had a very small bladder, a condition that was later verified medically. As a result, she required frequent trips to the restroom. In the first grade, Jane asked her teacher if she could go to the bathroom, and the teacher flatly refused. Jane continued to plead, but to no avail. After several minutes, Jane was no longer able to physically hold it and she urinated right there at her seat—which got her into further trouble with her teacher. Jane became the butt of her peers' cruel taunts, and it became an experience she was never able to live down throughout her school years. Yet as I treated Jane, she told me this story with a great deal of shame, crying the deep, profound tears that we may expect to see from someone who had experienced physical assault. Jane experienced assault at the level of her psyche, and because she was never able to talk about or make sense of the experience, she stayed stuck in the message that the experience gave her: *Jane, you are worthless and not good enough. You can't even wait to go to the bathroom.*

It is amazing how these experiences that may seem minor or silly on the surface can cause profound scarring—especially if our brains, hardwired for adaptive resolution of input, are not able to make sense of the wounding. For Jane, those early messages of "I am worthless" and "I'm

32

not good enough" stayed in her brain as file folders through which similar life experiences filtered. The table that appears at the end of this chapter is a list of the "greatest hits" of negative beliefs that may resonate for you and those you serve as a result of unhealed trauma.

Most of us have these small-t or adverse life experience stories somewhere in our past, each of them wounding us in their own distinct way. There were two such incidents that I needed to address in my early recovery. The first was when I was five years old and my pediatrician called me a "fatso." The other was when a boy at the Catholic school I attended made me think that he liked me. When I agreed to "go out" with him (as much as sixth graders can go out, mind you), he and several of the other popular girls who had put him up to it laughed in my face and called me pathetic. Both experiences solidified my own negative beliefs that I was ugly and pathetic. I needed to address both experiences clinically to move past these beliefs.

For both Jane and me, these events happened in elementary school—in our formative years. In his stages of psychosocial development, Erik Erikson identified the elementary school years (between ages seven and twelve) as the prime time for the development of self-confidence. In this elementary school stage (Erikson's "industry versus inferiority" stage), if children are ridiculed and punished for their efforts (as opposed to praised and encouraged, especially by adult figures), feelings and beliefs of inferiority can develop. As Alfred Adler contended, an individual's essential lifestyle patterns form in childhood as a way to cope with any feelings and beliefs of inferiority that emerge. Adler first introduced the concept of the "life style" as the pair of glasses through which an individual sees the world, glasses that we have designed to deal with our feelings of inferiority. Few will argue that lifestyle change is a critical component for successful addiction recovery, and trauma-sensitive approaches can give us (as professionals and sponsors) a better idea of where, when, and how faulty lifestyle patterns first developed.

Some of you may be nodding your heads yes in overwhelming agreement. This may upset those of you saying, "Okay, so you wet your pants in front of everyone when you were six years old, get over it already."

Getting over it may not be as easy for some as it is for others. I noted the importance of the elementary school years. We can take these discussions back even further to instances of birth trauma (e.g., breech births, losing a twin in childbirth) and other perinatal trauma (e.g., being in utero when the mother has a major traumatic experience; having a mother who drinks, smokes, or does drugs during gestation), and how these have the potential to shape the human experience. Many individuals who have a tough time getting over trauma can trace their traumatic experiences back to preverbal origins. The rest of this chapter puts the idea of trauma's impact across the lifespan into further view as we consider the tough question of why getting over trauma can be so hard to do.

Fundamentals of the Triune Brain

When we ask a person to just *think it through,* or *leave it in the past,* we may be asking a person to do something that is neurologically impossible. Paul MacLean's 1990 explanation of the human brain as triune in nature explains why. Psychiatrist Dan Siegel has made this model even more popular through his presentation of *the hand model* of the human brain (see photograph). The triune brain model acknowledges that the human brain operates as three separate brains, each with its own special roles—which include respective senses of time, space, and memory. The distinct brains are:

- ▶ The brainstem (R-complex or reptilian brain): includes the brainstem and cerebellum; controls instinctual survival behaviors, muscle control, balance, breathing, and heartbeat. The reptilian brain is very reactive to direct stimuli. Most associated with the freeze response and dissociative experiences.

- ▶ The limbic brain (mammalian brain or heart brain): contains the amygdala, hypothalamus, hippocampus, and the nucleus accumbens (responsible for dopamine release). The limbic system is the source of emotions and instincts within the brain, responsible for fight-or-flight responses. Emotion is activated by input in

34

this brain. According to MacLean, everything in the limbic system is either agreeable (pleasure) or disagreeable (pain). Survival is based on the avoidance of pain and the recurrence of pleasure.

▸ The neocortex (or cerebral cortex): is unique to primates and some other highly evolved species like dolphins and orcas. This newest region of the brain regulates our executive functioning—which can include higher-order thinking skills, reason, speech, and sapience (e.g., wisdom, calling upon experience). The limbic system needs to interact with the neocortex in order to process emotions.

When we encourage recovering people to put their intellect (I) over their emotions (E), we are asking them to use their neocortex. You may have heard the slogan "I/E, not E/I" in twelve-step recovery contexts. Although the intention is solid, the execution may be problematic.

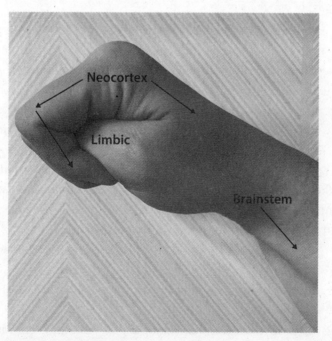

Hand model of the brain

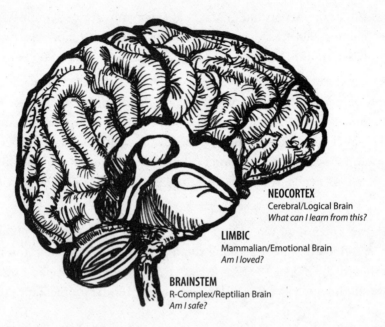

NEOCORTEX
Cerebral/Logical Brain
What can I learn from this?

LIMBIC
Mammalian/Emotional Brain
Am I loved?

BRAINSTEM
R-Complex/Reptilian Brain
Am I safe?

Diagram of the triune brain

Many twelve-step strategies and cognitive therapies target the neocortex. For a person with unprocessed trauma symptoms, the three brains are not optimally communicating with each other when the limbic system gets triggered or activated. During periods of intense emotional disturbance, a human being cannot optimally access the functions of the neocortex because the limbic, or emotional brain, is in control. Blood flow suspends to the left prefrontal cortex when the limbic system is overactivated to some degree. So we may have awareness of what's going on around us, and yet that disruption impedes our ability to process or make sense of it.

Have you ever tried to reason with someone in crisis?

Have you ever asked someone who has relapsed, "What were you thinking?"

Have you ever tried to be logical with someone who is newly in love or lust?

Trying to do any of this is like attempting to send an email without an internet signal. You may have wonderful things to say. You can keep clicking

Send, but it's not going to get through. Indeed, because the activated person has awareness, they may grow increasingly annoyed by your persistence—which can activate the limbic responses even further.

The visceral experiences of triggers—be they triggers to use an addictive substance or triggers related to trauma—are limbic-level activities that cannot be easily addressed using neocortical functions. Moreover, if something triggers a person into a reaction at the limbic level, one of the quickest ways to alleviate that pain is to feed the pleasure potential in the limbic system. As many traumatized addicts discover, alcohol use, drug use, food, sex, or other reinforcing activities are particularly effective at killing the pain. Continuing the email metaphor—when a person is in crisis, click Save on your metaphorical email for the rational material you have to share. Keep an open mind to the strategies I will teach you throughout the book, especially in chapter 6, for how best to work with a person in a high level of limbic activation. What you have to say is best shared when the person is less activated.

Author and cultural commentator Lily Burana, who has survived her own battle with PTSD, explains what happens in the brain of a traumatized person better than any psychotherapeutic professional or scholar I have ever encountered: "You can tell yourself, 'it's okay,' but your wily brain is already ten steps ahead of the game, registering danger and sounding the alarm… The long-range result is that the peace of mind you deserve in the present is held hostage by the terror of your past."[3] I recommend her book *I Love a Man in Uniform* if you want more explanation on this neuroscience delivered from the candid perspective of someone who has lived it.

The information I have presented to you about trauma is not without controversy, with some even calling the potential aftereffects of trauma a myth. Another major criticism is that people often use the diagnosis of PTSD, like addiction, to explain away unacceptable behavior. One reason people struggle to wrap their understanding around trauma's impact on functioning is that the horrible aftereffects do not happen to everybody. Indeed, many individuals who experience horrific traumas do not go on to develop PTSD or other problems in functioning.

No two people are wounded in the exact same way, and the conditions that exist immediately after the wounding can have a significant impact on how a person will heal (and deal) with the wound long term. Many variables play a role in determining how trauma will affect a person long term, including the severity of the original trauma, the severity and intensity of the initial trauma-related symptoms, the age at which the trauma occurred, the length of time that the trauma lasted, and the degree of positive sociocultural support that surrounded the individual at the time of the trauma. Cognitive or intellectual ability to comprehend a traumatic experience might also play a role in making an experience that may simply be stressful to one person traumatic to another.

A common question I get at workshops is, "Jamie, with this expanded definition of trauma, doesn't that mean we've all been traumatized?"

In short, yes.

Trauma affects all of us, even if we don't develop PTSD or other clinical symptoms.

This leads to another criticism—if we acknowledge that we are all traumatized on some level, aren't we demeaning or impugning the struggle of people who've really had it bad? Echoing a clever meme I saw swirling around Facebook, whether you drown in a tablespoon of water, a bathtub, or the ocean, you still drown. All of the variations can lead to suffering.

The Interplay between Trauma and Addiction

The statistical prevalence or comorbidity between trauma and addiction can be hard to pinpoint for several reasons. In their classic *Principles of Trauma Therapy,* John Briere and Catherine Scott explain that the term *trauma* only refers to the wounding experience itself. The manifestation of impact can be multi-faceted, ranging from diagnosable PTSD as defined by *DSM-5* to instances of depression, panic symptoms, or adjustment disorders that may result from small-t traumas. Sometimes a person can clearly see evidence in their lives and relationships that unhealed trauma is affecting them, and yet they may not meet a full clinical diagnosis. Thus, respective studies may define trauma-related aftermath in different fashions.

Terminology always makes comparing studies interesting due to the differences in operational definitions and inconsistent use of constructs among the studies (e.g., addictive disorders versus substance use disorders). *Addiction,* which derives from Latin, meaning "to be fixated on" or "to surrender to something," is not even a term used in the *DSM.* The term is largely accepted culturally and by the medical community. In this book, it's the easiest catchall term for me to use as I discuss various constructs (e.g., alcohol, drugs, other reinforcing behaviors) that fall under the same problematic umbrella. In the modern era, many dislike the term *addiction* and refuse to use it. Instead of *addiction,* the World Health Organization prefers the term *substance dependence*—even though this distinction was eliminated in the American *DSM-5,* opting for the continuum diagnosis of substance use disorders on a mild–moderate–severe scale. Additionally, there is no consensus in the peer-reviewed literature on what constitutes definitions of recovery or relapse.

Additionally, the inaccuracy in client (or study participant) reporting due to memory gaps or fear of stigmatization may also be a factor in some of the disparity in the numbers. For instance, the literature often reports that the comorbidity between substance use disorders and trauma or stressor-related disorders is higher in women than it is in men. My clinical experience continues to suggest that men in recovery struggle just as much with unhealed trauma as do women. While some of the manifestations and impact may be different based on cultural experience, to conclude that trauma is more of an issue for women in recovery than men would be inaccurate. I've come to learn that males can face an even higher degree of shame or stigma for disclosing abuse, especially sexual abuse. Many men find admitting to alcoholism or addiction an easier task than admitting to abuse. I discuss dynamics around gender further in chapter 11.

With some of these limitations noted, consider this general summary of the literature on the interplay among unhealed trauma, addiction, and the various ways they can show up clinically. Various studies have found a disproportionately higher percentage of abuse, neglect, or trauma histories in substance abusers than in the general population. Individuals with a history of PTSD were more likely to have a history of many other psychiatric disorders, an increased risk for alcohol dependence, and other significant psychosocial impairments. Substance abuse increases the likelihood of victimization, which can accelerate the vicious cycle of coping with trauma-related stress and self-medicating with addictive substances. The existing literature on co-occurring PTSD and addictive disorders also suggests improved outcomes when both diagnoses are treated concurrently. This crushes any antiquated notions that addiction must be treated first before trauma issues can be explored, and that unhealed trauma has little to do with addiction.

Complex PTSD and Developmental Trauma

We've established that trauma can seriously affect someone's life. But have you ever met a person who has grown up in a culture of trauma? Have you ever worked with a person who has so many wounds all over their psyche that you are really baffled as to where to begin the healing process? Have you ever met a person who, when you ask them if they have experienced any trauma in their life says, "Where do I even begin?" If so, you've likely encountered complex trauma.

Complex PTSD (C-PTSD) is a concept that psychiatrist Judith Herman first published in her 1992 landmark work, *Trauma and Recovery: The Aftermath of Violence—From Domestic Abuse to Political Terror*. Herman recognized the incomplete nature of the PTSD diagnosis as presented in the *DSM* at the time. She correctly called out the diagnosis as being very event-centric, and not accounting for the relational and intrapersonal torment that can result when traumatic experiences are repetitive, prolonged, or developmentally ingrained. Many of us working in trauma-focused care today laud Judith Herman as a pioneer. We recognize that most of the trauma and stressor-related disorders that we diagnose are rarely due to any singular event. There is usually a greater degree of complexity involved. Christine Courtois and Julian Ford express that the nature of traumatic experiences involved with C-PTSD is not sufficiently described by Criterion A in the current *DSM*. In C-PTSD, the traumatic experiences generally:

▸ Are repetitive or prolonged.

▸ Involve direct harm and/or neglect or abandonment by caregivers or ostensibly responsible adults.

▸ Occur at developmentally vulnerable times in the victim's life, such as early childhood.

▸ Have great potential to severely compromise a child's development.[4]

C-PTSD was not directly named in *DSM-5*, although it has been adopted for the most recent (2019) edition of the International Classification of Diseases (ICD-11). This will hopefully elicit an even greater push for continuing to validate and recognize the impact on human development of trauma that can get labeled with a variety of other names (e.g., personality disorders, conduct disorders, oppositional defiant disorder, reactive attachment disorder, disinhibited social engagement disorder).

Demystifying Dissociation

Beginning in adolescence, Susan used drugs and alcohol as a way of coping with the wounds of a traumatic childhood. She incurred numerous life consequences resulting from her addiction: inability to finish college despite her obvious intelligence, failed relationships, financial concerns, and problems in parenting her children. She relied on "zoning out" and letting her mind wander away from her body to deal with the brutal abuse that she endured at the hands of her mother.

When she entered inpatient treatment following a near-fatal overdose, Susan's motivation to change was very high. Already in her forties, Susan knew that her life needed to shift or she would end up dead. Although she felt treatment was working, on most days she found group work next to intolerable. She would usually check out or drift away during group sharing. Sometimes the disturbances were so great that she would break down and cry, needing to leave the room. As Susan shared, it was rarely what she said in group that caused these experiences. Rather, listening to others share or going too deeply into her own thoughts during the group process triggered this dissociative response.

When she had about thirty days sober, Susan arrived at my office. Susan reported a great deal of relief that I was able to affirm her struggle with group. Several counselors told her that what she was doing by zoning out and leaving the group was just her way of "getting attention." Through learning a series of simple, multisensory coping skills like using pressure points, the butterfly hug, and slow bilateral tapping while thinking about a pleasant color or sensation, Susan was better able to tolerate sitting in groups and twelve-step meetings. Susan's gaining consistency in using these skills became the foundation enabling her to effectively reprocess her past and move forward in sobriety.

In learning about the basics of trauma and how to address it, understanding dissociation is imperative. Susan's case is a classic example of how dissociation can show up in group settings or in meetings. Although dissociative disorders technically have their own diagnostic classifications in *DSM-5*, I have never treated a client for one of the dissociative disorders without uncovering a major trauma that could also qualify for a PTSD diagnosis. Within the PTSD diagnosis, flashbacks (Criterion B) are described as a dissociative response, and in *DSM-5,* there is a new subtype called PTSD with prominent dissociative features. A 2017 study indicated a high degree of co-occurrence between this new PTSD subtype and instances of substance use disorders, forcing us to take an even deeper look at the dissociative qualities of addiction.

Dissociation, trauma-related disorders, and addiction are interrelated because dissociation is a defense that the mind can call upon to handle intense disturbance. People dissociate in order to escape—to sever ties with a present moment that is subjectively unpleasant or overwhelming, stemming from unhealed trauma and its impact. The word *dissociate* comes from a Latin root meaning "to sever." People may dissociate to avoid being present with the fullness of self. For many survivors of trauma, this tendency to dissociate developed very early and may have taken the shape of activities like daydreaming, zoning out, developing imaginary friends, or even creating the most glorious imagined world.

Consider how, at some point in the developmental process, children who learn to dissociate discover that this experience can be amplified with chemical or behavioral assistance. As survivors age and become introduced to alcohol, drugs, and other behaviors helping them to sever, those objects of addiction may become even more appealing because the dissociative experience is familiar to them. Dissociative states help survivors protect themselves from the threats in life, no matter their form.

Adam O'Brien and I developed a model called Addiction as Dissociation to further expand upon these ideas and promote strategies for more effective treatment.[5] The most extreme forms of dissociation, such as dissociative identity disorder (DID, formerly known as multiple personality disorder), dissociative amnesia, and dissociative fugue can stump even the most seasoned professionals. These clinically significant dissociative disorders go hand in hand with complex trauma. Professionals can address these often-baffling disorders using many of the principles covered in this book and a sense of willingness to hear about the client's worldview. As one of my more memorable clients with DID shared with me many years ago, "People fear what they don't understand." In the spirit of his astute observation, I have learned that one of the first steps we as professionals can take to overcome dissociation is to deal with our own fears and concerns about people who dissociate.

At one time or another, we have all dissociated. If you've ever daydreamed, you've dissociated. If you've ever wished with every fiber in your being that you were somewhere else other than where you were—and the wish became so intense you actually brought another place into view—you've dissociated. If you've ever "zoned out" and stopped listening to someone speak because you were either bored or intensely disturbed, then you have dissociated. If you've ever done a visualization exercise or guided imagery like Calm Safe Place or Happy Place, you have dissociated in a therapeutic way! People who warrant a formal diagnosis of dissociative disorder, or people who experience dissociation as part of their PTSD, simply sever more intensely as a way to assuage the pain of disturbing stimuli that causes functional impairment.

Understanding dissociation takes on a new level of importance as we discuss addiction treatment. The complexities of group work and twelve-step or other recovery meetings can trigger dissociative responses in individuals. Think about it critically: A client may be sitting in group just listening to someone else share, and the other group member may say something that triggers an emotional response within the client—a response that she may not be ready to handle. Odds are, when someone seems checked out in groups or in a meeting, this is exactly what is happening. Although there are many benefits to treatment groups and recovery meetings, dissociation is a great risk for traumatized individuals who are early in their recovery process. If you are a group facilitator, acknowledging this risk is important, and making yourself available individually after a group to meet with someone who has dissociated is vital. Another preventative strategy is to teach clients and those new to recovery the multisensory stabilization skills in this book, especially those in chapter 9. If we can teach recovering individuals to listen to their bodies and emotional cues while they are in a group meeting and equip them with skills to address these disturbances, then tolerating groups or meetings with potentially disturbing subject matter becomes more realistic.

Addiction is a dissociative phenomenon. Once a person stops using or terminates a problematic behavior, even temporarily, we must recognize that their dissociative avenue is no longer available. Other forms of dissociation that I've described in this section may become more pronounced. In my own recovery journey, between one and two years of sobriety, I experienced an intense escalation in the dissociative escape behaviors I developed as a child. I even began noticing how different parts of experience were at war within me, even though amnesia between parts was never a factor in my experience. A colleague at my work and internship site noticed how difficult it was for me to stay present on the job, especially in the context of being a newly sober woman in graduate school and navigating some personal life challenges. The presence of those dissociative symptoms in early sobriety gave me the push to find a trauma-focused counselor who introduced me to EMDR therapy, meditation, and other holistic strategies. She was never afraid of my dissociation or my addiction, and I am grateful to this day.

The first step is overcoming your personal fears about encountering dissociation when you see it: Remember, the type of dissociation that freaks out professionals in sessions or in groups is simply extreme, maladaptive coping. Having an arsenal of multisensory grounding and stabilization skills at the ready is the simplest solution. Teaching clients prone to dissociation these skills ahead of time is vital to helping them if their dissociation becomes problematic or impairing. We thoroughly review the multisensory skills in later chapters, especially chapter 9.

Processing Trauma and the Culture of Healing

Processing is a psychological term for making sense of an experience. Processing is a way to achieve the resolution needed to move on from a traumatic experience or series of experiences. The nature of this resolution may vary from person to person. Some have even called processing the *digesting* of an unsettling event. As a colleague of mine presented in my 2014 book, *Trauma Made Simple: Competencies in Assessment, Treatment, and Working with Survivors,* when you process a trauma, it moves from being a hot, charged memory that controls your life to just being a bad memory.

If we are using the wound metaphor, processing occurs when the wound receives proper treatment within an appropriate time frame, and we give the individual space to heal. In a biological sense, referring once again to MacLean's triune brain model, processing occurs when the emotional material in the limbic brain can link up with the rationally oriented functions in the neocortical brain. The neocortex is a more efficient place for memories to be reconsolidated, integrated, and stored long term.

There is a variety of reasons that trauma remains unprocessed, undigested, unresolved, or unhealed. Pick whatever word makes the most sense to you. Earlier in the chapter I asked you to consider a girl who grew up in an alcoholic home while kids at school bullied her. The *don't talk, don't trust, don't feel* culture of that home completely thwarted the possibility of processing, making it easier for the traumatic memories to stay stuck in the limbic brain. Another reason trauma remains unprocessed is people tend to automatically assume that talking is the only way a person can process. In many treatment centers, talking is synonymous with processing. Although talking can help a person to process, talking is primarily a function of the neocortical brain and what Dan Siegel or Bessel van der Kolk would call a top-down intervention. A person can talk about the trauma all they want. Until they can address it at the limbic level, the trauma will likely stay stuck and impact one's quality of life.

Other healthy modalities of processing can include exercise, breath work, imagery, journaling, expressive arts of all kinds, or prayer. The physical act of picking up the phone to call your sponsor can be a form of processing because you are using the body for a healthy, adaptive purpose, even if no one is available to talk to you on the other line. Addictive substances and behaviors can be a traumatized person's attempt to process—to address the pain that is blaring in their limbic system. We can find them so effective because these substances and behaviors seem so pleasurable to the body. Our challenge is to help traumatized individuals seeking recovery to use their bodies in healthier ways that promote adaptive or healthy processing of information. Chapter 7 explores in depth why these body-based activities can actually be some of the most effective mechanisms for processing, digesting, resolving, or healing trauma.

The parallel between physical and emotional wounds appears throughout this book because there are so many salient connections. Many of us who entered the field of addiction treatment and the psychotherapeutic professions are familiar with the term "the wounded healer." This term, attributed to Dutch priest and writer Henri Nouwen, accurately describes many of our journeys. Nouwen once wrote: "When we honestly ask ourselves which person in our lives means the most to us, we often find that it is those who, instead of giving advice, solutions, or cures, have chosen rather to share our pain and touch our wounds with a warm and tender hand."[6]

This teaching helps me to remember, especially when I get overwhelmed by the clinical terminology of it all, that our task is to help heal the wounded. We can do this by remembering where we needed to be healed ourselves. And we must recognize that even in long-term recovery or in our professional lives, continuing to address our own wounds in a healthy way as life delivers them is vital. We deserve this level of care, and so do the people we serve.

A "GREATEST HITS LIST" OF PROBLEMATIC TRAUMA-RELATED BELIEFS

RESPONSIBILITY	VALUE
I should have known better.	I am not good enough.
I should have done something.	I am a bad person.
I did something wrong.	I am permanently damaged.
I am to blame.	I am defective.
I cannot be trusted.	I am terrible.
SAFETY	I am worthless/inadequate.
I cannot trust myself.	I am insignificant.
I cannot trust anyone.	I am not important.
I am in danger.	I deserve to die.
I am not safe.	I deserve only bad things.
I cannot show my emotions.	I am stupid.
CHOICE	I do not belong.
I am not in control.	I am different.
I have to be perfect/please everyone.	I am a failure.
I am weak.	I am ugly.
I am trapped.	My body is ugly.
I have no options.	I am alone.
POWER	
I cannot get what I want.	
I cannot succeed.	
I cannot stand up for myself.	
I cannot let it out.	
I am powerless/helpless.	

TOOLKIT STRATEGY: THE GREATEST HITS LIST

Take about five minutes to scan "A 'Greatest Hits List' of Problematic Trauma-Related Beliefs."

- Think about the last two or three people you have worked with who have specifically disclosed issues related to addiction or compulsive behavior. Which of these beliefs, in your assessment, might those folks "check off" as being relevant to them?

- Do you think these beliefs emerged from the person's addictive behavior, or did they predate the addictive behavior? Take a few minutes to jot down your responses.

- You can also do a reflection on this list for yourself. Scan down the list; which beliefs do you still struggle with in the present day? Looking back over the course of your own life, do you see them as originating in unhealed wounding?

What Twelve-Step Recovery Can Offer Traumatized Individuals

One day, Jeff and his friend were on their college campus, searching for a secluded spot so they could smoke a little weed. As they walked, they saw a girl with a physical disability on a nearby pathway, heading to class in a wheelchair. The friend, obviously uncomfortable, commented on how terrible it must be for that girl to maneuver around campus in a wheelchair. Jeff responded, "Well, it looks like she's been in a wheelchair most of her life. What would be even worse is if, all of sudden, you or I found ourselves strapped to a wheelchair. We wouldn't know what to do."

Within a couple of months, his words would prove chillingly prophetic. Following a near-fatal accident resulting directly from alcohol withdrawal, Jeff suffered permanent paralysis from the waist down. He was not even old enough to legally drink in his state. While he adjusted to the new realities of living life in a wheelchair, Jeff felt embarrassed and ashamed to enter a twelve-step recovery meeting—even though he knew deep down that he had to return to twelve-step meetings if he was going to stay sober. Jeff had attended twelve-step meetings during prior attempts at recovery, and he found the prospect of having to explain why he was in a wheelchair too overwhelming. Not to mention the taunts of old-timers saying things like, "It didn't get any easier out there, did it?" So, for nearly a year, Jeff managed to stay sober through close supervision by his mother and adjusting to his new physical existence. He also knew that something was missing.

Jeff eventually found his way back to a twelve-step meeting, and he was welcomed back without the taunts that he feared. In the midst of taking risks and beginning to work a program, a very interesting phenomenon occurred. Through sharing his story, the process of healing from his trauma was beginning to take place. Jeff found that as he shared one-on-one with people he connected to in the fellowship, took an inventory in the fourth step, and eventually shared his story in public at speaker meetings, the process of gradual catharsis took place.

Jeff believes that telling his story helped with the desensitization process that so often needs to occur in trauma recovery, noting, "Every time I told the story, I felt a weight lifting." Today, over two decades into his recovery journey, Jeff is able to share his message at twelve-step meetings and genuinely laugh when telling some of the same stories that used to bring him to tears. For Jeff, there is no doubt that recovery from his addiction and the healing of his traumas was an integrated process.

Healing Mechanisms in the Twelve-Step Approach

For someone like Jeff, a trauma survivor who came to embrace twelve-step programming and principles, the twelve-step approach offered more than just a recovery plan for alcoholism or addiction. The steps and the people he met helped him to heal. Jeff had a wonderful twelve-step support system and outside professional help was needed. He and many other trauma survivors working twelve-step programs are quick to credit the unquestionably important structure that the twelve steps gave them to guide their healing. Structure is one of the main benefits that recovery programs in general, not just twelve-step programs, bring to the healing process.

In this chapter, I explain what a twelve-step program can offer to someone with unresolved trauma who is also seeking addiction recovery. Special attention is paid to the benefits of positive sober support that recovery fellowships can provide, the opportunities for mutual support through listening, and the flexible structure offered by the twelve steps that can serve as a foundation for dual recovery. I also explore facets of twelve-step approaches that allow for catharsis (specifically fourth and fifth step work, and having the opportunities to share the story), and time-honored teachings of twelve-step programming (e.g., spiritual awakening, practicing acceptance, dealing with resentments) that may also prove helpful in trauma recovery. Attention is even paid to the well-established twelve-step alternatives that may fit the bill for addicted survivors of trauma who are in need of a structured program. Although this chapter presents a brief overview of the history and background of the twelve steps, I do not provide an intensive primer on twelve-step philosophy largely because other sources cover this extensively (see the Appendix if you are looking for such material).

Certain twelve-step purists may accuse me of stretching the boundaries of the program beyond where the originators intended them to stretch. A recovering professional challenged me once at a workshop, saying, "The twelve steps of (insert specific fellowship) are meant as a program of recovery from (insert specific substance or behavior), not trauma." In an orthodox interpretation of the recovery programs, these critics may have a point. However, if we use the broad definition of trauma offered in chapter 3, then just about everybody walking into a recovery meeting for the first time has some level of unresolved trauma that could prevent them from fully embracing a recovery program. Trauma recovery is a necessary aspect of addiction recovery. I often hear at twelve-step meetings that alcoholism, addiction, or the problematic behavior is merely the manifestation (or symptom) of a larger personality problem. Traumas can, and often do, play a critical role in shaping this larger personality problem, so approaching the twelve steps in a trauma-informed manner is more than relevant.

The other criticism I anticipate is from professionals or from people who have had negative experiences with twelve-step fellowships: this trauma-informed ideal is not how twelve-step programs are actually run in the real world. True, what I present in this chapter is my greatest wish for the full spectrum of what a twelve-step fellowship can offer an addicted trauma survivor. My wish is that every trauma survivor seeking recovery is provided with a welcoming, tolerant atmosphere at meetings or in treatment centers. Offering the addicted survivor of trauma proper, nonjudgmental support and guidance is critical. Unfortunately, many newcomers to twelve-step meetings are not greeted with the ideal. I address these criticisms and make some myself in chapter 5. For now, let's stay focused on the possibilities.

A Brief Overview of
How Twelve-Step Recovery Came to Be

When I first entered recovery, two ideas from the history of AA made an impression. The first idea was the power of one alcoholic helping another alcoholic. Through this mechanism of action upon which the program was founded in 1935, we can receive the support that we need to heal. I felt so uniquely crazy and warped coming into recovery, it was a relief to hear people say, "It's okay, Jamie. I get where you're coming from." From both addiction and trauma perspectives, that validation was incredibly healing. The second idea that appealed to me was the notion of a user-friendly spirituality as represented by the phrase God *as we understand Him.* Although some philosophical disputes took place among the early members of AA before they agreed upon this phrase, the wording eventually made its way into the twelve steps. I entered recovery craving some spiritual connection while finding myself wounded by the dogmas of denomination due to my religious upbringing. This phrase was embracing and welcoming for me, and I believe that this welcoming tone was the intention of the fellowship's founders.

The founding of AA traces back to 1935 when Bill Wilson, a former stockbroker from New York trying to recover his career, took a business trip to Akron, Ohio. Wilson had been sober for five months, largely using the ideas of the Oxford Group, a nondenominational Christian organization that embraced a charism of outreach to the downtrodden. Wilson, having experienced a sudden spiritual awakening while recovering from alcohol withdrawal in a New York City hospital, learned that the best way to retain what he gained was to share it with others through outreach. In the five months following his spiritual awakening, Wilson attempted to help scores of alcoholics, mostly by preaching to them, and found that not a single one stayed sober.

Except for him.

While in Akron awaiting the outcome of a proxy dispute, Wilson lingered in the lobby of the Mayflower Hotel. The lure of the bar seemed very appealing. He knew that in order to stay sober, he needed to talk to another alcoholic. Thus, using the pay telephone in the Mayflower lobby and the church directory posted nearby, he frantically began calling ministers to see if they could assist him in his quest. Eventually, he found a minister who put him in touch with a parishioner, Henrietta Seiberling, who knew just the right person for Bill Wilson to talk to: Dr. Bob Smith.

Smith, who lost his surgical practice as the result of his alcoholism, was still actively drinking during his first meeting with Bill Wilson in May of 1935. Having also tried the Oxford Group, Smith was initially resistant to talking to Wilson. After several hours of simple sharing, Smith and Wilson knew that they found something special, so they began their quest of reaching out to other alcoholics as a way to stay sober themselves.

A useful distinction is that the aim of the Oxford Group was to reach out to everyone who was down on their luck. However, the aim of this fellowship that would become Alcoholics Anonymous was to reach out only to alcoholics. In the early years of starting up meetings in both Akron and New York, in addition to incorporating several spiritual role models into their approach such as American philosopher William James and St. Francis of Assisi, Wilson and Smith continued to utilize a six-step plan from the Oxford Group:

- ▸ Admitted hopelessness
- ▸ Got honest with self
- ▸ Got honest with another
- ▸ Made amends
- ▸ Helped others
- ▸ Prayed to God *as you understand Him*

Wilson, with the help of others in the emerging fellowship, eventually expanded these ideas into what would become the twelve steps. In 1939,

Wilson put together a book that spelled out the twelve-step program, complemented by stories of those who had recovered using the approach that was emerging within the fellowship meetings.

The publication of the book *Alcoholics Anonymous* officially gave the fellowship a name, saw the publication of the first draft of the twelve steps, and provided the growing AA fellowship some uniformity. Bill Wilson (from New York) and the Akron groups wanted to keep the focus on spirituality. The New York groups wanted to keep the focus on the physical aspects of alcoholism. A combination of the two approaches emerged. *Alcoholics Anonymous* also featured a presentation of the disease concept of addiction by Dr. William Silkworth, the physician who treated Bill Wilson while he was in the hospital.

The groups hoped that the book's publication in April 1939 would propel the message of *Alcoholics Anonymous* into the mainstream. To the dismay of the groups, orders for the book only trickled in, following a nationwide postcard advertising blast. The Rockefeller Foundation, which provided limited support to the fellowship in its early stages, assisted with getting the four thousand non-purchased copies of the book out of storage. Jack Alexander's *Saturday Evening Post* article in March of 1941 was the turning point. This media attention resulted in an exponential growth of Alcoholics Anonymous membership throughout the United States. Famed writer Alexander set out to expose AA as a fraud. What emerged were six pages of praise about what he observed in the AA fellowship, necessitating a second printing of *Alcoholics Anonymous* in 1941.

Some fruits of AA's establishment included more widespread acceptance of alcoholism as a disease (including the American Medical Association's acceptance of the disease model by the early 1950s). Additionally, AA and the twelve steps inspired what would come to be known as the Minnesota model of treatment, which brought twelve-step approaches (although not the specific fellowship of AA) into hospital-based treatment centers around the country. By the 1950s, not only were treatment programs growing, but also a variety of other fellowships such as Narcotics Anonymous and Al-Anon Family Group began forming, using the twelve-step approach. To date, hundreds of recovery fellowships use the original twelve steps of Alcoholics Anonymous, including several that specifically target trauma, incest, and assault recovery. If you are interested in reading more about the history, development, and fruits of Alcoholics Anonymous and/or twelve-step recovery, see the Appendix.

Sober Support

When we treat trauma-related disorders, regardless of whether or not the person struggles with an addictive disorder, some degree of stabilization or preparation must take place. As discussed in chapter 2, a wise treatment provider would not expect a person who is new to recovery (whether that be from the addiction, the trauma, or both) to address the root disturbances associated with their traumatic stress unless a person has a set of skills to help them manage emotions and the unpredictability of life in a healthy way. Developing a mutual support network is a critical component of stabilization for so many addicted survivors of trauma. According to the literature, positive trauma-related social support is important in the development of a strong, early therapeutic alliance; lack of support is one of the strongest predictors in the development of PTSD.

The benefits of mutual support offered by twelve-step groups are twofold. First, many individuals entering recovery are surrounded by friends and family who are not sober or emotionally nourishing, so the meetings can offer an outlet to start building a network of people who support the individual's recovery. Second, isolation due to shame is such a common phenomenon with both recovering addicts/alcoholics and traumatized individuals. Many people enter recovery believing that the behaviors they engaged in or the feelings they experience are some unique brand of crazy or defective. Hearing others share similar experiences, thoughts, and feelings at meetings can facilitate the healing process. In hearing others share, many addicted survivors hear messages that help convey more positive beliefs in the vein of, "You are not alone."

For many, once they address some of the barriers about opening up to others (solutions for these barriers will be discussed in chapters 6 and 7), getting involved with people in a twelve-step fellowship becomes a powerful mechanism of action in the healing process. Mae is a woman in her late forties and the survivor of childhood sexual abuse. After she worked through the initial social barrier of getting involved with the groups, the benefits were astounding: "I am not a social butterfly, so that means that I have to put myself in the fellowship—my fellowship is Alcoholics Anonymous. I had to put myself in the middle and start interacting with people, and I kept missing that. I kept missing that it always got worse and never better."

At the time of a treatment follow-up interview in 2010, Mae credited the involvement in her fellowship and the receipt of outside counseling help as vital in her attaining six and a half years of sobriety, the most she had ever experienced in her long history of attempts. For JoElle, also a woman and survivor of domestic violence, involvement with twelve-step recovery groups allows her to measure her progress and remember where she has come from in her journey. Interacting with meeting newcomers makes this possible for her. As African-American women, Mae and JoElle's perspectives are valuable, particularly because the AA program has long been criticized as reflecting only the perspectives of white males.

People have differing reasons for wanting to make friends and support contacts within twelve-step fellowships. For Michelle, a young college student who grew up in a home with significant emotional abuse and family discord, most of her peer group consisted of people who drank, especially because she lived on campus. By coming to meetings, she was able to connect with other people who did not drink, and thus found a new social outlet for herself. Once she met her need for sober social interaction, she was gradually able to benefit from listening and sharing with the people in her new network of friends. I have even heard critics of AA admit that as long as a person can find a reasonable meeting, at the very least, AA offers a social outlet that is preferable to going to a bar. However, for people with social needs in early recovery, the opportunities for socialization that AA offers cannot be underestimated.

Flexible Structure

At first glance, the term *flexible structure* might seem like an oxymoron. Upon further exploration in this chapter, we will see how flexible structure is exactly what the twelve steps offer—provided that a person is not rigidly interpreting the steps. Flexible structure is what an addicted survivor of trauma may need, in order to obtain solid footing on the road to recovery.

In my investigation of addiction recovery programs—which includes programs informed by the twelve steps, programs that have nothing to do with the twelve steps, and programs that blend approaches—one common denominator emerges in what makes a successful recovery program: lifestyle change. Many individuals who have recovered from addictions contend that having structure was an absolutely critical element in making this change happen. Consider the case of Vince. A white male in his early thirties, Vince found himself in a place where he had lost everything as a result of his alcoholism: his girlfriend, his house, his business, and his driver's license. Without insurance, and having burned too many bridges at the community-based treatment facilities in his area, Vince's only choice for structured treatment was to go to a faith-based Christian facility in a nearby town. Vince was an agnostic, yet he somehow knew that he needed to go away for ninety days to get back on track. Vince credits the structure that the Christian facility gave him in initiating his sobriety.

"I didn't buy a word of what they were saying spiritually," said Vince. "But the structure I received there made all the difference."

While the importance of structure in bringing about lifestyle change is important, we must also consider that people growing up in traumatic environments may respond to structure in different ways. Some people like regimen because it is familiar to them or gives them a sense of control—be it actual or perceived. However, others feel completely turned off by structure, order, and being told what to do. That's the tricky thing about trauma: its effects on a person are varied and unpredictable. The flexibility concept allows us to meet people where they are during any given point in their recovery.

If not approached with a rigid mindset, many facets of the twelve steps are incredibly flexible. For instance, the traditions of Alcoholics Anonymous state that "the only requirement for membership is a desire to stop drinking." Thus, a person afraid to come to a meeting because they fear they will have to introduce themselves as an alcoholic or work the twelve steps can be assured that none of that is required. Most twelve-step programs are intended to be suggestive only. I'm the first to admit that some very rigid-minded sponsors lost this idea along the way and have turned the suggestions into absolute orders. If you are a person who encounters this absolutism and it's a deal breaker for working a program, search for other meetings or talk to other people. We flexible folks are out there! For a person resistant to structure and order, especially if this resistance is trauma related, being assured that the components of the program and the steps are *suggestive only* can make all the difference. From a trauma-sensitive perspective, it can actually help with one's sense of personal empowerment to make a choice to take the suggestions.

Flexible Language in the Steps

Flexibility is inherent in the language of the twelve steps if those of us guiding people through the steps choose to see the opportunities for framing them in this manner. Let's look at some specific examples:

- **Step 1: We admitted that we were powerless over alcohol, that our lives had become unmanageable.** While many survivors and otherwise resistant people struggle with the term *powerless,* the step does not say that we are powerless people. The step simply says that we are powerless when it comes to alcohol, drugs, etc. This means that if we put alcohol or drugs into our body, they will win every time. Behaviors can have a similar impact. By admitting defeat, we are carving the pathway to reclaim our power on the road ahead. The distinction is an important one in working with newcomers or new clients who may feel disheartened or even shamed by words like *powerless* or *unmanageable.*

- **Step 3: Made a decision to turn our will and our lives over to the care of God *as we understand Him.*** The italicized component of this step makes all the difference. It gives people who work a twelve-step program permission to fire their old concept of God and what

He/She/It/They means if that old concept has not helped them to stay sober. Some people who do not embrace Higher Power spirituality may choose to utilize "Good Orderly Direction," "Group of Drunks," or several other ideas I discuss in chapter 12. Although some twelve-step groups and sponsors may misinterpret the step, in its truest form the step leaves it up to individuals to decide how they will conceptualize their Higher Power—an idea that allows for flexibility and modification.

▶ **Step 5: Admitted to God, to ourselves, and to another human being the exact nature of our wrongs.** Many people get hung up on this step, discussed in greater depth in the next chapter. Let's first examine the flexibility inherent in this step. The step doesn't say that you need to voice your wrongs to a sponsor, a priest, a minister, a counselor, or to the whole world—it simply says "another human being." The person working the step is empowered to choose who that human being is, and it is a decision they can make based on their own comfort and safety levels.

▶ **Step 9: Made direct amends to such people whenever possible except when to do so would injure them or others.** The beauty in this step is that it is not an absolute step. Making things right, or making amends, is part of the suggested twelve-step process. However, this step acknowledges that there are certain cases in which seeking people out to make amends might make things worse. Most people interpret this step to mean that the person working the step is also included in the phrase "injure them or others."

▶ **Step 11: Sought through prayer and meditation to improve our conscious contact with God *as we understand Him*, praying only for a knowledge of His will for our lives and the power to carry it out.** Once again, italics highlight the flexible property of this step. Those working the steps have the right to decide how they see God, Higher Power, or Inner Power (a commonly used alternative). More ideas for how spiritual flexibility and diversity can be applied to the step appear in chapter 12.

Opportunities for Catharsis

Catharsis, often defined as the purging of emotions, comes from the Latin root meaning "to cleanse." This process is required on some level for meaningful recovery to occur. Processing trauma implies some form of catharsis—be it verbal, physical, emotional, spiritual, or a combination. Many individuals dread the cathartic aspects of recovery because they fear it will make them worse. Sometimes the process is what people dread. This process requires work and patience, which can be challenging for people used to instant gratification.

Letting unresolved emotions, thoughts, and experiences accumulate is like never emptying out the garbage can in your kitchen. You may continue to stuff them down into the garbage can. Eventually the can will overflow and start to stink up the kitchen. Temporary fixes like air freshener and pushing the garbage down farther into the can may help the state of the kitchen in the short term; nothing is going to help like getting that garbage out to the curb. In real life, the garbage collector does not come into your house to take your garbage out for you. It is up to you to take the garbage out to the curb. Only then can the metaphorical garbage collector, be it your Higher Power, your support group, the universe, or however you choose to see the power greater than yourself, take the stuff away, freeing you of its power.

There are many opportunities within twelve-step and other recovery programs to engage in catharsis. In a twelve-step model, steps four and five provide a golden opportunity for such catharsis. In chapter 5 we explore how these steps can be a gauntlet for so many people in recovery. However, with proper preparation and guidance in working the first three steps (with outside help if needed), steps four and five do not have to be frightening. In fact, they can be quite healing. Steps four and five ask the recovering individual to take a searching and fearless moral inventory and share that inventory with God/Higher Power, themselves, and just one other human being. If done sensitively, steps four and five can be a powerful form of narrative-style therapy that allows the addicted survivor of trauma to get all of the garbage out.